4th edition

The Index for Inclusion:

a guide to school development led by ir

Tony Booth and Mel Ainscow

Index for Inclusion: a guide to school development led by inclusive values

Written by Tony Booth and Mel Ainscow

Third and fourth editions radically revised by Tony Booth
First edition published March 2000
Second edition published September 2002
Third edition published May 2011
Fourth edition published January 2016

Published by Index for Inclusion Network (IfIN)
3 Norwich Street, Cambridge, CB2 1ND.
Tel: 07813 974694
email: info@indexforinclusion.org

Design adapted for the 4th edition by Jannie Brightman

Printed and bound by Colchester Print Group

A catalogue record for this book is available from the British Library

ISBN 978-0-9935122-0-9

The Index for Inclusion Network was established in 2012 to promote work with the *Index for Inclusion* around the world and other activities that share its aim of putting inclusive values into action.

Contents

Acknowledgements

The ideas for this book have been developed in dialogue with a large number of people over the last decade. Some people deserve special mention. Judith Carter's encouragement and comments have been sustaining, not least through her gentle expertise in co-ordinating the work with Norfolk County Council and her commitment to make the Index work with the current schools inspection framework. Sue Buckingham introduced me to planetary rights which I resisted then embraced. A group from Transitions Cambridge, Anna McIvor, Mark Skipper, Myriam Thomachot and Margaret Parker gave of their time and expertise. The experience and comments of Stephen Scoffham, Gill Hope, Jill Matthews, Jonathan Barnes, from Canterbury Christ Church University gave me confidence that the work on the curriculum had theoretical and practical use. Andreas Hinz and Barbara Brokamp gave their perspective as people who have worked for a long time with the Index in Germany and Kari Nes did this for Norway. Kari Nes made a special contribution on a European tradition off didactics for asking questions about curriculum content and Barbara with her insightful ideas about the Index process and ways to support it through 'process companions'. Susan Hart's suggestions and particularly her approval for what I was attempting to do were important. Em Williams provided useful insistence on a rethinking about gender binaries and Artemi Sakellariadis gave critical comments during the writing process. Jannie Brightman, Mary Young, Jane Carpenter, Alison Peacock, Peter Pope, Hannah Booth, Katie Booth, Ben Greig, Astrid Greven, Mark Antopolski, Nigel Pickford, Pat Yarker, also provided very useful comments.

Thanks are due for the photographs from schools: Burston and Tivetshall, Caister Junior, Diss High School, Edward Worlledge, Hanover Primary and Nursery, Hemsby Primary, Hemsby High School, Highgate Infants, Holloway, Parkside, Roydon Junior, Wroxham School and Tom and Clair Mein for the Olive Tree. Stuart Beard provided some stunning pictures of adults and children at work and play as did Hannah Burns of activities in Tyrrels Wood. Thanks to the Candoco dance company for the picture on page 47. Jill Eastland drew the lovely fern and flowers in Part 1, Denise Knowelden stepped in with some timely copy-editing and Jannie Brightman drew on one of her many skills in adapting the design for this edition. Thanks to our Spanish colleagues for allowing us to imitate the cover on their translated version of the *Index*: Gerardo Echeita, Cecila Simon, Marta Sandoval and Yolanda Munoz.

Schools in the Norfolk *Index* pilot project.
Infant and nursery school: Clover Hill.
Infant schools: Colman, Costessy, Lodge Lane, Recreation Road.
Junior schools: Caister, Edward Worlledge, Lingwood, St. Michael's, Wroughton.
Primary schools: Bignold, Bishop's, Bluebell, Cawston, Colby Ditchingham Fairstead, Hapton, Heartsease, Roydon, Sporle, Tacolneston, Terrington St John, Tilney St Lawrence, Walpole Highway, Whitefriars, Wicklewood.
Secondary schools: Broadland High, Downham Market High, Hewett Comprehensive, Hobart High, King Edward VII High, Springwood High.
Special schools: Churchill Park, Sidestrand.

Background to the fourth edition of the *Index*

The first edition was published in 2000 with the subtitle: developing learning and participation in schools. The first *Index* team was set up by Mel Ainscow and Mark Vaughan. The final content of the first edition was shaped particularly by the work of Tony Booth and his colleagues, Patricia Potts and Will Swann at the Open University linking inclusion to the development of a system of comprehensive community pre-school, primary and secondary education and by Mel Ainscow's work on school improvement.

The government provided a copy of the first edition to all primary, secondary, special schools and local education authorities in England. A second edition, broadly similar to the first, was published in 2002 and was distributed to every school in Wales, in Welsh or English, by the Welsh Assembly.

Versions of the *Index* for early years and childcare were developed in 2004 and 2006.[1] Besides extending the *Index* for very young children and babies, the revisions took the overall project forward by adding the significance of well-being for children and adults and emphasising the importance of play.

While the book is produced for English schools it is not a typically English document. It reflects countless dialogues with colleagues around the world. It sees educational improvement as pushed forward by attention to the flourishing of teaching, learning and relationships rather than by a sole focus on attainment outcomes. Its approach to development has been seen as relevant for many countries and it has been translated and adapted for use in about fifty countries. An international team supported by UNESCO looked at how versions could be developed for economically poor areas of countries of the South.[2]

I made radical changes for the third edition published in 2011 and dedicated it to the decade of biodiversity 2011 to 2020. It reflected experience in England[3] and and other countries over a ten year period. It introduced a framework of inclusive values as an answer to the question; 'how should we live together?' It drew together principled interventions to do with environmental sustainability, national and global citizenship, non-violence, democratic education and health promotion within a single approach. It included concern for the environment as an imperative for education to set alongside the imperative for fostering non-violent relationships locally and globally. It invited dialogue about the content of curricula by outlining a 21st century answer to the question: 'What do we need to know in order to live together well?' This helped the *Index* to fulfill more honestly than previously the claim that it set out the implications of inclusive values for all aspects of schools.

I have made relatively minor modifications for this fourth edition. The subtitle is new: *a guide to school development led by inclusive values*. This makes clearer that the *Index* is about school development and improvement involving adults and children and all aspects of settings. It should help to further overcome the widespread view that inclusion is about a particular group of children seen as 'having special educational needs'. It contrasts 'values-led' with 'outcomes-led' development', an approach that has dominated thinking about 'school improvement' in England and other countries over many years. In doing this it aims to increase the sustainability of a widened array of outcomes.

Values are now represented in a three-dimensional structure without any suggestion of hierarchy. I have introduced the idea of 'values literacy' to name the process of exploring the connections of values to actions. I have contrasted inclusive with excluding values. Many colleagues see these latter values as reflected in aspects of their schools. The task for development is to put inclusive values into action and disconnect action from excluding values. I have provided indications of how a values-led approach can help to prepare for, and respond to, inspections. The *Index* is supported with a website indexforinclusion.org which provides information about its use in England and other countries, further resources and opportunities for feedback.

1 Booth, T., Ainscow, M. and Kingston, D. (2004, 2006) *Index for inclusion: developing play, learning and participation in early years and childcare*, Bristol, CSIE.

2 Booth, T. and Black-Hawkins, K., (2001, 2005). *Developing learning and participation in countries of the South; the role of an Index for inclusion*, Paris, Unesco.

3 Rustemier, S. and Booth, T., (2005). *Learning about the Index in use: A study of the use of the Index* for inclusion *in schools and LEAs in England*, Bristol, CSIE.

Getting started

This book is a comprehensive guide to the development of your school.

Colleagues in Germany have been amongst the most inventive in getting people working with *Index* materials. Although some schools use the *Index* to support whole school development from the beginning, this is often not the case. Small changes can develop into whole school commitments as others see the benefits their colleagues derive from working with the *Index* materials. The following encouragement to get started is adapted from a list of hints given to people in Germany[4]. Point 9 comes from Australian colleagues who worked with *Index* materials in equally flexible ways, in Queensland[5] and from the experience of working with schools under pressure in Norfolk. Ideas for getting started with the *Index* are developed further in Part 3.

1. Get started – starting anywhere, even by finding and sharing one interesting question, is much better than not starting at all.
2. Keep brief records of your work with a note-book and camera.
3. Involve others with like minds.
4. If you are not a senior member of staff try to involve someone who is.
5. Ask a young person or adult who you do not usually consult about their priorities for development in the setting.
6. Start by making a small change that is within your power.
7. Make a list of current initiatives in the school. How can the *Index* connect them together?
8. Explore the framework of values in Part 2 of the *Index*. What activity could you change in the school so that actions more closely reflect your values?
9. Consider a change that you and/or others are hoping or trying to make. Perhaps this is already in your development plan. Find the most relevant indicator. Use it to refine your plan.
10. If you are working on your own, find someone with experience of working with the *Index* to support you.

4 Barbara Brokamp, Montag Stiftung Jugend und Gesellschaft, *Practical Hints*.

5 Suzanne Carrington and Robin Robinson, personal communication

1 Overview of the *Index*

"Working with the Index *has revitalized our school improvement planning enabling us to look at issues and concerns in a very different way. We have loved working with it and will continue to do so..."*

– June Sewell, George White Junior School

"The Index *has been like a critical friend, asking the questions which help you to look at an issue differently and then drive forward improvements."*

– Elly Roberts, Highgate Infant School

"The Index *has provided a framework for looking at how everyone gets involved in our school community. It has given us structures and prompts to seek views and opinions about how we can make our school better. By focusing on the values of participation and community it has allowed us to work together to achieve the best outcomes for all."*

– Nick Southgate, Colman Infant School

"The Index *has led to a collaborative working relationship with two other schools, to improve outcomes for children. We have used the Index as a vehicle for exploring pupil voice and community participation in worthwhile projects. It has been fantastic to see the enthusiasm of pupils when exploring and discussing ways of working together. I believe this partnership working will continue to grow."*

– Coral Brinklow, Caister Junior

"I have used the Index as a vehicle to help to refocus on the school values; it has… given the scaffolding to enable stake-holders to become actively involved in school improvement. I would recommend the Index to any school that is starting on the journey of school improvement, it has really helped me."

– Jane Jewson, King Edward VII High

"The Index *has led to collaboration between our primary school, Caistor Junior and Caistor High. The pupils have particularly enjoyed working with those older than themselves… They are proud to be represeneing our school but also the new interschool 'Councils" they have become part of.*

A brilliant experience for both pupils and staff." – Edward Savage, Hemsby Primary

Overview of the *Index*

How can the Index help you to develop your school?

The *Index for inclusion: a guide to school development led by inclusive values* is a set of materials to support the review and development of all aspects of a setting; in playgrounds, staffrooms and classrooms and surrounding communities and environments. It encourages wide participation in the development and implementation of inclusive improvement plans.

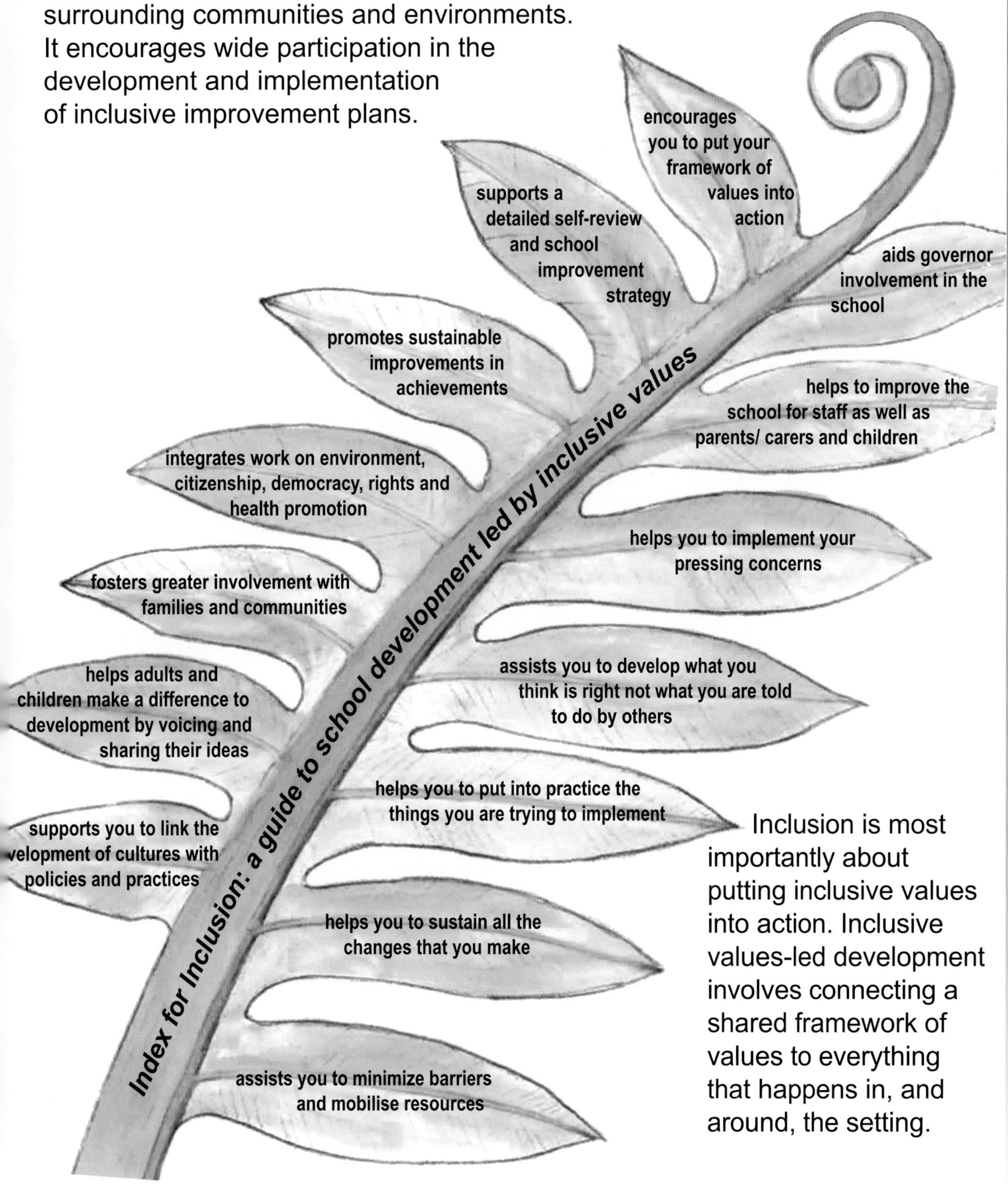

Inclusion is most importantly about putting inclusive values into action. Inclusive values-led development involves connecting a shared framework of values to everything that happens in, and around, the setting.

How are schools changed?

Schools are always changing, in all sorts of ways for all sorts of reasons. Only some of these changes happen as a result of an agreed plan to which everyone is committed.

Changes may not be consistent with each other or with development according to inclusive values …

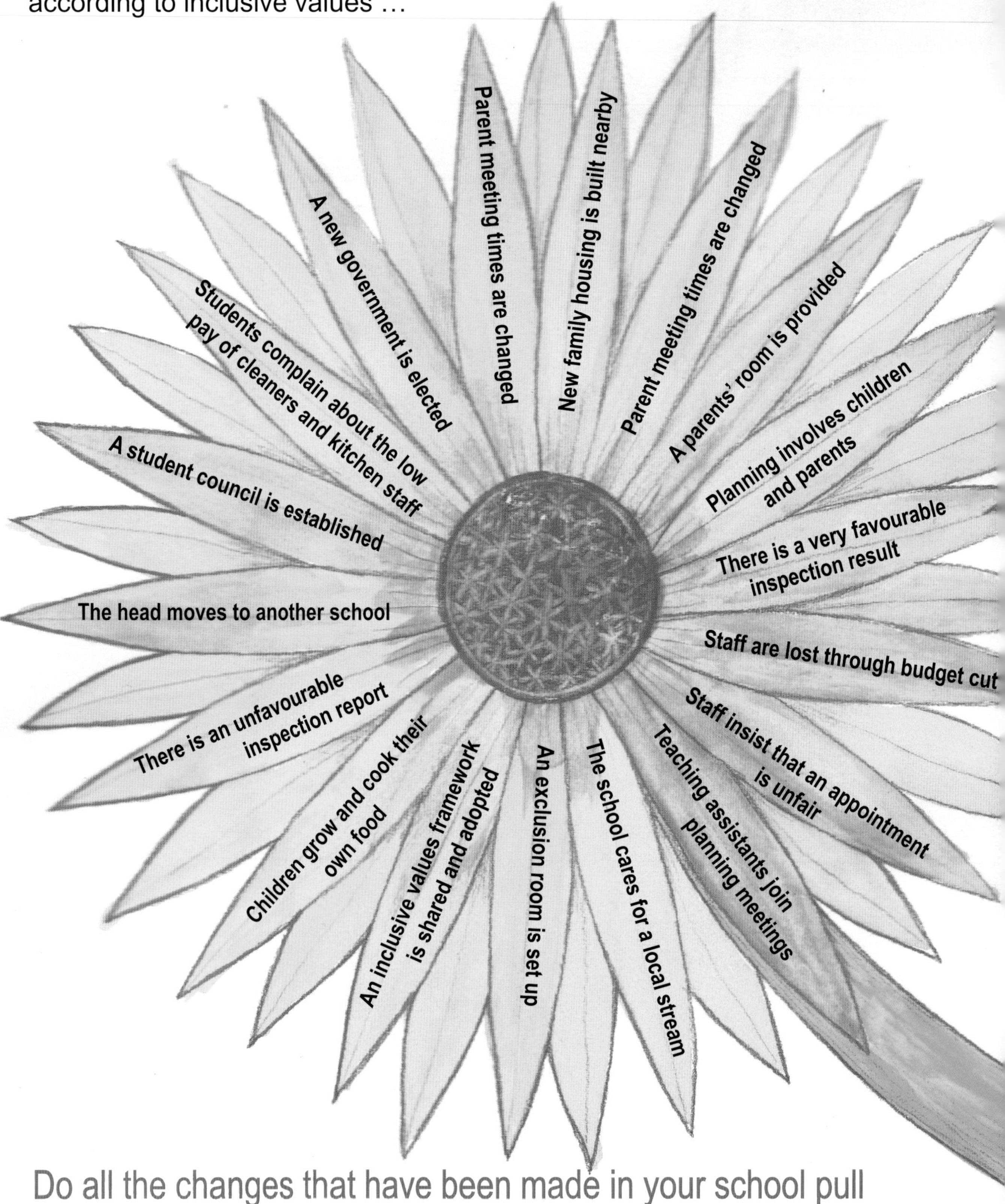

Do all the changes that have been made in your school pull in the same direction?

What is inclusive development?

We recognise change as development or improvement when it reflects our values. It becomes inclusive development when it is led by inclusive values.

Doing the right thing involves connecting actions and values. Relating our actions to values can be the most practical step in developing your school.

Values are deep-seated beliefs that push us to act. We understand values through actions rather than words. Fine words become headings for values when we connect them to our deep beliefs, give them detailed meaning and then act upon them.

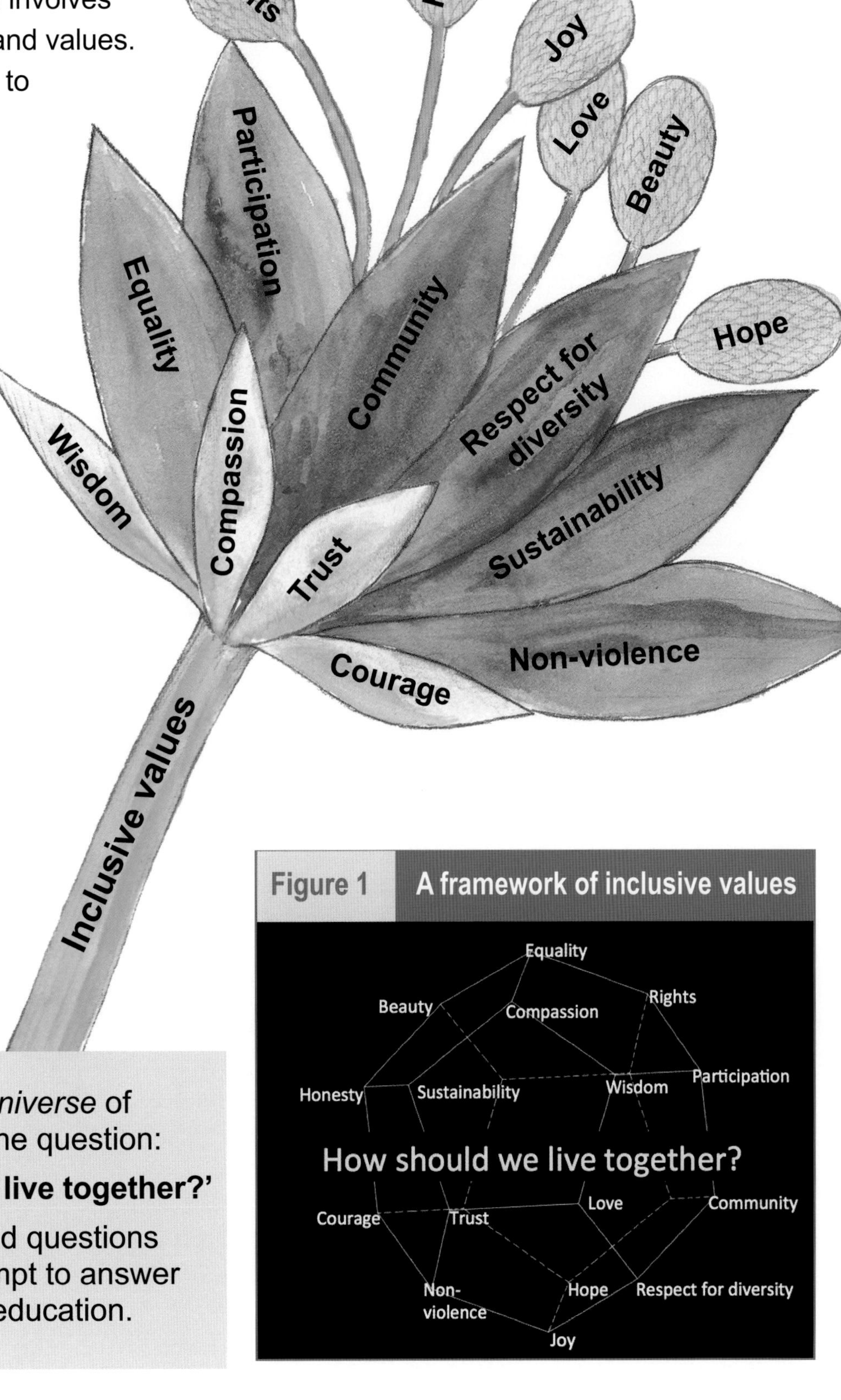

Figure 1 A framework of inclusive values

A framework or *universe* of values answers the question:

'How should we live together?'

The indicators and questions of the *Index* attempt to answer this question for education.

The dimensions, sections and indicators of the *Index*

Dimension A: Creating inclusive cultures

A1: Building community

A2: Establishing inclusive values

Dimension B: Producing inclusive policies

B1: Developing the school for all

B2: Organising support for diversity

Dimension C: Evolving inclusive policies

C1: Constructing curricula for all

C2: Orchestrating learning

Each indicator, or aspiration for development, is given meaning by questions which tie down its meaning and provide ideas for development.

C2.3 Children are encouraged to be confident critical thinkers.

C2.4 Children are actively involved in their own learning.

Each indicator starts with suggestions about its relationship with other indicators.

a) Do staff support each other to be confident critical thinkers?

b) Is it understood that dialogue works best when people set aside differences of power and perceived status?

c) Do staff demonstrate that they respect and value alternative views?

d) Are children and adults encouraged to express their point of view assertively without aggression?

e) Are debates encouraged so that people get to hear, and practise expressing, points of view other than their own?

f) Are children encouraged to develop and express views and feelings about important local, national and international events, such as when their country is at war or there has been a catastrophe in their own or another country?

g) Are children encouraged to ask challenging questions?

h) Do those on different sides of arguments recognise the importance of other views in clarifying opinions and reaching joint solutions to problems?

i) Do children learn to detect contradictions in their own and other people's arguments?

j) Do children and adults learn to weigh up the strength of arguments including their own?

k) Do children learn when the truth of an assertion or argument requires supporting evidence?

l) Do children learn how to use examples to support an argument?

m) Do children learn how carefully chosen examples can show the limits to generalisations?

n) Do children learn to ask 'to what extent..?' and 'under what circumstances...?' questions when people assert that something is true about the world (for example about differences between genders)?

o) Do children learn how to assess the audience to which a piece of writing is intended to appeal?

p) Do children learn how people take for granted that certain arguments are correct, even when they are not, because they seem to carry the voice of authority?

q) Do children and adults identify the beliefs and values that underlie differences of view?

r) Are children and adults helped to increase their fluency in argument?

s) Do children learn about the pressures on them to think and act in particular ways?

t) Do children explore the reasons for the opinions they express?

u) Are all those taking part in dialogue supported to retain their self-esteem?

v) Do people avoid triumphalism when they feel they have won an argument?

w) Do child and adult mentors help others to contribute their views?

x) Is particular attention paid to helping those who are shy about speaking up, to make a contribution?

aa) ____________________

ab) ____________________

ac) ____________________

This is to show that you can add your own questions. There is no limit to the questions that could be asked.

Support for curriculum development

Section C1 in the *Index* outlines a novel way of dividing up teaching and learning activities under 13 subject headings. It offers additions to, and re-combinations of, traditional subjects as a curriculum for the 21st century. It is being used to help schools to expand their curricula so that they better connect with the experience of children, young people and their families. It arises from the values, principles and imperatives promoted within the *Index*.

It is intended as an international and interconnecting curriculum, making sense in any area of the world. It is a way of dividing up knowledge for everyone – inside and outside schools – throughout life.

It provides an answer to the question:

'What do we need to know in order to live together well?'

Figure 2 Subjects for a 21st century curriculum

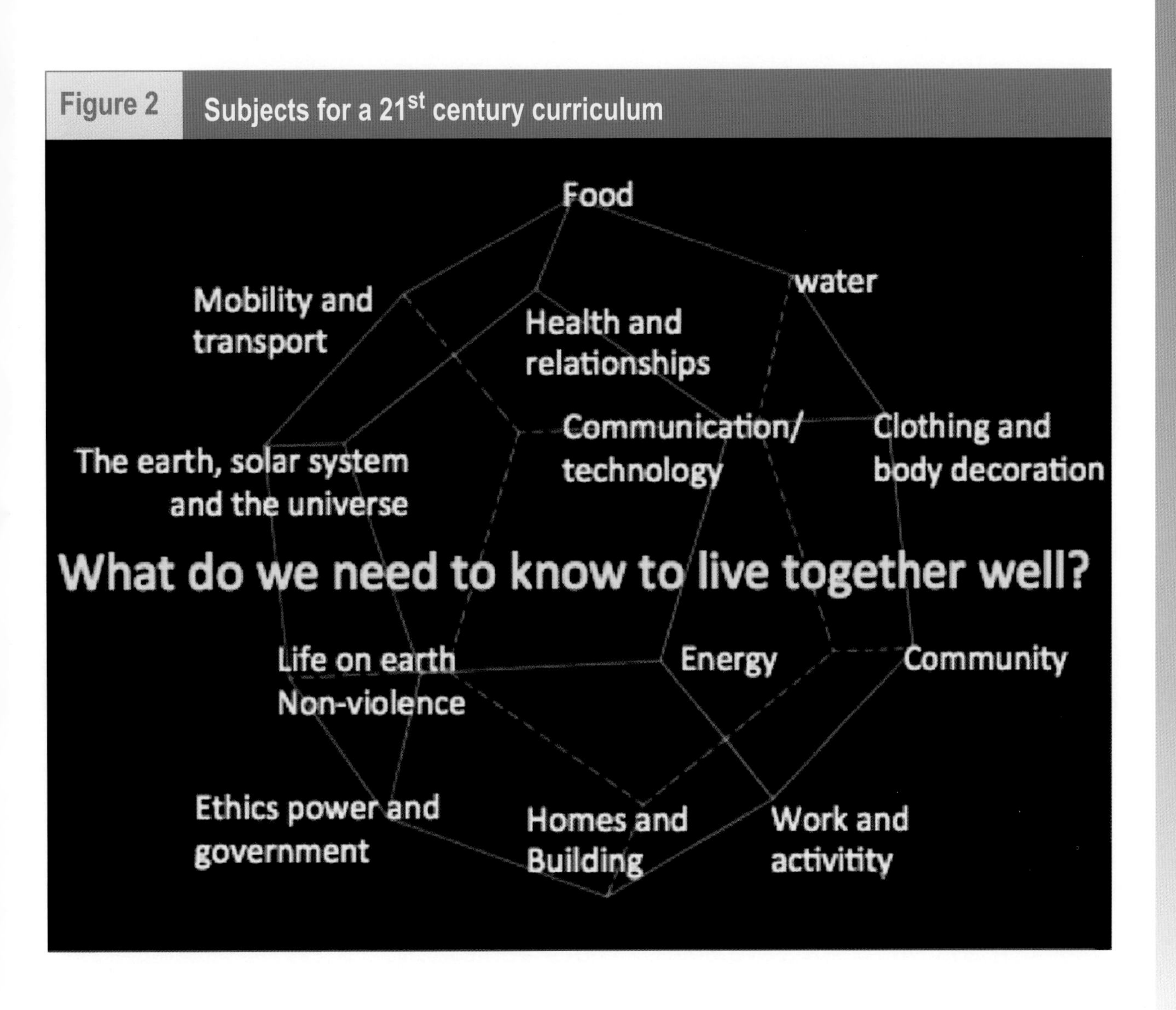

Development led by inclusive values draws together all principled approaches to the development of schools ...

Schools are involved in many activities to promote their development which share values with the *Index*. The *Index* helps to draw these together into a single approach; a single tree drawing strength from many roots.

Making these connections reduces policy fragmentation and initiative overload. It builds alliances for working together on inclusive values-led development. But it does not matter if 'Inclusion', 'Inclusive values into action', 'democratic education', or some other word or phrase is chosen to express this common purpose. This choice is far less important than making explicit the links between activities arising from shared values so that they reinforce each other. And for us it is of greater significant that you guide development with a framework of inclusive values than that you use the *Index for Inclusion*.

How do you work with the *Index*?

Your use of the *Index* can start anywhere: with the changes in practice that arise from a focus on values into action; examining the implications for development of an indicator and its questions that were already of special concern to you or have become so following an inspection; with a focus on a single question to prompt dialogue; an interest in reviewing aspects of the curriculum; or as a way to make sense of a number of separate interventions in a school.

The *Index* encourages wide involvement in review and improvement activities from staff, children, families and governors. Broadening involvement is itself part of inclusive development. It helps to release the mass of knowledge and energy for action within the communities of the setting.

But while you can start anywhere, the *Index* may be used most powerfully when it helps to develop, and then becomes integrated into, routine planning and development processes.

The *Index* is divided into three dimensions to structure development of the setting:

Cultures reflect relationships and deeply held values and beliefs. Changing cultures is essential for sustained development.

Policies are concerned with how the school is run and plans to change it.

Practices are about what is learnt and taught and how it is learnt and taught.

Each dimension is divided into two sections. The dimensions and sections can form a planning framework so that attention is paid to all areas that need to be developed if changes are to be sustained.

Figure 3 **Index dimensions of development**

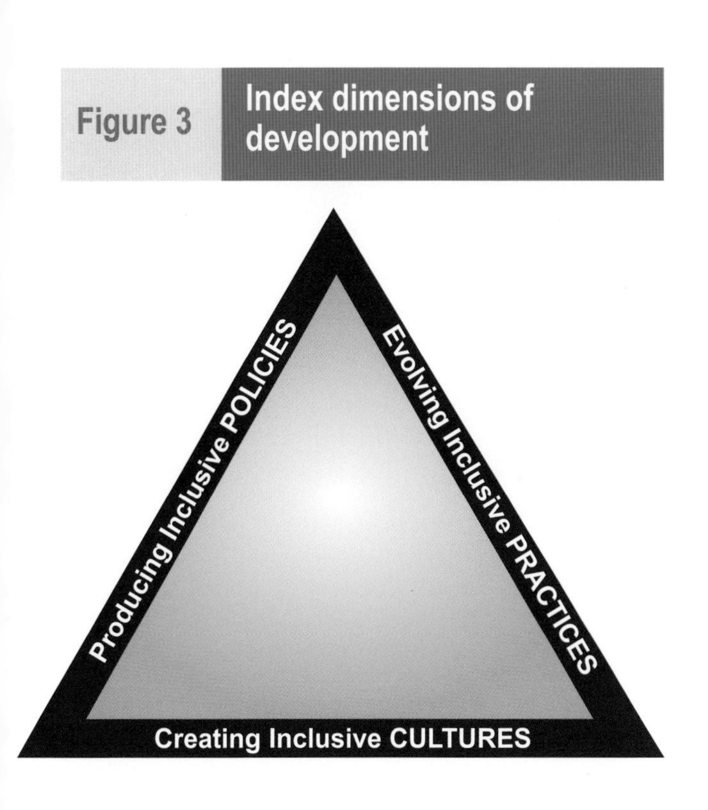

Figure 4 **Planning Framework**

Dimension A:
Creating inclusive cultures
A1: Building community
A2: Establishing inclusive values

Dimension B:
Producing inclusive policies
A1: Developing the school for all
A2: Organising support for diversity

Dimension C:
Evolving inclusive practices
A1: Constructing curricula for all
A2: Orchestrating learning

How can the index help you to respond to external pressures?

All schools are subjected to external pressures including Inspection, national tests and government policies and guidance. The *Index* can help schools to respond to such requirements in ways that reflect their values.

Responding to inspection

We have mapped the *Index* indicators onto the Ofsted inspection framework showing how they address all its concerns as part of a coherent approach to development. See our website for the latest version of this document: indexforinclusion.org. Participatory self-evaluation supported by the *Index* can be used to provide convincing evidence of activities for the self-review required by the framework. After an inspection the *Index* can supply ideas for immediate action on the recommendations of Ofsted reports. This is particularly valuable when, following an unfavourable report, morale can be low. As one head teacher remarked "the *Index* adds clarity and focus to Ofsted".

Dealing with numbers

Comparisons of performance on tests and examinations, between schools, and over years in the same school, have been most significant in determining the rating schools receive after an inspection. This happens even when they are statistically dubious because the numbers for comparison are small or the cohort being measured has changed, because of communities joining or leaving the school.

Reconsidering appraisal

Where relationships are collaborative, appraisal - the regular review of how staff are working and being supported - builds on the detailed everyday knowledge that staff already have of each other's work and should rarely throw up new information or tasks. Yet in other settings people may be handed targets that do not make sense to them and may not reflect their deepest aspirations for the wellbeing and progress of children. Performance related pay linked to the successful meeting of targets can also undermine staff relations when decisions seem unfair. The *Index* approach can be used to ensure that an appraisal policy is consistent with the schools values.

Producing development plans

Development plans can be written in such a way as to be real working documents that are accessible for staff. children and their families and lift everyone's spirits. They do not need to be written according to a formula supplied by a national website or local authority. The involvement of children and young people in shaping the schools development priorities can be integrated into valuable teaching and learning activities. Pictorial plans designed by adults and children at the school might be produced as was done on a course on the *Index* for colleagues from Ukraine.

2 A singular approach to the development of your school

A singular approach to the development of your school

In Part 2 we introduce a distinctive approach to inclusive school development. We define inclusion as **putting inclusive values into action**. We provide a framework of values as a foundation for principled, practical intervention in education – an answer to the question 'how should be live together?'. We offer a set of inclusive pedagogical principles. We outline a curriculum, or way of dividing up knowledge, for the 21st century linked to *Index* values, principles and imperatives. This provides an answer to the question: 'What do we need to know in order to live together well?' It fills a longstanding gap in discussions of values-led development and inclusive teaching and learning.

We show how the approach in the *Index* can draw together principled views of educational development to do with rights, democratic participation, environmental sustainability, global citizenship, health promotion, non-violence and anti- discrimination. We argue that these overlapping concerns are best implemented when co-ordinated into a single approach.

The concepts of 'barriers to learning and participation', 'resources to support learning and participation' and 'support for diversity' are a way to direct a shared open exploration of the knowledge already possessed within a school and to raise ideas for further investigation. We introduce the review materials of the *Index* structured into three dimensions for development to do with *cultures, policies and practices*. The indicators and questions invite reflection on what inclusive values imply for activity in all aspects of a school, its environments and communities. They also help to identify barriers and resources. Together with the questionnaires these materials provide a further means to build on what is already known by shaping a review of the fine detail of what is going on, in order to produce and implement an inclusive development plan. The *Index* thus brings together more systematic development planning with the changes improvised as adults and children live out their shared values, moment-to-moment, in collaborating communities.

A guide to school development led by inclusive values

The *Index for inclusion: a guide to school development led by inclusive values* offers a supportive process of self-review and development as an alternative to one based on inspection, competition and fear of failure. The *Index* provides you with an opportunity to develop your school in collaboration with others in accordance with your principles. It can be used in many different ways. It can help to clarify thinking and prompt individual and collective action as well as structure educational development for a school and its communities. It can be used by teachers, non-teaching staff, governors, parents/carers and young people as a way of examining and improving their schools. It can prompt new dialogues about what children might learn inside and outside schools.

The materials are designed to build on the wealth of knowledge and experience of staff, children, young people and their families about the nature of their setting and how it can be improved. The process of working with the *Index* allows these rich resources to be shared and to make a difference. It is a comprehensive document that can help everyone to find their next steps in developing a setting. However successful and inclusive a school is thought to be currently, the *Index* can be used to support the unending processes involved in developing learning and participation for all and reducing all exclusionary pressures.

When people first open the *Index* they can find the amount of ideas within it overwhelming. Yet as they learn to focus on one or a few issues at a time, they realise the significance of having such a comprehensive document. Like a guide book to a city or a country, the *Index* enables people to select the places that they wish to visit, leaving open the possibility of a return trip when other places might be explored. The *Index*, then, can assist people in working together to decide what they want to develop next, draw up a plan and carry it out. However, just as some people do not plan a visit to a country in minute detail in advance and just land up in a place and then start to explore, so people can find a part of the *Index* that interests them, perhaps even a single question, and spread their enquiries and action from there.

The *Index* is not an additional initiative but a way of improving schools according to inclusive values. It is not an alternative to raising achievements but is concerned with all the achievements of all children, young people and adults. It encourages active learning in which children integrate what they are taught with their own experience and engage with the realities of their worlds. It is a practical document, inviting reflection on what putting inclusive values into action might mean for all aspects of schools: in staffrooms, classrooms, playgrounds, in relationships within the school and with families and communities. It emphasises changes in cultures, so that developments are sustained.

The entrance hall to many schools contains a statement of values and documents, shields and plaques certifying that the school has achieved a standard in the promotion of such issues as environmental sustainability, rights, health, good organisation. We have wondered whether there is an incompatibility in granting an award for inclusion, since the putting into action of inclusive values might be its own reward. We would not wish any certificate to suggest that a school has reached a final destination of development. Schools are always changing; children and staff arrive and move on; new forms of exclusion arise; new resources are mobilised. Inclusive development is a never-ending process. The only sense in which a school is 'inclusive' is when it is committed to a development journey guided by inclusive values. However we do support the idea of schools celebrating the completion of a period of work with the *Index* by designing their own record of their achievements with contributions from staff, parents and children.

Inviting dialogue

At the heart of the *Index* are many hundreds of questions any one of which might become the start of extended reflection and provoke further questions and answers. The materials of the *Index* therefore do not prescribe what people should do or think but are there to promote dialogue. When two or more people are in dialogue there is a mutual exploration of each other's opinions and assumptions on the basis of equality, honesty and trust. Listening becomes more important than talking. Attachment to previous positions is loosened, at least temporarily, so that shared investigation is felt as genuine by all those involved. What counts as movement in conversation is negotiated and such movement becomes a shared responsibility. Dialogue has been contrasted with discussion, derived from the same root as 'percussion' and 'concussion'.[6] Though discussion can also have a gentler meaning, the contrast can be instructive.

Figure 5 Inclusion in education involves:

- Putting inclusive values into action.
- Viewing every life and every death as of equal worth.
- Supporting everyone to feel that they belong.
- Increasing participation in learning and teaching activities, relationships and communities of local schools.
- Improving schools for staff and parents/carers as well as children.
- Reducing exclusion, discrimination, barriers to learning and participation.
- Learning from the reduction of barriers for some children to benefit children more widely.
- Restructuring cultures, policies and practices to respond to diversity in ways that value everyone equally.
- Linking education to local and global realities.
- Viewing differences between children and between adults as resources for learning.
- Acknowledging the right of children to an education of high quality in their locality.
- Emphasising the development of school communities and values, as well as achievements.
- Fostering mutually sustaining relationships between schools and surrounding communities.
- Recognising that inclusion in education is one aspect of inclusion in society.

Clarifying inclusion

Inclusion in the *Index*, then, is a principled approach to the development of education and society. It is linked to democratic participation within and beyond education. It is not about an aspect of education to do with a particular group of children. It is concerned with bringing coherence to development activities that take place under a variety of headings so that they encourage the learning and participation of everyone: children and their families, staff and governors and other community members.

Everyone has their own meaning for inclusion. Complex concepts like inclusion, cannot be captured within a single sentence. In fact, many people find that their notion of inclusion becomes clearer as they engage with the indicators and questions of the *Index*. Examining these practical implications of inclusion can lead to greater consensus than extensive theoretical discussions divorced from a consideration of action.

Some features of our approach to inclusion are summarised in Figure 5. We see inclusion as a never-ending process concerned with the involvement of individuals, the creation of participatory systems and settings, and the promotion of inclusive values. In each case it involves increasing participation for everyone in the cultures, communities and curricula of local settings, and reducing all forms of exclusion and discrimination. It is concerned with listening to the voices of children and acting on them. But it is as much concerned with families and with staff in schools as it is with children. We cannot see how support for the participation of children can be embraced to any great extent if the adults who work with them have no say in decisions about the detail of their working lives. Yet people commonly think of inclusion as concerned with the participation of children with impairments or those categorised as 'having special educational needs'. We see this view as problematic, not least because we could define inclusion in this narrow way in relation to any one of a number of advocacy issues, to do with age, gender, sexual orientation, ethnicity, class as well as disability. We discuss this further on pages 40-43 in addressing the idea of using

6 Boem, D., (1996) *On Dialogue*, London, Routledge.

'barriers to learning and participation' to replace the notion of 'special educational needs'.

Ideas about inclusion are confused by the way the term 'social inclusion' has been used. It is sometimes used to mean 'overcoming deprivation', such as poverty and inadequate housing, though at other times it seems to mean overcoming the stigma associated with disadvantage rather than disadvantage itself. Social inclusion is also used in government documents and by educators to mean overcoming 'difficulties with behaviour'. One teacher taking part in a research project[7] introduced herself and a colleague with the words: 'I'm inclusion – special needs, and she's social inclusion – naughty boys'. But the idea that 'inclusion' should refer to one group while 'social inclusion' refers to another is unhelpful. Since inclusion is often seen to refer to people with impairments it can encourage a belief that they are subjected to a kind of non-social exclusion which arises naturally as a direct result of their impairment. All forms of inclusion and exclusion are social, arising in interactions between people and environments.

Increasing inclusion involves reducing exclusion. It involves combating the exclusionary pressures that impede participation. Since we are trying to promote a coherent view of how to develop schools, we prefer to define our concepts for ourselves. Yet 'exclusion' is often used in a specific way following the 1986 Education Act to refer to 'disciplinary exclusion', the temporary or permanent removal of a child from a school over breaches of school rules. Yet, the removal of children from schools for disciplinary reasons generally marks a particular stage in the playing out of exclusionary processes..

Increasing participation for everyone cannot be accomplished by a focus on individuals. The participation of individuals who have been subjected to exclusionary pressures will be limited unless a school is welcoming and responsive to diversity *in ways that value everyone equally*. It is not sufficient to require our systems and settings to simply respond to the diversity of children since this can be satisfied through the creation of a hierarchy of value within and between schools. Schools may respond to diversity, for example, by selecting children according to attainment, disability, religion and wealth. Divisions on the basis of attainment within and between schools, is generally bolstered by the ascription of ability labels to children from a very young age. This constrains thinking about future achievements and affects self-expectations[8]. When they value everyone equally, schools welcome all children within their surrounding communities. Inclusion is therefore linked to the development of the common school for all; to comprehensive community education in nursery, primary and secondary schools.

However, in addition to focusing on the wellbeing of individuals and the responsiveness of settings, inclusion is most importantly seen as putting inclusive values into action. This linking of school improvement to the putting into action of a framework of values can transform schools. It is a commitment to particular values which accounts for a wish to overcome exclusion and promote participation. If it is not related to deeply held values then the pursuit of inclusion may represent conformity to a prevailing fashion or compliance with instructions from above.

Values are fundamental guides and prompts to action. They spur us forward, give us a

7 Ainscow, M., Booth, T. and Dyson, A. (2006) *Improving schools, developing inclusion*. London, Routledge.

8 Hart, S., Dixon, A., Drummond, M.J. and McIntyre, D. (2006) *Learning without limits*, Buckingham, Open University Press. http://learningwithoutlimits.educ.cam.ac.uk

Developing a framework of values

sense of direction and define a destination. We cannot know that we are doing, or have done, the right thing without understanding the relationship between our actions and our values. For all actions affecting others are underpinned by values. Every such action becomes a moral argument whether or not we are aware of it. It is a way of saying 'this is the right thing to do'. In developing a framework of values we state how we want to live and educate each other together, now and in the future. Values are part of cultures. As people in schools develop a shared framework of values and understand their connection to detailed action then this helps to sustain the changes that they make in their policies or classroom practices.

Most schools already have a statement of values. The distinguishing feature of values in the *Index* is that they are meant to influence the detail of practice and to become a force for pushing forward school development. Being clear about the relationship between values and actions is the most practical step we can take in education. We are guided to know what we should do next and to understand the actions of others. The *Index* invites you to derive educational development in your schools from actions arising from your own deeply held values rather than from a series of programmes or initiatives designed by others underpinned by values that you may reject as they become apparent.

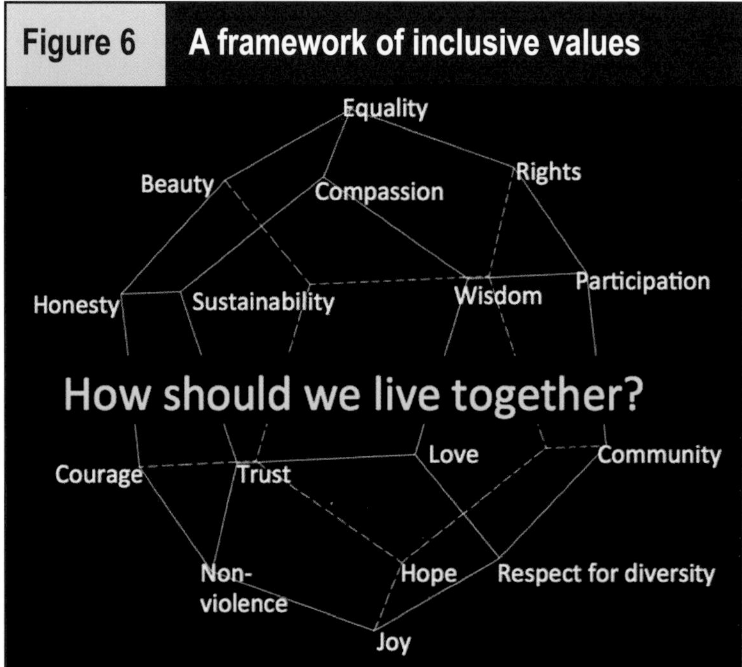

A careful piecing together of a framework of values which together support the inclusive development of education has resulted in a list of headings concerned with *equality, rights, participation, community, respect for diversity, sustainability, non-violence, trust, compassion, honesty, courage, joy, love, hope/optimism, beauty and wisdom*. Each of these words stands for a value, which is only to be understood through a more detailed exploration of its meaning as begun below. Each value summarises an area of action and aspiration for education and society more widely. The list the result of numerous discussions with teachers, students and others in the UK and around the world. For example, a final decision to include the linked values of honesty, trust and courage arose from a series of workshops with a previous edition of the *Index* in which colleagues in senior positions in schools described the process of building the courage to be honest about weaknesses as well as strengths in their schools and how this was helped in the workshops by engaging on a common task with others who were trusted to be supportive and not to criticise and blame.

Many have said how much they like the values flower on page 11, but we also like to represent a framework of inclusive values three dimensions as in Figure 6. This helps to create an image of a an all encompassing universe of mutually supporting and interacting meanings.

In the last edition of the *Index* we suggested that some values make a greater contribution to inclusive development than others. We now see this as unhelpful. In the very many discussions we have had in schools in the last years we have been struck by how different people choose different starting values for their explorations of how to put values into action. Commonly they end up by pointing out the interconnections between all the values in the framework. If you doubt the contribution of a particular value, try subtracting it from education. What would education be like without trust, honesty, courage compassion, joy, love, hope or beauty? We like to think that schools can strive to be places that nourish the human spirit. But it would also be strange to argue for a concern with the inclusion of everyone in schools and then omit from one's framework the headings of equality, rights, participation and community. Rights arise from valuing equality but are included separately because of the strategic importance of the concept of rights in promoting recognition of the equal worth of people and countering discrimination.

During the development of this work it was argued by some that a concern for environmental sustainability and the reduction of environmental degradation such as is happening through global warming, were unconnected to the idea of inclusion. This may be because we tend to think about issues in their own separate boxes, which is itself an exclusionary tendency. But once one recognises the fundamental significance for the survival of present and future generations of living in viable environments then the link becomes clear. The inundation that will affect large areas of land around the world unless global temperature rises are severely restricted will take away communities, their homes, their schools and ways of life. We give some values such as, sustainability, the status of imperatives for educational development.

Equality

Equality and related notions of equity, fairness and justice are central to inclusive values. Inequality, inequity, unfairness and injustice are forms of exclusion. Equality is not about everyone being the same or being treated in the same way but about everyone being treated as of equal worth. This has implications for how adults and children behave towards each other in schools. It affects the way children are grouped between and within schools and classes, so that hierarchies of worth are avoided. It concerns, too, the way schools are managed. An inclusive view of equality is not about 'equality of opportunity' to unequal status, wealth and living conditions but about reducing such inequalities.

Reflection on the acceptability to people of inequalities nationally and globally, in wealth or living conditions, reveals deep disagreements about inclusion. Often, people do not behave as if 'every life and every death are of equal value' not just because they are naturally more concerned about those closest to them but because they do not think that the suffering of others outside their own families, neighbourhoods or country should prompt action to reduce it.

Rights

A focus on rights builds on a concern with equality. It is a way of expressing the equal worth of people since they hold rights equally. To invoke rights is to argue that everyone has equal entitlements to freedom from want and freedom to act. So everyone has an equal right to food, shelter, protection and care and to participation as citizens. Where actions lead to inequality then they cannot involve a right. This is a constraint on any idea of rights of choice or property ownership if this exacerbates inequality for others to exercise their rights. Children and young people have a right to free, public (that is state provided) education of high quality in their locality. The promotion of human rights within education encourages the development of reciprocal and caring relationships.

People sometimes wish to link rights and responsibilities, but this is mistaken if there is any implication that the granting of rights is conditional on behaving in a certain way. Rights are unconditional, possessed by virtue of our humanity. But rights can conflict and this can mean, for example, that one person's right to safety can involve restrictions on the freedom of another. It is evident that like equality, rights are also disputed in practice, despite an apparent commitment to abide by their expression in United Nations documents. This is evident from widespread disregard for them around the world and lack of attempts to address breaches of them. A consideration of human rights can also lead to questions about the treatment of non-humans and the idea of extending rights to all forms of life and even to the integrity of the planet (see page194). Rights are the starting point for school improvement in the UNICEF 'Rights respecting schools' award.[9]

Participation

Participation in education settings for staff, young people and their families is also frequently not sought. Participation goes beyond, but starts with, simply being there. Participation involves two elements to do with participatory action or activity and the

9 http://www.unicef.org.uk/rights-respecting-schools/

participating self. A person participates not only when they are involved in common activities but also when they feel involved and accepted. Participation is about being with and collaborating with others. It is about active engagement in learning. It is about involvement in decisions about one's life, including education and links to ideas of democracy and freedom. It also entails the important right not to participate, to assert one's autonomy against the group by saying: 'no'. This may involve courage. When we are conscious of the source and nature of our actions, intentions and feelings, this can help us to actively participate. Participation involves dialogue with others on the basis of equality and thus requires the deliberate setting aside of differences of status and power. Participation is increased when engaging with others reinforces a sense of identity; when we are accepted and valued for ourselves.

Respect for diversity

Inclusive respect involves valuing others and treating them well, recognising the contributions they make to a community because of their individuality as well as through their positive actions. It does not mean deferring to people because of their position of status or authority. 'Diversity' includes seen and unseen differences and similarities between people: diversity is about difference within a common humanity. Diversity encompasses everyone, not just those seen to depart from an illusory normality. However, its use is sometimes corrupted so that 'diversity' becomes linked with 'otherness'; those not like us. Groups and communities are seen as homogeneous when differences within them are unrecognised.

An inclusive response to diversity welcomes the creation of diverse groups and respects the equal worth of others regardless of their perceived difference. On this view diversity is a rich resource for life and learning, rather than a problem to be overcome. This response contrasts with a selective view which attempts to maintain uniformity by categorizing and dividing people and assigning them to groups arranged according to a hierarchy of value. But the valuing of diversity has its limits. It does not mean that we accept or value the destructive efforts of people towards others or the environment, involving the infringement of rights, even if this is firmly integrated into their identities.

A rejection of difference commonly involves the denial of otherness in ourselves. So, when people do not want to acknowledge their own potential for impairment and old age this can reinforce their wish to separate themselves from and discriminate against old or disabled people. An inclusive approach to diversity involves understanding and opposing the profoundly destructive dangers in equating difference or strangeness with inferiority. When this becomes deeply embedded in a culture, it can lead to virulent discrimination or even genocide.[10]

Community

A concern with building community involves a recognition that we live in relationship with others and that friendships are fundamental to our wellbeing. Community is built through cultures which encourage collaboration. An inclusive view of community extends attachment and obligation beyond family and friendships to a broader fellow feeling. It is linked to a sense of responsibility for others and to ideas of public service, citizenship, global citizenship and a recognition of global interdependence. An inclusive school community provides a model of what it means to be a responsible and active citizen whose rights are respected outside school. Inclusive communities are always open to, and enriched by, new members who contribute to their transformation. In education, inclusion involves developing mutually sustaining relationships within schools and between schools and their surrounding communities. A concern with community is about acting collaboratively, with collegiality and in solidarity; it leads to an understanding of how progress in changing institutions can be best achieved when people join their actions together.

Sustainability

The most fundamental aim of education is to prepare children and young people for sustainable ways of life within sustainable

10 This last sentence requires a reference to Primo Levi 1996, *Survival in Auschwitz*, New York, Collier Books, p9: "Many people – many nations – can find themselves holding, more or less wittingly, that 'every stranger is an enemy'. For the most part, this conviction lies deep down, like some latent infection; it betrays itself only in random, disconnected acts and does not lie at the base of a system of reason. But when this does come about, when the unspoken dogma becomes a major premise in a syllogism, then at the end of the chain there is [the death camp]."

communities and environments, locally and globally. A commitment to inclusive values must involve a commitment to the well-being of future generations. Discussions of inclusion always beg the question: 'inclusion into what?' Schools developing in inclusive ways are places that encourage the sustainable development of everyone's learning and participation and the lasting reduction of exclusion and discrimination. They avoid making unco-ordinated changes only for the short-term, signing up to programmes and initiatives which are not linked closely into their own longterm commitments. Environmental sustainability is central to inclusion at a time when environmental degradation, deforestation, and global warming threaten the quality of the life of us all and are already undermining the lives of millions around the world. Schools developing inclusively have to be concerned with maintaining the physical and natural environment inside and beyond their boundaries. But 'ecological literacy' has to grow out of an understanding of, and respect for, nature, rather than a terror of catastrophe. It has to be linked to hope and optimism that hazards can be overcome. To be sustainable, all changes have to be integrated into cultures and through them to the development of changed identities.

Non-violence

Non-violence requires listening to, and understanding, the point of view of others and weighing up the strength of arguments, including one's own. It requires the development of skills of negotiation, mediation and conflict resolution in children and adults. It requires adults to model non-violence in their own conduct. Within communities of equals, disputes are resolved through dialogue rather than coercion derived from differences in status and physical strength. This does not mean that people avoid challenging or being challenged and deny disagreement, but that they use challenge to provoke reflection and invention.[11] Bullying happens when people abuse their power in order to make another feel vulnerable, physically or psychologically. The harassment and bullying of people because of their ethnicity, gender, disability, age, sexual orientation, beliefs and religion are all forms of violence. A commitment to non-violence may involve challenging ways of resolving conflicts associated with some versions of masculinity and hence a need to offer alternative routes to a robust male identity. It leads to a dissection of notions of 'losing face' and 'losing respect' and their links to 'revenge'. It necessitates a balance to be found between assertion and aggression. Anger is seen as an important indication of the strength of one's feelings about a person or event but is to be directed into productive action and away from aggressive response. Institutional violence or institutional bullying may occur when the humanity and dignity of those within institutions are not respected; when people are treated as a means to an end. This can happen when schools or other educational institutions are treated as businesses or are so concerned with results that the well-being of students or staff is neglected. Non-violent institutions are developed in harmony with the needs of the people within them, with the environment and with their surrounding communities.

Trust

Trust supports participation and the development of relationships and secure identities. It is required to encourage independent and unobserved learning and the establishment of dialogue. Education can help to build trust for children and young people in others outside their families, and may involve considered discussion of the nature of safe and unsafe encounters with others. This can be especially important for those who feel vulnerable at home or have been made to feel distrustful in the past because of an experience of routine discrimination. Trust is closely related to ideas of responsibility and trustworthiness. Trust is needed for the development of self-respect and mutual respect in professional practice. The less people are trusted, the less trustworthy they may become.[13] Trust that others will listen and respond fairly is required if difficult issues which impede educational development are to be uncovered and addressed: people feel free to speak their minds when they trust that others will engage in respectful dialogue without seeking an advantage.

11 This owes a reference to John Dewey, in Boydston, J. (ed) (1988) John Dewey, Human Nature and Conduct 1922, *Morals are human , Middle Works 1899-1924*, Vol.14, p. 207. Also see DEWEY-L archive posting by Richard Hake (2005): 'Conflict is the gadfly of thought. It stirs us to observation and memory. It instigates invention. It shocks us out of sheep-like passivity, and sets us at noting and contriving.

12 O'Neill, O. (2002) A question of trust, Reith Lectures

Honesty

Honesty is not just the free expression of the truth. Dishonesty may have more to do with the deliberate omission of information than with direct lying. Purposely withholding information from, or misleading, others impedes their participation. It can be a means for those with power to control those with less power. Honesty involves avoiding hypocrisy in advocating one thing while doing another. It involves keeping promises. While honesty is linked to integrity and sincerity, it is also related to values of courage and trust. It is harder to be honest when it requires courage and easier where others can be trusted to be supportive. Honesty in education involves sharing knowledge with young people about local and global realities; encouraging them to know what is going on in their worlds so that they can make informed decisions in the present and future. It involves encouraging the asking of difficult questions and a preparedness to admit mistakes and the limits to one's knowledge.

Courage

Courage is often required to stand against the weight of convention, power and authority or the views and cultures of one's group; to think one's own thoughts and speak one's mind. Greater personal courage may be necessary to stand up for oneself or others where there is no culture of mutual support or it has been eroded. But the extent of courage that is required to offer an opinion depends on one's personality and the extent to which one has developed a fear of speaking up in public.

What is called whistle-blowing, speaking out about malpractice in one's organisation and risking loss of advancement, employment or friendship, generally requires courage. Whistleblowing may be seen as disloyal by those with power, though inclusive loyalty is to the wider community and to the most vulnerable within it. Courage may be involved in counteracting discrimination, first by acknowledging it, and then naming it and acting against it.

Joy

Inclusive values are concerned with the development of whole people, including their feelings and emotions; with enhancing the human spirit; with joyful engagement in learning, teaching and relationships. They involve seeing schools as places to 'be', to live well in the present, as well a preparation for what one will 'become' in the future. A joyful education encourages learning through play, playfulness and shared humour. It fosters enjoyment in acquiring new interests, knowledge and skills as the best way of sustaining them. Education settings which focus only on a narrow set of core attainments, or on the role of education in securing personal status and economic benefits, can be joyless, humourless places. This can diminish adults and children by constricting their self-expression and can lead to disaffection and disengagement.

Compassion

Compassion involves an understanding of the suffering of others and a wish for it to be alleviated. It requires a deliberate attempt to know the extent of discrimination and suffering locally and globally and a willingness to engage with other people's perspectives and feelings. Compassion means that personal well-being is limited by a concern with the well-being of everybody, though not to the extent that we should encourage misery until everyone around the world is smiling. Embracing compassion involves replacing punitive approaches to the breaches of rules through caring and resourcefulness. It involves adults in taking some responsibility when there is a breakdown in relationships with children and young people. However fractured the relationship between a young person and a setting might seem, it remains the duty of professionals to continue to ask: how can this young person be best supported to develop relationships and engage in learning in this school? A compassionate education is one where mistakes can be acknowledged, irrespective of the status of the person involved, apologies can be accepted, restitution made and forgiveness is possible.

Love

Compassion is closely linked to the value of love or care. Love as ' a deep caring for others, which asks for nothing in return', is a core motivation for many educators and a basis for a sense of vocation[13]. It involves

13 Noddings, N (2005) The challenge to care in schools; an alternative approach to education, New York, Cambridge University Press.

nurturing others to be and become themselves in recognition of the way people flourish when they are valued. This fosters a sense of identity and belonging and promotes participation. A willingness to care for others, and be cared for that children display in return, underlies the creation of communities connected by fellow feeling as well as common activities. But as a value for educators, 'love' or 'care' is a feature of an asymmetric relationship. It may be a professional duty that educators should care equally for all children and young people within their settings, without regard to any warmth, gratitude or progress that they display in return.

Hope/optimism

A value concerned with hope and optimism may also be seen as a professional duty for educators and a personal duty for parents and carers: we may have an obligation to convey a sense that personal, local, national and global difficulties can be alleviated. It involves showing how people can make a difference to their own and other people's lives. This does not mean that we fail to engage with the realities of the world, or the cynical motives of others, and only 'look on the bright side of life'. For hope and optimism require an eagerness to engage with reality as the foundation for principled action. Clarity over inclusive values can provide a framework for action, connecting together those with similar values but with different labels for their activities. This can increase collective power to counteract the formidable exclusionary pressures that are manifest locally and globally. It can make change for the benefit of people and the planet more likely. Thus hope supports the possibility that a future can be sustained in which people can flourish.

Beauty

A concern with creating beauty may seem contentious since it is evident that beauty is in the eyes and mind of the one who sees or conceives it. It is also evident how oppressive and excluding the marketing of particular notions of beauty is for many people. Although it is clear that doing what we can to bring beauty to the environment of our schools is important for the wellbeing of everyone. It is also part of this list of values headings since people sometimes identify their most rewarding achievements in education, a particular sequence of learning activities for example, as involving the creation of something beautiful and their most motivating encounters or observations in their day as containing moments of beauty. Its inclusion also allows people to connect values with their interpretation of spiritual fulfillment. Beauty can be seen in gratuitous acts of kindness, in precious occasions where communication has transcended self-interest, in collective action and support to demand rights, when people find and use their voice. Beauty is there when someone loves something that they or someone else has crafted, in an appreciation of art and music. Inclusive beauty is to be found away from stereotypes in the diversity of people and in the diversity of nature.

Wisdom

Wisdom involves choosing between courses of action by weighing up the justification for, and consequences of, each: we allow time for reflection, and the gathering of alternative perspectives before forming an opinion of a person or situation: we reflect on our own and other people's experience so that we avoid repeating mistakes: we resolve disputes through mediation, dialogue and restitution rather than punishment, aggression or power. In learning to be wise we connect values to actions and try to act according to the values we espouse: we base our arguments and decisions on values, reason and evidence: we are honest about the limits of our own knowledge and value the the knowledge of others, both children and adults: we question and listen: we understand that we are bodies as well as minds and are part of the natural world: we attempt to face, rather than deny, difficult realities in ourselves and the world, in order to find sources of improvement: we do not take for granted the truth of accepted ways of thinking; we make connections between areas of thought that are commonly separated: we explore what is important in our own lives and for others in theirs: we seek the knowledge that helps us to live well together in our homes, communities, schools, societies and on our planet.

Responding to the framework of values in the *Index*

The framework is not intended as a prescription but an invitation to dialogue. Not everyone will agree with it although sometimes they may agree with the descriptions of values taken together – the universe of meanings - while preferring to use different headings for them which relate more strongly to threads of thought, motivation and experience in their own lives. Since values should prompt action, the words used to summarise them will differ between different people. When some people first consider the list they may say that one or other of their core values like 'responsibility', 'freedom' and 'collaboration' are omitted. They may want the list to be altered even though on closer examination they find that their concerns are covered by the meaning of the values. For example, 'freedom' is linked with 'rights' and 'participation', and 'responsibility' and collaboration' with 'community'.

They may also find that they hold different values. This may be a matter of detail. People have very different ideas about the extent to which inequality between people should be reduced or how far the participation of people within schools and society should be encouraged. Setting out the meaning of inclusive values is meant to draw out such differences. The more we share the detail of our values, the more likely it is that differences in our positions will emerge.

A negotiated framework of values may result from dialogue with staff, children, families and governors. This might be expressed as simple statements, as in Figure 6, that are more readily accessible than our framework. They might be written under the headings devised at one primary school[14] in Figure 7. One school working with the *Index* used the values heading respect to frame a policy on conduct in the school: 'respect for self, respect for others, respect for the environment and respect for belongings'[15]. Nevertheless, a more detailed engagement with the meaning of values is necessary if they are to provide a framework for action for children and adults sufficient to engage with the complexity of life in schools.

However, it is clear that some people act on the basis of radically different values from the inclusive framework described here. There is ready evidence that not all people try to act on a belief that every life and every death is of equal value in their own community, country or other countries. Some people are keener than others on pursuing revenge and retribution for perceived wrongs or on the unprincipled pursuit of money and other possessions, on short-term self-interested ends.

Figure 7 Values in our school

- We want everyone to be treated fairly and to feel part of a community.
- We care about children and adults in our school.
- We enjoy finding out about each other, what we have in common and how we differ.
- We act on the understanding that we share a planet with all other living things
- We are concerned when people suffer hunger, disease and poverty.
- We learn from each other and share what we know.
- We connect what we learn at home and at school.
- We sort out problems by listening to each other and finding solutions together.
- We speak up when we see that something is wrong.
- We celebrate all the different plants and animals in the world.
- We try to save energy and avoid waste.
- We help to make our school and the world better places to live in.

14 Values from Harbinger school, Tower Hamlets, London.

15 Behaviour policy, Dereham St. Nicholas Junior School, Norfolk.

Figure 8 Our values in Harbinger School

Together	Well-being	Learning
See a diverse community enjoying working together	See compassionate actions	See everyone eagerly engaged in learning
Hear people contributing comfortably	Hear confident, courageous voices	Hear times of quiet and times of bustle
Notice high levels of participation	Notice everyone being heard	Notice confidence and willingness to try
Feel valued and at home	Feel safe and secure	Feel proud of our individual and school success

It is important to recognise as values, those pushes for action that we view negatively for there are many different values frameworks which equally answer the question: "**How should be live together?**' There is no set of universally held values. Inclusive values can be contrasted with excluding values. A framework of excluding values is depicted in Figure 9 although the headings are not strictly opposites of inclusive values. People recognise these values as operating in many schools in the UK and elsewhere. In this framework *equality* is replaced by *hierarchy*, *rights* in practice by *opportunity* in theory, *participation* by *consumption* of goods and 'knowledge', obligations to an ever widening *community* by allegiance to an *in-group, respect for diversity* by a desire for a *monoculture,* environmental *sustainability* by continued *exploitation, non-violence* by *discrimination, trust* by *surveillance* through continual observation, assessment and inspection, *honesty* by a preoccupation with *image, courage* by *compliance* with majority or official opinion, *joy* in learning and teaching by seeking *reward* and administering or avoiding *punishment, compassion* by *self-interest, love* by *authority, hope/optimism* by *fatalism, beauty* by *efficiency* and *wisdom* by the exercise of *power*.

Figure 9 A framework of excluding values

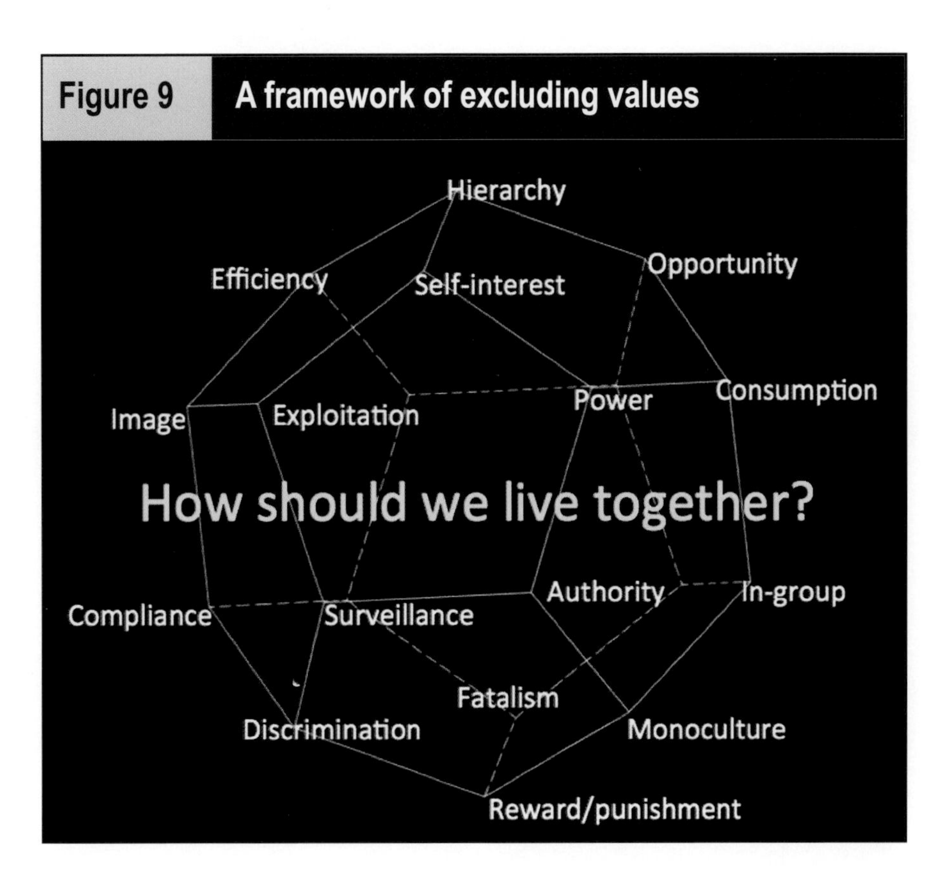

Developing values literacy

The process of putting inclusive values into action involves connecting our actions to inclusive values and disconnecting them from excluding values. We call this a process of acquiring 'values literacy' – to describe what people do as they investigate the difference a deep understanding and implementation of a value can make to what happens within their schools. Groups of governors, teachers, parents and children have worked together to make such connections, identifying a value of interest, thinking about its meaning and then challenging themselves and each other to work out what difference it would make to actions in the school if such a value were really put into action (see Part 3, Activity 6 page X). 'Learning walks'[16], can be used in schools as part of a collaborative strategy to support teaching and learning. One of the schools with which we have worked came up with the parallel idea of 'values walks', where adults and children observe school activities, buildings and displays, note the values they seem to embody and then engage in dialogues about them. Other schools have engaged children and young people in a day of activities around values and have been surprised by the sophistication young people have shown in their values discussions.

In one school their day was given a focus by a painting by a teaching assistant of the framework of inclusive values from the *Index* on the branches of a tree, an echo of their cherished cherry tree in providing shelter, shade and a meeting place in the school grounds.

> *"I love your book ... I've been talking about it with my family ... its about making the school a better place ...when you love one another so that everyone has friends, and if you come from another country then you are ok because people can just be friends with you ... its about what is important for you ... how you love your family."*
>
> – Travis, aged 8 during a day of work with values.

Linking to other values-based schemes

Our basing of educational development on secular inclusive values has much in common with other approaches to values-based education, including 'Living-Values'[17] emanating from the religious/spiritual group Brahma Kumaris and Imaginor, a Christian Organisation also linked with writings on 'living values'[18]. Figure 10 compares the values headings in the *Index* with these two schemes. This exercise is limited without a comparison of the deep meanings given to each heading. But while there is some overlap, there is an absence in the other lists of ideas of participation and sustainability. The only shared headings in all three schemes are to do with community, respect and honesty. In fact we first introduced the value of non-violence into our scheme after engaging with Living-Values and then developed it as an imperative for education. In 'Living-values' values are seen as universal whereas we see values as disputed with very different frameworks influencing the actions of different

16 https://www.teachingchannel.org/videos/the-learning-walk https://creativeteachersupport.wordpress.com/2012/11/18/lets-go-for-a-learning-walk/

17 Hawkes, N. (2003) *How to inspire and develop positive values in your classroom*, Cambridge, LDA. Frances Farrer (2000): A quiet revolution, The story of the development of values education at West Kidlington Primary School in Oxfordshire, Oxford, Rider.

18 http://www.imaginor.co.uk/values/ Vickery, S, Ed. (2011) Living values, a practical guide to rooting your school in Christian values,

groups of people. Also the *Index* is unique in setting out through its seventy indicators and 2,000 questions what its framework of values mean for the detail of practice.

In both other schemes adults and children are invited to engage in values literacy exercises, too, through a focus of attention on a different value heading each month, which forms a constant reference point in formal and less formal activities. In practice some of the schools adopting this approach negotiate their own framework of values with staff and/or children. A few regard the results of such negotiation to be a set of values applying only to children in order to improve their conduct. Our framework of values, as well as the other schemes I have mentioned are intended to apply to everyone.

Figure 10 Comparison of values heading

Index for Inclusion	Imaginor	Living values
Equality	Justice	Responsibility
Rights	Friendship	Freedom
Community	Respect	Cooperation
Respect for diversity	Perseverance	Tolerance
Sustainability	Trust	Respect
Participation	Compassion	Humility
Trust	Forgiveness	Peace
Compassion	Thankfulness	Honesty
Non-violence	Truthfulness	Love
Honesty	Courage	Happiness
Courage	Generosity	Simplicity
Beauty	Service	Unity
Love		
Joy		
Hope		
Wisdom		

Adding pedagogical principles

There are implications for how and what we teach and learn arising from inclusive values. Inclusive values can be used to produce inclusive pedagogical principles – rules to guide teaching and learning with diversity. In some cases this is relatively straightforward, so that ideas of joyfulness, care and participation, for example, have clear implications for teaching and learning interactions as reflected within the indicators and questions. But we and others have found it helpful to define some additional inclusive teaching and learning principles that do not arise in a straightforward way from the *Index* values framework but are important to bear in mind in developing our schools. Like the values framework such principles have been pieced together from reading and reflection over many years as a support to developing schools in inclusive ways. Whereas the values are a broad answer to the question: How should we live together?, the principles have a narrower focus on 'how we should teach and learn together'. Figure 11 was produced by cutting down a long list of principles until what was left provided a guide to action that was additional to the values framework.

Like each of the values, the principles can create a starting point for thinking about educational development. For example the idea of schools fostering immediate and lifelong activities and interests (14) is a theme carried through the *Index*. It is about recognising that it is an aim of schools to develop interests in children and young people which contributes to a life of activity. For most, paid work will be significant alongside other interests and activities.

Figure 11 Inclusive pedagogical principles: Teaching and learning with diversity

Education should:

1 set no limits on what children and adults can achieve.
2 build learning from personal and shared experience.
3 involve learning activities outside classrooms.
4 draw on diversity as a resource for learning.
5 develop the capacity for dialogue.
6 build theoretical knowledge from the development of practical skills.
7 view practical skills as of equal value to academic knowledge.
8 make connections between understandings in different subjects and contexts.
9 view good relationships as important in themselves as well as a support for learning.
10 recognise the significance for learning and well-being of secure identities.
11 connect learning with emotion.
12 link school activities with social, cultural, political and economic life beyond schools.
13 connect what happens locally to what happens globally.
14 nurture immediate and lifelong activities and interests.
15 make living well in the present as important as preparing for the future.
16 recognise that learning in earlier life shapes who we are and what we do in later life.
17 focus on enabling play, learning and teaching to flourish, more than attainment outcomes.
18 conceive of schools as a support for all in their communities.
19 support active, democratic, local and global citizenship.
20 emphasise the interdependence of people, other animals, plants and environments.

Listening to imperatives

A framework of values or a set of pedagocial principles is a gentle way of expressing commitments and determining how and what we should teach and learn. But sometimes it may be important to breathe some fire into them. Towards the end of his life, Theodor Adorno, a social theorist, gave a speech expressing concern at the way education had responded to the lessons of the Holocaust:

> "The premier demand upon all education is that Auschwitz not happen again. Its priority before any other requirement is such that I believe I need not and should not justify it. cannot understand why it has been given so little concern until now."[19]

Adorno used the Holocaust as a metaphor for the destructive, soul-breaking conflicts in the world that education might have a role in avoiding. He asks us to allow our knowledge that societies can descend into barbarism, to make a difference to the way we educate our children. The *Index* has indicators directly related to values of non-violence and respect for diversity, which may be most closely linked to Adorno's concern.

Arguments for bringing people into a new relationship with their environment, if the sources of their life are to be preserved, are as compelling as the need to avoid racism and other conflicts. This involves learning about the effects of what we consume and how we can make new choices about it. In its literature, a past government encouraged the development of sustainable, environmentally aware and active schools and, like us, suggested that sustainability could become a guiding principle for revising the whole curriculum.

> "Sustainable development is a cross-cutting dimension of the National Curriculum...A curriculum designed to achieve...a future where nothing can be taken for granted... would differ from that which is taught in many schools."[20]

We have used inclusive values, principles and imperatives to create a curriculum – a way of dividing up knowledge for the 21st century.

19 Adorno, T. (1966) First presented as a radio lecture on 18 April 1966, under the title 'Padagogik nack Auschwitz'. English translation 'Education after Auschwitz' in Adorno, T. (2005) Critical Models: Interventions and Catchwords, New York, Columbia University Press. Available online at http://ada.evergreen.edu/~arunc/texts/frankfurt/auschwitz/AdornoEducation.pdf

20 Department for Children, Schools and Families (2009): S3: Sustainable school self-evaluation, London, DCSF.

Attending to the curriculum

What are the implications of inclusive values, principles and imperatives, for how and what we learn and teach? If values are about how we should live together, then curricula are about what we might learn in order to live together well. After earlier editions of the *Index* were published, we sometimes made claims that the *Index* set out the implications of inclusive values for all aspects of a school. But we left a large gap for we had failed to specify the implications of our values framework for the content of learning and teaching activities. In a long period of rigidity about curriculum planning in schools following the introduction of the National Curriculum in England at the end of the 1980s, it seemed impossible to consider alternatives to counter the weight of government determination of what should be taught.

We have now tried to fill the curriculum gap even though we do so at a time of continued restriction on curricula innovation particularly in secondary schools. Curriculum suggestions form a new section in Dimension C in this revised edition of the *Index* (See pages 124-158). We hope this will stimulate dialogues in the UK and elsewhere about the nature of inclusive curricula, what is taught in schools and why, and what an appropriate curriculum should be for the 21st century. We see the need to change the way knowledge and skills are structured in schools as an urgent matter if education is to be part of the solution to pressing environmental and social problems nationally and globally. So we hope that our curriculum ideas will make ripples and that these will gather force, joining with the waves created by others.

The meaning of the 'school curriculum' has two elements. It can refer to teaching intentions, planned learning activities and how these are structured under subject headings. It can also denote everything else that is learned by children and adults through their experience of being in school. How we learn and how we teach may be part of this less formal curriculum. It gives opportunities for adults and children to take some control over the less formal and sometimes most influential aspects of the curriculum. For example, in challenging the creation of hierarchies through which children and adults learn their place, the *Index* promotes dialogue about how education can transform rather than simply reproduce existing patterns of social relationships.

But we have also looked closely at the implications or our framework of inclusive values, principles and imperatives, our experience and reading, for thinking about the more formal aspects of the curriculum, the structure and content of teaching and learning activities. Our framework prompts thinking about the nature of curricula so that it links to the experience of children and their families a critical move in breaking down barriers to learning and participation in schools. We wanted to design a resource for adults and children in schools that would give children some control over their lives by preparing them to be active national and global citizens, would reflect human rights, encourage action on sustainaility, links people globally and breaks down distinctions between academic, practical and vocational education, and connect them to the realities of the world, including the way people earn money.

We were influenced by many conversations with teachers and other colleagues. For example, a colleague in Hong Kong responded to a draft scheme relating the curriculum to human needs for food, water, clothing, shelter and health and care that 'Sun Yatsen [21] had said that basic needs were for food, clothing, shelter and transportation'.[22] Through this conversation, transport has been incorporated as an essential curriculum subject broadened to encompass 'when, why and how people move around their locality and the world'. It includes modes of transport, trade and migration within and between countries. It enables curricula to address one of the most important inclusion questions for all countries: 'what is an ethical immigration policy?' In exploring such a question children might be helped to reflect on the levels of distrust shown to many of those who flee conflict or poverty and seek asylum, or work, in a new country.

We see the creation of curricula as an expression of how we, adults and children,

21 A mid 20th century Chinese political leader.

22 Heung, V. (2000) personal communication

Figure 12	Comparing curriculum headings
A global rights-based curriculum	**A traditional curriculum**
Food	Mathematics
Water	Language and Literature
Clothing	Modern Foreign Languages
Housing/building	Physics
Transport	Chemistry
Health and relationships	Biology
The environment	Geography
Energy	History
Communication and Communication Technology	Design and Technology
Literature, arts and music	Art
Work and activity	Music
Ethics, power and government	Religion
	Physical Education
	Personal, Health and Social Education

structure our learning and knowledge about the world. So curricula are not simply a feature of formal schooling but are about knowledge for everyone. They reflect the resource that teacher-citizens bring to the support of children's education.

Curriculum headings and outlines

We have set out the headings for two curricula in Figure 12. On the right is a traditional set of subject headings. They would have been recognisable to schools at any time in the previous hundred years and are familiar to most countries. In thinking about their origins, one might conclude that they were not designed to capture the interest of all children now but to prepare a past elite group for a traditional university education. On the left are headings for a rights-based, global, sustainability, curriculum. These headings are not topics but are intended to be given the same status as traditional subjects or disciplines.

The headings on the left of Figure 12 capture common concerns of people everywhere. They could be used to construct a curriculum in cities and villages in China, Burma or the Democratic Republic of the Congo as well as England and Germany and so link people between these countries and circumstances. They provide the basis for a curriculum for people from three to one hundred and three, for pre-school, primary, secondary and higher education. They are headings which can be linked to shared experiences for all children, irrespective of their attainments. They are concerned with the activities of people in the communities around schools and so reinforce the contributions that can be made to curricula of all children's families. Activity and work, as suggested earlier, are considered together, so that schools prepare children to think of waged work as a paid activity amongst other fulfilling activities in their lives. In reflecting the kinds of work in which people commonly engage, such a curriculum can break down distinctions between vocational and academic education. The rights based curriculum in Figure 9 is sketched out through the indicators and questions in Dimension C section 1: Constructing curricula for all (see Figure 10). You might wish to have a quick flick through the curriculum section now. We have given its pages a distinctive tint, in recognition of its special status as an area of the *Index* that schools may treat differently. These provide a few pages of initial guidelines on each indicator, which can be extended and adapted to the circumstances of any school. Each area is divided under a number of headings and this is a further distinctive feature of this area of the *Index*. The result is an outline curriculum presented in sufficient detail for a school to create its own curriculum; to recreate the way schools used to work before they were subjected to the central direction of a national curriculum. Each area has been checked as much as possible with experts and through consulting a wide literature.

Figure 13 **Indicators for Dimension C, Section 1: Constructing curricula for all**

1. Children explore cycles of food production and consumption.
2. Children investigate the importance of water.
3. Children study clothing and decoration of the body.
4. Children find out about housing and the built environment.
5. Children consider how and why people move around their locality and the world.
6. Children learn about health and relationships.
7. Children investigate the earth, the solar system and the universe.
8. Children study life on earth.
9. Children investigate sources of energy.
10. Children learn about communication and communication technology.
11. Children engage with, and create, literature, arts and music.
12. Children learn about work and link it to the development of their interests.
13. Children learn about ethics, power and government.

But you may well find omissions and issues that you feel are inaccurately expressed. Your involvement is positively welcomed.

Please contact us on **info@indexforinclusion.org**

Each area follows a pattern of relating issues locally and globally, considering ethics and politics and linking the past with the present and future.[23] In most subject areas, questions are raised about connections to business and the economy. Although governments think they are boosting economic activity by a focus on pushing up scores in mathematics, science, and literacy on the Programme for International Student Assessment (PISA) tests this could be questioned given the weak relationship between the content of what is taught in schools and the economic activities that actually take place in our societies. We ask people to also consider the balance between the contribution economic activity makes to human well-being and the health of our planet.

The form of the curriculum reflects a long tradition of encouraging the development of learning activities from children's shared experience. A major place is given to environmental issues. Every school is encouraged to link itself to a water source: a local stream or river and also to a river in another part of the world.[24] An understanding of the rivers of others, provides insights into their lives, their climates and perhaps to the origin of their conflicts.

Adapting traditional curricula

Primary and secondary schools in England extend their curricula, as we have suggested through 'cross-curricular' activities, and topics from the headings on the left. Many schools have already integrated aspects of the proposals into teaching and learning activities about citizenship, sustainability, health promotion, and adding a global dimension in cross-curricular topics, projects and problem-solving. Schools establish green days and

23 Kari Nes has described a related discussion of a principled curriculum developed in Norway: Nes, K. (2003) Why does education for all have to be inclusive education? In Allan, J. (ed.) Inclusion, Participation and Democracy: What is the purpose? London, Kluwer Academic Publishers.

24 The idea for connecting to a local river comes from 'Ecological Literacy': Stone M. and Barlow, Z. (2005) Ecological Literacy: Educating our children for a sustainable world. San Francisco, Sierra Club Books. It also pays due respect to the Maori practice of identifying one's river, a source of one's life, as a first move in a formal introduction.

sustainability weeks and follow the sustainability decade, use the Olympics or drama to explore global interdependence, finance, food, ethics, power and government. They set up technology projects to convey information and to explore recycling and energy conservation. They may use the material to further relate a more traditional curriculum to the lives and experience of children, picking up ideas in areas that have received less attention such as 'clothing and decoration of the body' and 'transport'.

Travelling in time to create 21st century curricula

However, there are two arrows in Figure 13. In outlining an alternative curriculum we were concerned to ensure that knowledge associated with traditional curricula is included within the new scheme. The content of physics and chemistry might be seen to fit within an understanding of the earth, solar system and universe, but they also arise in several other areas and particularly for physics in a consideration of energy. Biology arises in understanding food cycles and health but more coherently in the context of an understanding of life on earth. Of course any school will wish children to be literate and numerate. In this scheme, literacy is given attention in the communication area and across all other curriculum areas.

History appears in every area through the requirement to link past, present and future, a move seemingly in accord with the History Association's position given to the government review of the primary curriculum in 2009:

> "We fully support ...the development of a less prescriptive and a more flexible National Curriculum that draws upon subjects like history as tools for learning."[25]

Mathematics too, becomes a cross-curricular theme. Concerns have been expressed that the hierarchical nature of Mathematics knowledge requires that it is taught as a separate subject and that seeing it as informing many different subjects would impede understanding. At the same time, disquiet is voiced about children's motivation for acquiring mathematical understanding, and possible limited achievement, when mathematics is taught as a subject disconnected from the real world. Seeing mathematics as a cross-curricular resource is not incompatible with children pursuing mathematics as a complex system of thought as they progress through school. When we do things differently we are faced with new problems to resolve.

Making comparisons

The *Rose Review* was one of three primary reviews making proposals for a revised curriculum at the end of the first decade of the 21st century. Their proposed structures are shown in Figure 14. All these reviews are based on principles which overlap with the values framework of the *Index*. However, they are structured around more familiar curriculum headings. Despite emphasising cross-cutting themes, the headings carry the weight of traditional expectations. Each was concerned to 'dovetail' primary curricula with a subject based secondary curriculum and this limits their aspirations.

What can be achieved by proposing changes to the curriculum?

Neither the *Rose Review* nor the more extensive *Alexander Review* have been implemented by the government so we are not expecting our suggestions to be immediately nationalised. Our only power is through the strength of our ideas to engage others in dialogue. We are encouraged by the knowledge that the curriculum we propose is much closer than a traditional curriculum to what people generally learn outside school and in education beyond school. It is the curriculum which more closely reflects the lives, experience and futures of children. We believe as strongly that the school curriculum needs to change as that people need to wean themselves from a dependence on oil, from beliefs that they can continue to increase consumption of the other finite resources of their planet, and that their planet can healthily absorb ever increasing amounts of their non-biodegradable waste. We believe these issues are connected. We remain optimistic.

Figure 14 New curricula for old?

Independent (Government Initiated) Review of Primary Curriculum (Rose Review)	Cambridge Primary Review (Alexander Review)	International Baccalaureate Primary Years Programme[26]
Understanding English, communication and languages	Language, oracy and literacy	Language
Mathematical understanding	Mathematics	Mathematics
Scientific and technological understanding	Science and technology	Science
Historical, geographical and social understanding	Place and time	Social studies
Understanding physical development, health and wellbeing	Physical and emotional health	Personal, social and physical education.
Understanding the arts	Arts and creativity	Arts
Religious education	Faith and belief	
Citizenship	Citizenship and ethics	

26 www.ibo.org/pyp/curriculum/*Index*.cfm

Forming alliances

The *Index* helps to draw together all activities which promote inclusive values and so reduces policy fragmentation and initiative overload. Figure 15 contains a list of activities which can be connected under a heading of inclusive development.

So the school actively promotes democratic education and education for citizenship and global citizenship, based on a recognition of human rights. Schools reach out to all in their communities so that communities and schools form a mutually supportive relationship. This is the best contribution they can make to 'community cohesion'. Breaking down divisions between groups within their communities, they become health promoting, attending to the wellbeing of adults and children and to the health of their bodies. They become part of international movements for developing schools such as those promoted by UNICEF 'child-friendly school' or the UNESCO led global push for quality education for everyone called 'Education for All'. They integrate 'spiritual, moral, social and cultural education' as well as 'social and emotional learning' into the way relationships, and teaching and learning activities are conducted. There is a concern to reduce all forms of discrimination so that they exceed the requirements of 'equalities' legislation. Teaching and learning activities respond to an environmental imperative that connects children into local and global environments and joins these up with the schools' use of their grounds, energy, food, and approach to waste. All these are linked into the school curriculum. Forest school becomes an option for promoting environmental sensitivity, cooperative learning, spiritual engagement and a reevaluation of risk. This recognition of the importance of 'learning outside the classroom' links learning with experience, which expands the connections children and young people make in their thinking, talking, writing and artistic expression. Both children and adults develop their powers of critical thinking which can be supported through dialogues encouraged within the enquiry based learning approach of 'Philosophy for Children'. When they shift away from the identification of children's difficulties as arising only from their 'special educational needs' to a concern with from barriers arising anywhere within a school's cultures, policies and

Figure 15 Alliances for inclusive educational development?

- Values-based education
- School improvement/school development
- Democratic education
- Citizenship/Global citizenship education
- Rights-based education[27]
- Comprehensive community education
- Community Cohesion[28]
- Peace/non-violent education
- Health-promoting schools[29]
- Child-friendly schools[30]
- Education for All[31]
- Spiritual, moral, social and cultural education[32]
- Social and emotional learning (SEAL)[33]
- Anti-discrimination/anti-bias education[34]
- Equalities education
- Environmental education, education for environmental sustainability
- Learning outside the classroom[35]
- Forest School[36]
- Co-operative learning
- Experience-based learning
- Philosophy for children[37]
- Dialogic Education
- Innovative thinking[38]
- Learning without ability labelling[39]

27 www.unicef.org.uk/rrsa
28 The Education and Inspections Act 2006 inserted a new section 21(5) to the Education Act 2002 introducing a duty on the governing bodies of maintained schools to promote community cohesion.
29 http://www.who.int/school_youth_health/gshi/hps/en/
30 http://www.unicef.org/cfs/
31 http://www.unesco.org/new/en/education/themes/leading-the-international-agenda/education-for-all/
32 http://www.doingsmsc.org.uk
33 http//:www.sealcommunity.org
34 Derman-Sparks, L. and Olsen Edwards, J. (2010) Anti-Bias education for young children and ourselves, Washington, National Association for the Education of Young Children.
35 http//:www.lotc.org.uk
36 www.forestschoolassociation.org/what-is-forest-school/
37 http://www.philosophy4children.co.uk, http://p4c.com/
38 Hart, S. (1996) Beyond special needs: enhancing children's learning through innovative thinking, London, Paul Chapman Publishing. Hart, S. (2000) *Thinking through teaching: a framework for enhancing participation and learning*, London, David Fulton.
39 Hart, S., Dixon, A., Drummond, M.J. and McIntyre, D. (2006) *Learning without limits*, Buckingham, Open University Press., Swann, M., Peacock, A., Hart, S and Drummond, M. Buckingham, Open University Press.

practices they release resources to find imaginative resolutions of barriers to children's progress as indicated within 'innovative thinking'. They avoid labeling children with ability tags which can lead to a hierarchy of value of children, encourage disaffection, limit expectations of others and negatively influence the identities of children themselves.

'Inclusive Educational Development' is used in the title for Figure 14 because 'inclusive' can be used as a super-ordinate concept standing for a framework of values which promote a wide range of educational activities usually designated by other labels. Other words can be used for the same purpose – such as 'democratic' or 'values-based' or 'sustainable' or 'anti-bias' to imply an overall approach. We do not mind what word is chosen to perform this integrative function, provided the need for drawing these activities together is recognised.

Many organisations offer their 'programmes' or initiatives about one or other of the areas in Figure 14 to assist the development of schools. Teachers are meant to integrate the issues raised and lessons learned into their own future plans for teaching and learning. Many such programmes are carefully considered and inspiring. Yet their own sustainability may be questioned if there is not already space and commitment to integrate them into the learning activities of the school. The timing of such involvements is critical, so that they are incorporated into a school at a point when they can give a further push to what is already beginning to take place. It may be that a smaller scale innovation in the area, researched by staff and firmly established within their curricula and timetables, may make more lasting impacts. The *Index* shows how such activities can be linked together as illustrated in the examples that follow.

Learning about rights

The *Index* encourages similar developments to the Rights Respecting Schools Award initiated by UNICEF UK but embeds this within wider changes in school cultures, policies and practices that may lead to more long lasting changes. It identifies the idea of 'rights' as a heading for a value linked into a framework of fifteen other values. Learning about rights may not be a familiar activity in some schools, so it is introduced in indicator A2.2 'The school encourages respect for all human rights', pages 192–193 introduce human rights documents and page 194 refers to planetary rights or 'the rights of mother earth', linked to indicator A2.3, 'The school encourages respect for the integrity of planet earth'.

Joining up sustainability, global awareness and values-led development

Figure 16 shows the connections between the way government documents divided up the concerns of the National Framework for Sustainable Schools and the Global Dimension for Schools. Figures 17 and 18 then list the *Index* indicators which link to each of these programmes showing the comprehensive way they are represented. Other interventions listed in Figure 15 can be similarly reflected in particular indicators.

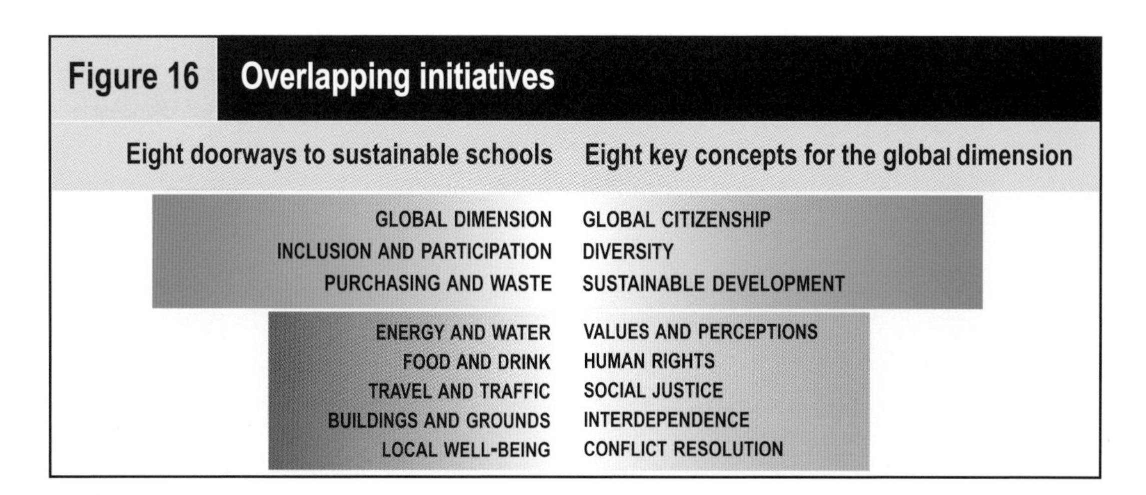

Figure 16 Overlapping initiatives

Figure 17 Indicators for eight doorways to sustainable schools[39]

Global dimension

A1.8 The school encourages an understanding of the interconnections between people around the world.

C2.6 Lessons develop an understanding of the similarities and differences between people.

C1.7 Children investigate the earth, the solar system and the universe.

C1.8 Children study life on earth.

Inclusion and participation

A2.4 Inclusion is viewed as increasing participation for all.

All other indicators

Purchasing and waste

B1.13 The school contributes to the reduction of waste.

Energy and water

B1.12 The school reduces its carbon footprint and use of water.

C1.2 Children investigate the importance of water.

C1.9 Children investigate sources of energy.

Food and drink

C1.1 Children explore cycles of food production and consumption.

C1.8 Children study life on earth.

Travel and traffic

C1.5 Children consider how and why people move around their locality and the world.

Buildings and grounds

B1.11 The buildings and grounds are developed to support the participation of all.

C1.4 Children find out about housing and the built environment.

Local well-being

A1.10 The school and local communities develop each other.

A2.9 The school encourages children and adults to feel good about themselves.

A2.10 The school contributes to the health of children and adults.

C1.6 Children learn about health and relationships.

Figure 18 Indicators for eight key concepts for the global dimension[40]

Global citizenship

A1.7 The school is a model of democratic citizenship.

A1.8 The school encourages an understanding of the interconnections between people around the world.

Dimension C, where all indicators are to be linked locally and globally

Diversity

A1.9 Adults and children are responsive to a variety of ways of being a gender.

C2.6 Lessons develop an understanding of the similarities and differences between people.

Sustainable development

A2.3 The school encourages respect for the integrity of planet earth.

B1.12 The school reduces its carbon footprint and use of water.

B1.13 The school contributes to the reduction of waste.

C1.7 Children investigate the earth, the solar system and the universe.

C1.8 Children study life on earth.

C1.9 Children investigate sources of energy.

Values and perceptions

A2.1 The school develops shared inclusive values.

Human rights

A2.2 The school encourages respect for all human rights

Social justice

A2.7 The school counters all forms of discrimination.

Interdependence

A1.8 The school encourages an understanding of the interconnections between people around the world.

C1.1 Children explore cycles of food production and consumption.

C1.2 Children investigate the importance of water.

C1.3 Children study clothing and decoration of the body.

C1.5 Children consider how and why people move around their locality and the world.

C1.7 Children investigate the earth, the solar system and the universe

Conflict resolution

A2.8 The school promotes non-violent interactions and resolutions to disputes.

39 http://esdgc.escalate.ac.uk/doorways

40 https://globaldimension.org.uk/pages/8444

Barriers, resources and support

'Barriers to learning and participation', 'resources to support learning and participation' and 'support for diversity' are three key concepts in the Index. They can help to direct the shared knowledge of adults and children. The questions in Figure 19 connect them together. When shared through a participative process and linked to the development of inclusive values, they can generate ideas for review, planning and implementation even without the help of the indicators and questions in Part 4. Sometimes there are huge issues known by almost everyone to be holding back the improvement of a school but remain unspoken. They become the elephants in the room.

Barriers to learning and participation

Barriers to learning can occur in interaction with any aspect of a school: its buildings and grounds, the way it is organised, the relationship amongst and between children and adults and in approaches to teaching and learning. Barriers may be found, too, outside the boundaries of the school within families and communities, and within national and international events and policies. But we may have to resist the temptation to see barriers to learning and participation only in places that lie outside our responsibility and power to act. Our attempts to remove school barriers should focus on those that staff, children and their families can do something about, especially when they work together.

Identifying barriers to learning and participation is not about finding fault with a school. Inclusion is a never-ending process, which involves the progressive discovery and removal of limits to participation and learning within co-operating communities. Uncovering barriers and devising plans to reduce them are always positive moves.

Replacing special educational needs

Using 'barriers to learning and participation' to help to resolve educational difficulties can replace the identification of children as 'having special educational needs'. The idea that educational difficulties can be resolved by labeling children in this way and then intervening individually has considerable limitations. Seeing the impairments of children as the main cause of their educational difficulties, deflects us from barriers in all other aspects of settings and systems and obscures the difficulties experienced by children without the label. It encourages children to be seen through a lens of 'deficiency' rather than as whole people who may be subjected to a range of exclusionary pressures.

Figure 19 Barriers, resources and support

- What barriers to learning and participation arise within the school and its communities?
- Who experiences barriers to learning and participation?
- How can barriers to learning and participation be minimised?
- What resources to support learning and participation are available?
- How can additional resources to support learning and participation be mobilised?
- How should the resources to support learning and participation be deployed?

In categorising children as having 'special educational needs' we may ignore over-representations in the category by gender, class and ethnicity. For example, in England almost twice as many boys as girls are categorised as 'having special educational needs'.[41] This imbalance is similarly marked in those not so identified but seen to be relatively low in attainment or to have difficulties in their behaviour. These figures have persisted for decades, yet have been given relatively little attention. They suggest that educational difficulty may have something to do with the interaction between gender and the way children learn in schools and that reducing barriers depends on thinking and acting differently about gender. The *Index* urges staff in schools to reconsider how they promote, and respond to, forms of masculinity and femininity and other gender identities.

Labelling children as 'having special educational needs' can also lead to lowered expectations. When linked with the categorisation of children as 'gifted and talented', it can be part of the creation of a hierarchy of value of children seen as 'less than normal', 'normal' and 'supernormal' learners. This can happen even though in practice some children are categorised both as 'having special educational needs' and as 'being gifted and talented'. Many schools work hard to value all children equally despite the labels and are working to overcome the very perceptions that categorisation helps to foster.

We should reflect carefully before we label someone as 'having special educational needs' or 'SEN' or any of the acronyms for categories of 'abnormality' such as 'EBD' (emotional behavioural difficulty/ disorder, sometimes prefixed with S for Social) or 'ADHD' (Attention Deficit Hyperactivity Disorder) and the more recent suggestion that children who do not conform 'have ODD' (Opposition Defiance Disorder). Reducing a child to an acronym, a common practice, involves a particularly disrespectful act.

A stereotypic response to educational difficulty has arisen in terms of separate, 'differentiated' individualised curricula and close attention from teaching assistants that can impede relationships with other children and adults. When a class activity requires group work a teaching assistant, usually less qualified than a teacher, may often be found working with children grouped together because they are thought to experience the most difficulties. The persistence of a close-coupling model for assisting children seen to experience difficulties, despite a considerable amount of advice to engage in other approaches, is a tribute to the power of the 'special educational needs' concept to restrict creative thinking about how support should be provided.

The concept of 'individual educational needs' has replaced the notion of 'special educational needs' in aspects of the practice of some Local Authorities and some schools. This has the virtue of drawing together policies and practices for all children vulnerable to exclusionary pressures. But it retains a focus on an individual response rather than the removal of barriers and mobilisation of resources in the cultures, policies and practices of the setting as a whole.

The notion that educational difficulties are to be overcome by 'removing barriers to learning and participation' became used more widely in the decade following the first publication of the *Index* for inclusion in 2000, partly through its influence. However, the use of this idea within official documents has not been accompanied by a corresponding challenge to former ways of thinking, and so pressures to continue using the term 'special educational needs' have remained. The language is used in the advice on writing 'Education, Health and Care Plans'[42] , in the identification of student difficulties in the Special Educational Needs and Disability Code of Practice[43], in the use of Individual Education Plans and in the information that schools have to provide about their expenditure. Although they do not have to use the title by law, schools are encouraged in the 'Code of Practice' to designate someone as 'a special educational needs co-ordinator' usually abbreviated to the acronym 'SENco'. The alternative terms 'learning support coordinator', 'learning development

41 Office for standards in education, (2010) The special educational needs and disability review, London, Ofsted.

42 Department for Education (2014) Children and families Act, London, HHSO.

43 Department for Education, Department of Health (2015) Special educational needs and disability code of practice: 0-25 years, London, HMSO

co-ordinator' or 'inclusion co-ordinator' are preferable because they encourage a more imaginative and flexible response to barriers to learning and participation, how they can be reduced and how resources can be mobilised.

If staff are to take control over the way they think about educational difficulties, then they might use the language of 'special educational needs' only when they are fulfilling official requirements and allow the alternative thinking based on barriers to learning and participation to permeate the cultures, policies and practices of their school. This reflection on how concepts are used is important if old ways of thinking are to be prevented from reasserting themselves. 'A child who is experiencing barriers to learning and participation' can easily be eroded into 'a child with barriers' as a euphemism for 'a child with special educational needs'.

Social and individual models of disability

The use of the concept 'barriers to learning and participation' for the difficulties that children encounter, rather than the term 'special educational needs', contrasts a social with 'a medical' or 'individual deficit' view of educational difficulties. This can be linked to social and medical models of disability. Impairment can be defined as a long term 'limitation of physical, intellectual or sensory function',[44] though the notion of an intellectual impairment is problematic and may suggest an unwarranted physical basis to difficulties in learning. Disabilities can be seen as barriers to participation for people with impairments, chronic pain or illness. A medical or individual model of disability views the barriers faced by people with impairments as a direct consequence of their impairments. A version of the social model views disability as constructed from the experience of people with impairments of the interactions between their bodies and the social and physical environment. Often, disabilities are entirely created within the environment in the form of discriminatory attitudes and practices and a failure to remove obstacles to access and participation. At other times, they arise from the interaction between the environment and a person with an impairment, pain or chronic illness.

There may be relatively little that schools can do to overcome impairments, though the prevention of disease and attention to a safe environment can help to avoid them for some children. However, schools can considerably reduce the barriers produced by discriminatory attitudes and actions and institutional barriers put in the way of children and adults with impairments. Schools are required by law to make 'reasonable adjustments' to support the participation of children with impairments.[45] Changes in school cultures can be helped immeasurably by ensuring that staff with impairments are welcomed as employees.

Institutional discrimination

Barriers that affect the participation of particular groups, and arise in the way institutions are structured or run, involve 'institutional discrimination'. The Macpherson Report[46] following the inquiry into the way the murder of black teenager Stephen Lawrence had been handled by the police, focused attention on the 'institutional racism' within police forces and education, health and social services, though of course such discrimination is not confined to the public sector. Institutional racism was defined as discriminatory service 'through unwitting prejudice, ignorance, thoughtlessness, and racist stereotyping, which disadvantages minority ethnic people'[47] following a definition by Stokely Carmichael in the US forty years earlier. But institutional discrimination is wider than racism. It includes the ways institutions disadvantage people because of their poverty, gender, impairment, class, ethnicity, sexual orientation, gender identity, religion, beliefs and age. Institutional discrimination becomes deeply embedded within cultures and influences the way people are perceived and the responses that are made to them. Institutional discrimination is the responsibility of all members of institutions. So although it may predate the joining of the institution by a particular

44 Adapted from Disabled People's International, (1982) Proceedings of The First World Congress, Singapore: Disabled People's International.
45 Department for Education and Skills (2006) Implementing the Disability Discrimination Act in schools and early years settings, London, DFES.
46 Macpherson, W. (1999) Stephen Lawrence inquiry (Macpherson report) Command Paper 4261, vol 1, London, Stationery Office.
47 Ibid para 6.34

member and may act as a pressure on their actions, each person is still responsible for any resulting discrimination and hurt caused by discriminatory practices they may unreflectively inherit. Institutional discrimination creates barriers to participation and in education may impede learning. Serial discrimination may create an impoverished educational history and reduced qualifications which make people less able to obtain work. It may lead to staff in schools being unrepresentative of their local communities. The development of inclusion may involve people in a painful process of challenging their own discriminatory practices, attitudes and institutional cultures.

Racism, sexism, genderism, classism, homophobia, transphobia, disablism, ageism and discrimination in relation to religion and belief, share a common root in intolerance to difference and the use of power to create and perpetuate inequalities. Because people are often more familiar with discussion of racism or sexism than disablism, they may be less aware of the involvement of people and institutions in the creation of disability. The uncritical general acceptance within a school of the exclusion of children because they have an impairment or are categorised as 'having learning difficulties' amounts to institutional discrimination.

Intolerance to difference is linked to 'mono-culturalism' whereby institutions, or groups of people, define a particular way of life and the identities it supports as the only acceptable way of being. When people do not feel accepted within mono-cultural institutions they may experience this rejection as racism, disablism, sexism etc. In the first decades of the 21st century the voices of European politicians, but also a number of people and organisations otherwise concerned with reducing inequality, were raised against 'multi-culturalism'.[48] It was suggested that multiculturalism had failed as a way of bringing people of different ethnicities together. But in rejecting a particular form of multi-culturalism, they were wittingly or unwittingly promoting the continuation of monoculturalism and the institutional discrimination that it engenders.

The *Index* assists schools to develop complex open multi-cultures sustained by the development of anti-discrimination policies. The nature of these policies might go beyond, but be informed by, government instruments such as the Equality Act 2010. All such requirements might be set in the context of a school determinedly responsive to the valued diversity of all its members. Anti-discrimination policies would then be put into place because they promote the values shared within a school, not in order to comply with legislation.

48 Alibhai-Brown, Y. (2000) *After multi-culturalism*, London, Foreign Policy Centre.
Phillips. T (2004) *Guardian*, May 28th, 2004

Resources to support learning and participation

Reducing barriers to learning and participation involves mobilising resources. When values are made clear and shared across a school's communities, this becomes a large resource for a school. It creates a common direction for development, shapes decisions and helps to resolve conflicts. Inclusive values become a constant prompt to increasing participation in learning and in the wider life of a school. Similarly the drawing together of principled interventions in a school, involving programmes with a variety of titles within a single approach to development, becomes a resource through increased clarity and coherence. Just as with barriers, resources can be found in every aspect of a school; in its cultures, policies, and practices; in buildings, classroom equipment, books, computers; in its teaching and nonteaching staff, children and young people, parents/carers, communities and governors.

There are always more resources to support learning and participation than are currently used within any setting. There is a wealth of knowledge within a school, about what impedes the learning and participation of children. One of the main purposes of the *Index* is to help schools to draw on this knowledge to inform their development. The idea that diversity can be a resource for learning permeates the indicators involving collaboration between and amongst children and adults. The resources in children, in their capacity to direct their own learning and play and to support each other's play, learning and participation may be particularly under-utilised, as may the potential for staff to support each other's development.

The proposals for a restructured curriculum based on inclusive principles link each curriculum area locally and globally and this leads schools to draw on local resources to support the curriculum. Since the new curriculum relates closely to children's lives and the lives of people in their communities, it becomes clear how the local human and physical environment becomes a resource for the curriculum. The boundaries of the classroom take in the locality and beyond that the world.

Support for diversity

When educational difficulties are thought to arise from the 'special educational needs' of children and young people, it can seem natural to think of support as about providing additional people to work with individual children to overcome their problems. We adopt a far broader notion of 'support' as 'all activities which increase the capacity of a school to respond to the diversity of children and young people in ways that value them equally'. So efforts to uncover and reduce barriers to learning and participation, and the mobilising of resources, are support activities.

Since, on our definition, the inclusive development of teaching and learning are support activities, support involves all staff, children and their families. If learning activities are designed to support the participation of all children, the need for individual support is reduced. Support is provided when teachers plan lessons with all children in mind, recognising their different starting points, interests, experience and approaches to learning. It is given when children help each other. There is an equivalence between sitting with a child who struggles to understand the terminology of a lesson on biodiversity, and revising the activity so that it is rooted in a common experience for children, extends everyone's learning and the language can be generally understood. Individual support to children should always be given with the intention of encouraging greater independence: of increasing a child's capacity to learn and the capacity of adults and children to include them within learning activities.

The review materials

Developing a school by drawing on a framework of values, or through identifying barriers, resources and opportunities for support, can be done more or less systematically. It can involve individuals, groups or whole schools. The dimensions, sections, indicators, questions and questionnaires of the *Index* provide a further set of supports that can contribute to far ranging dialogues about what adults and children want to do next in developing their school. They can also be used systematically to review the setting, draw up an inclusive development plan and implement it. If you have not already done so, it might be an idea to skim through the list of indicators on pages 12–13 and the indicators with questions in Part 4, noting how they are structured, and how they serve as headings for the questions which give them meaning.

Dimensions and sections

The review of a school using the *Index* materials explores possibilities for development along three interconnected dimensions: ***creating inclusive cultures, producing inclusive policies and evolving inclusive practices***. Figure 20 repeats the triangle from the overview which illustrates the way the dimensions are connected and Figure 21 overleaf provides a summary of the content of each.

Experience with the *Index* in many schools in many countries confirms that these dimensions are widely seen as having significance for structuring school development. Although each represents an important area of focus for development, they do overlap. It is only from the evidence of practice that we can detect the influence of cultures and policies. Just as values are to be understood from an observation of actions, so understanding the nature of policies depends on observing attempts to influence practice. Putting the word 'policy' on the cover of a document does not make it a policy in any important sense, unless it represents a clear intention to regulate practice. Without an implementation strategy a so-called policy document becomes rhetoric, perhaps used only to impress inspectors and visitors.

Figure 20 The *Index* dimensions of school development

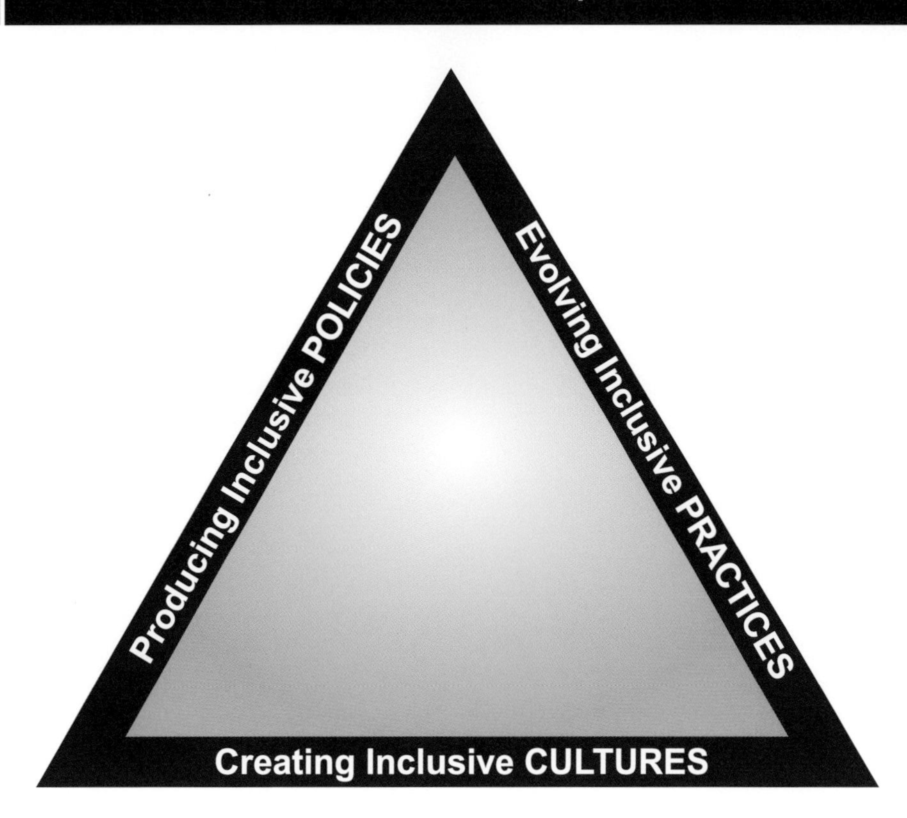

Figure 21 Explaining the Dimensions of the *Index*

Dimension A: Creating inclusive cultures

This dimension is about creating secure, accepting, collaborating, stimulating, welcoming communities, in which everyone is valued. Shared inclusive values are developed and conveyed to all staff, children and their families, governors, surrounding communities and all others who work in and with the school. The values of inclusive cultures guide decisions about policies and moment-to-moment practice, so that development is coherent and continuous. The embedding of change within school cultures ensures that it is integrated into the identities of adults and children and is passed on to new arrivals to the school.

Dimension B: Producing inclusive policies

This dimension ensures that inclusion permeates all plans for the school and involves everyone. Policies encourage the participation of children and staff from the moment they join the school. They encourage the school to reach out to all children in the locality and minimise exclusionary pressures. Support policies involve all activities which increase the capacity of a setting to respond to the diversity of those involved in it, in ways that value everyone equally. All forms of support are connected within a single framework aimed at ensuring everyone's participation and the development of the school as a whole.

Dimension C: Evolving inclusive practices

This dimension is about developing what is taught and learnt, and how it is taught and learnt, so that it reflects inclusive values and policies. The implications of inclusive values for structuring the content of learning activities are worked out in a section called 'Constructing curricula for all' (see pages 125-162). This links learning to experience, locally and globally, to rights and environmental sustainability. Learning is orchestrated so that teaching and learning activities are made responsive to the diversity of young people within the school. Children are encouraged to be active, reflective, critical learners and are viewed as a resource for each other's learning. Adults work together so that they all take responsibility for the learning of all children.

The importance of cultures

We have placed cultures along the base of the triangle in Figure 20 and their significance is underlined. It is when policies and practices make a difference to the cultures of a school that they are likely to be sustained. But the relative permanence of cultures makes the development of communities, institutions and systems both possible and difficult. It is through cultures that change is not only sustained but also resisted.

Cultures are relatively permanent ways of life which create, and are constructed by, communities of people. Cultures are established and expressed through language and values, in shared stories, histories, knowledge, skills, beliefs, texts, art, artefacts, formal and informal rules, rituals, systems and institutions. Cultures may bestow, reinforce or contest differences in power. They establish a collective sense of how things are done and should be done. They contribute to the formation of identities so that people see themselves as reflected in, and affirmed by, the activities of a group. An identification with a group's activities provides a motive to show the ways of the community to new arrivals. Like identities, cultures are formed from multiple interacting influences and so are complex. They reflect the different as well as similar influences acting on people and so generally involve networks of overlapping sub-cultures. We use 'cultures' in the plural to reflect this plurality. We generally avoid the word ethos or institutional climate which can reflect a limited view of a school, an image conveyed by the managers of the institution rather than a reflection of the shared experience of everyone.

Cultures involve explicit or implicit rules for identifying and responding to visitors and outsiders. Inclusive cultures encourage a recognition that a variety of ways of life and forms of identity can co-exist, that communication between them is enriching and requires differences of power to be set aside. Where flexibility and variety in activities is ruled out, any change may be experienced as a loss of identity by community members and be resisted. Inclusive cultures meshed together through shared values are welcoming to new members and therefore always involve a preparedness for change.

Each dimension in the *Index* is divided into two sections as illustrated in the Planning Framework in Figure 22 overleaf and on page 179. The Framework can encourage schools attempting to develop one aspect of their school relating to one dimension of the *Index* to look at what needs to be developed in other areas if their hoped for change is to be implemented and then sustained.

Indicators and questions

The indicators and questions in Part 4 of the *Index* make up the bulk of its pages and are our contribution to answering the question: 'what do inclusive values imply for the activities of all aspects of schools?' Indicators are suggested aspirations for development. Each section contains up to 14 indicators. They can be used to review existing arrangements in order to set development priorities. They are headings designed to capture an important possible aim for a school committed to developing inclusively. Sometimes the importance of an issue such as ethnicity, or impairment, is reflected by being spread through the indicators as a whole, rather than being given its own indicator. Gender concerns are both given their own indicator but are also raised in many other places. The permeation of issues through the questions limits the extent to which priorities for development can be determined by focusing on the indicators.

The questions define the meaning of indicators. They challenge thinking about a particular indicator and draw out existing knowledge about the school. They sharpen the investigation of the current situation in the school, provide additional ideas for development activities and serve as criteria for the assessment of progress. Often, it is when people begin to engage with the detail of the questions that they see the practical power of the *Index*. Some schools using the *Index* start from dialogues around one or a very few questions chosen by a group of colleagues working together. Indicators and questions can be used to initiate dialogues about values and the connection between values and actions. At the end of each set of questions there is an invitation to add further questions. In this way adults and children in every school may make their own version of the *Index* by adapting and changing existing questions and adding their own.

Some indicators and questions refer to matters for which schools share responsibility with local authorities, such as access to school buildings, Education, Health and Care Plans and admissions policies. We hope that schools and local authorities will work constructively together to produce building plans, procedures for developing Education, Health and Care Plans, and admissions policies, which encourage the participation in the mainstream of all students from a school's locality.

In some schools, staff and governors may conclude that they do not wish to engage with particular indicators at present, or that these do not point towards a direction in which they wish to travel. Schools are expected to respond in different ways and to adjust the materials to their own requirements. However, adaptation should be resisted if it is proposed because an indicator or question poses an uncomfortable challenge.

In other schools, indicators and questions may not apply because of the character of the school. Single-sex schools and many religious denomination schools do not set out to include all students from their locality. Nevertheless staff in such schools often do wish to plan for the inclusive development of their school and may wish to adapt the indicators and questions to suit their purposes. When the *Index* was first published it was not anticipated that it would be used to prompt the development of special schools. The index is clear in encouraging schools to include all children within their localities. However, several special schools have used it to remove restrictions on the participation of children and staff within their schools.

Figure 22 Planning Framework

Creating inclusive cultures	
Building community	Establishing inclusive values
Producing inclusive policies	
Developing the school for all	Co-ordinating support
Evolving inclusive practices	
Constructing curricula for all	Orchestrating learning

Questionnaires

There are four questionnaires in Part 5 of the *Index*, which can be used to stimulate dialogue and initial expressions of the priorities for development from children, parents/carers, governors and staff. The first is based on the indicators and is for anyone involved in the school. It should be used with reference to the questions, so that the meaning of any particular indicator can be explored. The other three are for parents and children. They, like the indicators and questions, were constructed by thinking about the implications of the *Index* framework of values for the nature of schools. In doing this task the questionnaires quickly became very extensive and had to be cut down. We were encouraged by the way the values framework translated into such practical statements. Schools may wish to shorten them further or otherwise adapt them for their own purposes.

Engaging with the materials

The use of the questionnaires is further discussed in the next part of the *Index* describing the way it can be used in participatory processes. We have stressed that there is no right way of using the materials. Inclusive development of schools may be sparked by: engaging with values; seeing the importance of integrating overlapping initiatives; questioning the nature of planned and experienced curricula; using concepts of 'barriers to learning and participation', 'resources to support learning and participation' and 'support' to change the way educational difficulties are considered; drawing on the role of cultures in sustaining and resisting change. All these activities can be done separately. But they are the issues which have prompted the development of the indicators and questions of the *Index*. So they are brought together in employing the review materials to enable a detailed exploration of what is going on at the school and what might be changed to promote inclusive development.

3 Using the *Index* to take action

Using the *Index* to take action

In Part 3 we suggest ways to work with the *Index* materials. Thousands of people have used the *Index* so we know what varied use they make of it. It is used as a source of ideas in many contexts from schools to university student assignments and to shape university courses. One way of using the *Index* in schools starts from a shared commitment to put inclusive values into action and leads on to the production of a comprehensive inclusive school development plan produced and implemented through collaboration with all those involved in the school's communities. But *Index* use can also focus on a single aspect of a school or even the work of a single teacher though this may contribute to dialogues that will eventually result in inclusive values spreading more widely and deeply. But whatever way the *Index* is used, the aim should be sustained development, not the completion of an inclusion project.

We include a number of accounts of the experience of others who have used the *Index*. Like everything else in this book they are there to stimulate ideas, not because they represent perfect practice.

Routes to inclusive values-led development

You are involved in values-led development from the start of your engagement with the *Index*, when you consider how it can help to resolve your most pressing concerns, connect actions to inclusive values, pedagogical principles and imperatives, think how to remove barriers and mobilise resources, integrate programmes and initiatives and collaborate with others in development planning and implementation.

The *Index* indicators and questions promote all these activities as depicted in Figure 22. At the base of this diagram is a reminder that any development is the result of the efforts of adults and children and belongs to them. The diagram combines a systematic approach with the way development is improvised as inclusive values and *Index* concepts affect moment-to-moment practice.

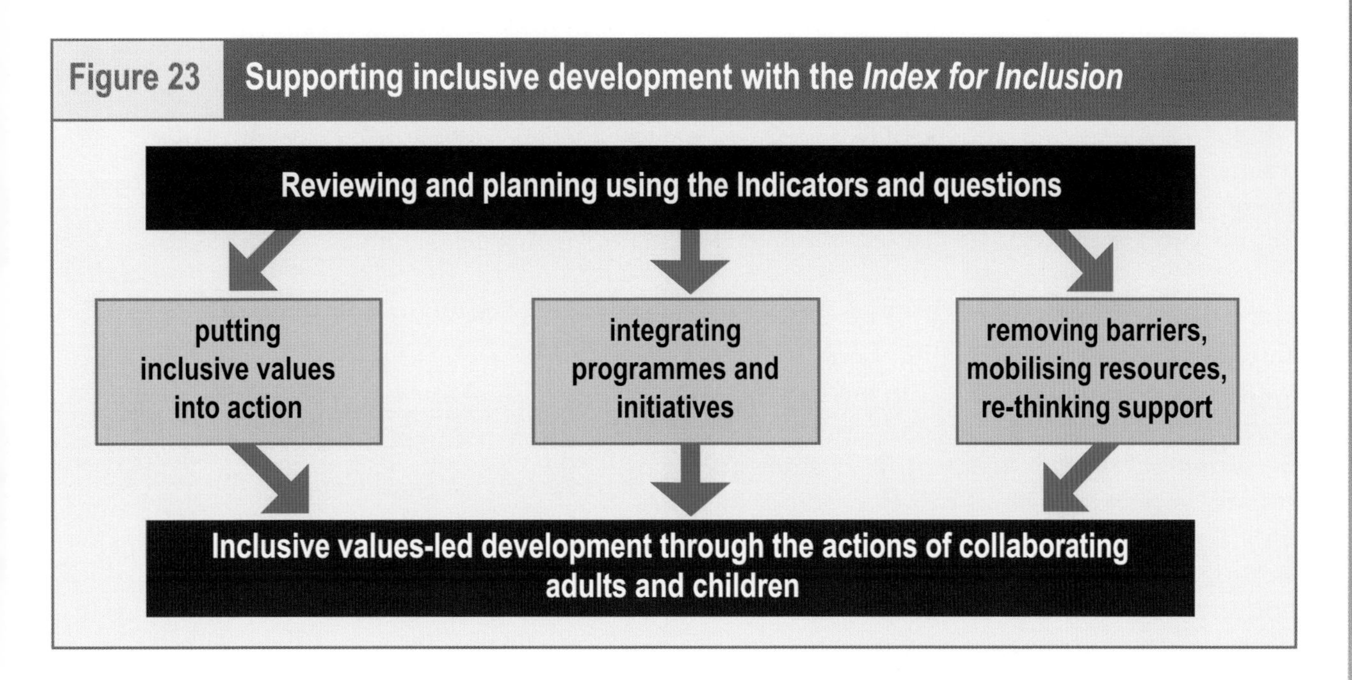

A values-led school development process can be depicted in the cycle shown in Figure 23 though in schools developing continuously, activities under each Phase may be happening simultaneously. Phase 1 is concerned with a development planning group learning how to work with the *Index*, which includes engaging with the values framework. We have broken down each Phase into a set of tasks as shown in Figure 24 each of which we elaborate further.

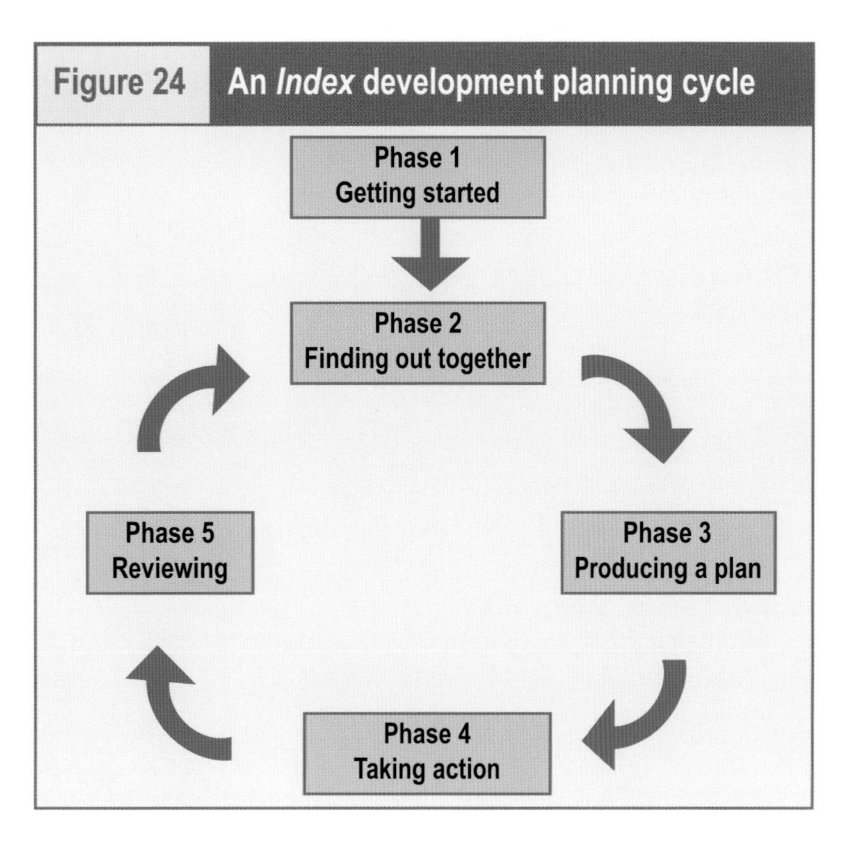

Phase 1: Getting started

Start where and how you can

A push for development in a school may not only come from senior teachers, it can come from parents/carers, governors or a children/young people's school council. Index account 2 is a report of the first meeting of a teacher working as an inclusion co-ordinator, nominated by her school to work with a draft of the Index. Previously we might have seen the opportunistic way she gathered her Index group together as having limitations as a way of beginning work with the Index. But because it makes a start it is ideal. One meeting, in which some dialogue takes place, is an achievement and may make a permanent impression.

Develop your planning group

Nevertheless, as the teacher's report implies, it is an aim in work with the Index that a single, inclusive, approach to school development is put in place. Adding a group to work in a school that is running parallel to ordinary review and development activities increases the overall work of staff. It raises concerns over coherence of the school's activities and the sustainability of any changes that are made.

Sometimes work with the Index is initiated by members of an existing school development planning team. However it starts, membership of a group may need to be widened so that it represents teaching and non-teaching staff, parents, children and young people and governors. It is important that a group reflects the gender and ethnic composition of the school. New people may be co-opted as the work progresses. In a large secondary school each department might have its own planning group, linked to a central group.

The *Index* materials need to be accessible to all those working with it. Schools are encouraged to photocopy any of the materials for their use; these can also be circulated in electronic form and made available for example on a computer in the foyer or a parents' room.

Figure 25 Index phases for development

Phase 1: Getting started

- Start where and how you can
- Develop your planning group
- Find support
- Work inclusively
- Put yourselves in the picture
- Keep a record
- Use the indicators and questions
- Attend to dialogues about values
- Develop a common language: inclusion, barriers, resources and support for diversity
- Review change and development in the school
- Consider the integration of interventions
- Explore the Planning Framework
- Address barriers to using the Index

Phase 2: Finding out together

- Raise awareness
- Make the Index materials available
- Explore the ideas of staff and governors
- Explore the ideas of children
- Explore the ideas of parents/carers and members of local communities
- Negotiate priorities for development
- Integrate consultations into everyday life

Phase 3: Producing a plan

- Put priorities into the development plan

Phase 4: Taking action

- Put priorities into action
- Maintain development

Phase 5: Reviewing development

- Review and celebrate progress
- Reflect on work with the Index
- Consider next steps

Find support

It can be particularly helpful to have the advice of someone with experience of using or introducing the Index in schools. Such a supporter can help to devise the best way to get things moving and to engage staff and others in the process. He or she can ease access to the materials and allay fears about extra workloads. This can help to get a collaborative process of values-led development, moving in the school.

Some have also found it helpful to include a 'critical friend' in their planning team. This, too, can be someone from outside the school who knows the school well and is supportive and challenging. People who have been asked to fulfil the role of critical friend include teachers from other schools, educational advisers, governors, educational psychologists and academics. A primary and secondary school chose to use the opportunity provided by the Index to establish closer links between them by having the learning development co-ordinator in each school as the other's critical friend.

However, anyone from outside the school will need to be committed to seeing the process through for a considerable period and it is better for members of the planning group to become critical friends to each other than to take on as a critical friend someone who cannot take an interest in the way work with the Index is developing in the school over time. All members of the group can be willing to gently challenge their colleagues to produce evidence for their opinions and conclusions about the school.

Index Account 1 — Seizing an opportunity to start in Winterburn High School

I had a fascinating first meeting. I was opportunistic in who I had asked to come. My line manager was there, representing the Senior Management Team. I had a looked after child who had statemented support. I had an Asian girl on the 'gifted and talented' register and a parent of sporty laddish boys, a governor involved in work placements and the child protection governor who is on our admin staff. I invited teachers who were free at the time.

I wanted it to be informal so I supplied basic refreshments – it's amazing what you can do with a packet of party rings and a bag of grapes. I gave a simple introduction and I used the idea from the launch of the project in our area where, in threes, people tell each other two truths and a lie about themselves as an icebreaker, just to get everyone talking. I got them to share their ideas of inclusion – and there was a consensus that it meant 'involving everyone'.

When we discussed barriers, the children said it was unfair the 6th form students could get away with behaviour not tolerated lower down the school and the parents and teachers agreed. It was also remarkable that teachers, parents and pupils all came up with the same concerns around communication. If a child was sent out of the classroom it could be a week before a letter went home to the parents. The school had moved to a largely paper free system and this assumed that parents had internet access whereas many did not have computers at home. Although screens were available in school, they did not have the confidence to use them. Even on parents' evenings nothing was given to parents about their children – they were expected to look on-line at home. The issue of smoking came up. Some of the cafeteria staff go to smoke in the same place as 6th formers.

There were positives as well as negatives, for 'special educational needs' issues it was agreed that communication was good, and the student house councils and school council were thriving. There were lots of good resources at the school though these were under pressure as the school expands because it is popular.

We agreed on half-termly meetings to take things further. They realised that this was just a beginning and work with the Index would involve deeper changes following more detailed engagement with the materials. I showed it to the person who leads the school self-evaluation reporting who thought it was a really good self evaluation tool. It was giving us an opportunity to move away from the top-down way the School Development Plan has been produced. This is the other way round. We wouldn't have done this without the support of the Index. We could have done – and we should have done – but it's given us a reason for working this way and I like it.

– Inclusion Co-ordinator, Winterburn High School

Work inclusively

Becoming critical friends to each other, moving from discussion to dialogue, is an inclusive process. The planning group has to be a model for inclusive practice within the school, operating collaboratively, ensuring that everyone is listened to carefully irrespective of gender, background or status, and that no one dominates interaction. The group members will need to feel that they can trust each other and that it is possible to speak freely and in confidence. Each member of the group needs to offer their opinions in a way that invites dialogue. Differences in view should be welcomed as a resource to carry the group forward in its thinking.

Keep a record

A record will be invaluable when it comes to reflect on any progress made in the previous three months, six months or year. It can help to keep in mind the idea of collecting evidence to present to others including inspectors, about progress. It might contain accounts of meetings and interventions, reflections, questions, photographs, films. As the work progresses several people might contribute to an overall log. It is important to be specific, mentioning the indicators and questions that were used to prompt development. Work with the Index in a school can be given a boost when staff doing degrees or other courses use the work to complete dissertations and assignments that they share with colleagues. In keeping a record of any intervention the questions can be useful.

Figure 26 — What changes were made as a result of using the *Index* in the school

- What was the area of activity or concern
- Who was involved
- What was it like before using the *Index*?
- What was done?
- What changes resulted from using the *Index*?
- What is the evidence for the change?
- What barriers were encountered?
- How were they overcome?

Use the indicators and questions

At a first meeting it can be good to get to the heart of the Index early on by introducing the indicators and questions in Figure 26 can be useful. *Index* Account 3 tells how one assistant head introduced the *Index* to sceptical teachers in a large secondary school, while *Index* Account 4 tells how teachers' views of inclusion changed rapidly as they engaged with the indicators by discussing their responses to an Index indicator questionnaire.

Index Account 2 — Facing reality

In St Simon's School, the assistant head presented the Index to staff following an initial local authority training session. A co-ordinating group was formed which included the head, the assistant head, a teacher, the assistant who provides physiotherapy and other support for children, the link worker for the deaf, a lunchtime supervisor who was also a parent, and the caretaker who was also a governor. A colleague from the local education authority acted as a critical friend. The school had engaged in little overt discussion about inclusion, which previously had been taken to mean that children categorised as having 'special educational needs' should be educated in mainstream classrooms. The assistant head reported on the introduction of the Index:

"At the first meeting I explained the whole process. We did a small exercise [with indicators]... and then we went through questions connected to indicator A1.1 Everyone is welcome and talked about them. When we first started we were saying we are certainly inclusive, we'd never turn anyone away, and we could think of lots of things that we did. But when we started looking at the Index questions, we began to see as well, what we didn't do …"

Index Account 3 | Transforming views of inclusion

At Garside Comprehensive School, the deputy head addressed a staff meeting after questionnaires had been circulated to all staff. She began by suggesting that the Index process was a way of reinforcing and sustaining achievement:

"I started off by saying that inclusion isn't where we want everybody to be happy all the time and where nobody has any rules to obey. I presented [the Index] as an opportunity for a school to take a hard-edged look at where we were as a community facilitating inclusive achievement… The presentation was done. The head then added her bit and then walked away and let it happen. If you can imagine all these 140 people in this assembly hall arguing about what they were going to put down. From a situation where inclusion had been very, very sidelined, it became mainstream. Some people were still sitting there at a quarter to six having debates, having gone into the group at twenty past three, because something in the process had triggered an intellectual response which said 'Hey, this actually belongs to us – this is about me as well as that girl over there [categorised as having special educational needs]. It's actually about all of us'."

During the *Index* work in Norfolk, Judith Carter, Senior Adviser, developed the five-minute introduction to the Index. This bypasses the concern people have expressed about the amount of issues raised by the *Index* and moves straight to its main purpose – to help teachers, governors, children and their families to take action in the areas that concern them. In recognising that it can provide help in meeting an immediate concern people feel encouraged to integrate it into longer term planning. It is a good idea for those co-ordinating work with the Index to become confident in this task. Figure 27 can help with this quick summary.

Figure 27 The Index Structure

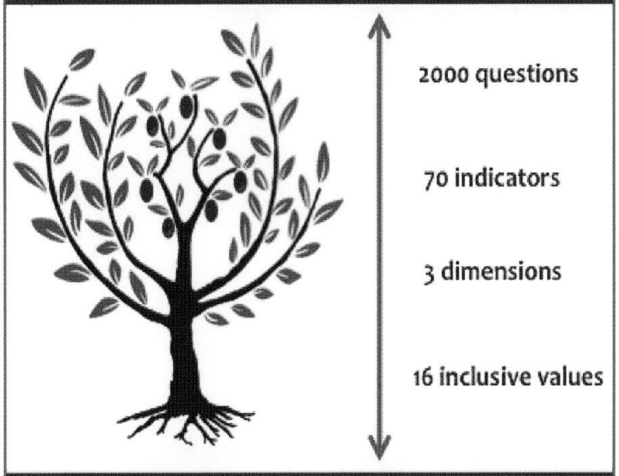

2000 questions

70 indicators

3 dimensions

16 inclusive values

From Values into Actions

Activity 1: A five-minute introduction to the Index

Look at the values framework in the Index on page 11 as the basis of the Index. The task of work with the Index is to put a values framework like this into action. Turn to the indicators on pages 12-13, noting the way they are organised into dimensions and sections. Choose an indicator because it relates to a pressing concern or to a particular interest for development, then turn to its page(s) of questions to deepen your exploration.

Activity 2: Favourite questions

Group members might be asked to look through some of the indicators and questions in Part 4 of the Index before an early meeting and arrive with a favourite question for discussion that they think raises an important issue for the school. Each person can introduce their question, where it is to be found and why it is important. Alternatively the person leading the group can come having selected three or more questions from different parts of the Index that they think will provoke discussion and draw people into getting to know the materials better. Some people have found that whatever questions are selected, discussion of them generally leads on to a consideration of the main challenges facing a school.

Activity 3 provides an opportunity to discuss the value of using questionnaires. Detailed analysis of questionnaires, compiling graphs, bar charts and tables, can be time consuming and can delay the start of development work. It may be important to remember that when used in consulting with staff, parents or children, it is the priorities which summarise what people feel needs to be developed in the school that need to be collated rather than the whole questionnaire. All the questions are written so that agreement that they are true of the school can be viewed as a positive evaluation. People sometimes represent their school as more inclusive than it is. As group members develop trust and feel able to be honest with each other then inclusion in the school may appear to lessen. This limits the extent to which Index questionnaires can be used without further investigations to assess progress in the development of inclusion.

Activity 3: Using the indicators questionnaire to identify priorities for change

The purpose of this activity is to use indicators to identify concerns that might need to be examined further. The complete list of indicators from page 12-13 is also in Questionnaire form on pages 180–181. People can work individually to answer questionnaires and then compare their responses with others in the group, so that differences can be discussed. Each indicator is responded to in one of four ways: 'definitely agree', 'agree and disagree', 'disagree' and 'need more information'. Alternatively the indicators can be written on cards and sorted into piles with these same headings. 'Need more information' is chosen when the meaning of the indicator is unclear or insufficient information is available to make a decision.

At the end of the questionnaire there is space to mention three things that are liked and three priorities for development in the school. The group should share and discuss their priorities for change.

Activity 4: Responding to Section C1: Constructing curricula for all

The group might consider specifically how they responded to the indicators in Section C1. This is likely to differ in primary and secondary schools though both work under curriculum constraints. They might review the arguments for an alternative curriculum on pages 36-40 in Part 2.

- *To what extent do the indicators and questions in C1 offer a sensible way to structure curricula?*
- *To what extent can aspects of C1 be used to improve a more traditional curriculum?*
- *How could the group use the Index to engage others in dialogue about curricula content?*

Activity 5: Discussing evidence

The group might agree on an indicator where they think the school is performing well and another where they think there is considerable room for development. In each case they might provide evidence to support their view. They should use the questions under each indicator to help to find relevant areas of evidence.

Activity 6: Reviewing remaining indicators and questions

This activity might be carried out between meetings. The members of the co-ordinating group all need to familiarise themselves with the indicators and questions of the Index if they did not do so for the first activity. They will see how sometimes questions suggest an aspect of the school which can be easily changed, while other questions may spark off thinking about deep and widespread changes that need to be made. They might share what they have considered at the next meeting.

Index Account 4	From questions to answers at Gregory White Junior School

At Gregory White Junior School, a senior teacher and teaching assistant led the Index work. They started with staff agreeing to look at Indicator C2.9, 'Staff plan, teach and review together', and particularly at two of the questions d) and e): 'Do teachers plan activities so they make use of each others' knowledge and skills?', and 'Do teachers use collaborative teaching as an opportunity for learning from each other?' This prompted the teacher to share her strength in ICT with a colleague who was a PE specialist by teaching each other's classes. Colleagues soon began to work in a similar way 'drawing on each other's strengths'.

The questions in the Index were particularly appealing:

> "One of the most useful things with this resource, as opposed to any other we've worked with, is everything is a question. Just the fact that it's written as a question makes you properly consider it."

The Index questions were also helping 'a core group of governors to get much better at challenging' and in turn the questions were helping teachers to support what they said was happening with evidence.

They had started to use the Index to support the environmental focus of the school. Staff had already made great use of the schools' extensive grounds, transforming the playground with fitness machines, developing the adjourning green space with an orchard, wild area, mud kitchen, massive story chair and a theatre. Indicator: 'A1.7 The school is a model of democratic citizenship' prompted them to link activities in the environment with citizenship and parent participation. The staff had been discussing question l) 'Do children engage in jobs which contribute to the development of the school?'

> "It isn't an obvious eco-link but everyone looking after your environment that has to be about citizenship. And then we looked down the list of jobs and immediately there's composting, cooking of food, tree planting, there are lots of things in there... Or in question b) under that indicator –'Do staff, children and families deliberately create a culture of participation and collaboration?' I think we've got much better at engaging parents but predominantly that's mums, so maybe doing stuff in the garden, practical outdoor stuff, maybe that's where we can get our dads in and involved... "

But the biggest contribution of the Index was in helping them to take control of their own development:

> "We've had to make a conscious choice over the last few years to stop being told what to do and to start looking at what we think works for our children and where we want to go. Interestingly at the point where we started to develop for ourselves and looked at the Index and at other schools, that's when we stopped being Satisfactory and became Good. We're moving rapidly towards doing outstanding things. The Index has really helped us to do that thinking for ourselves."

Attend to dialogues about values

Exploring indicators and questions is likely to have raised discussion of values even if this has not been part of group discussions from the start. The group might continue that discussion with the support of indicator 'A2.1, The school develops shared inclusive values.' They can look at the framework of values on pages 24-33 and the way this is translated into statements for a school in Figure 7 on page 30.

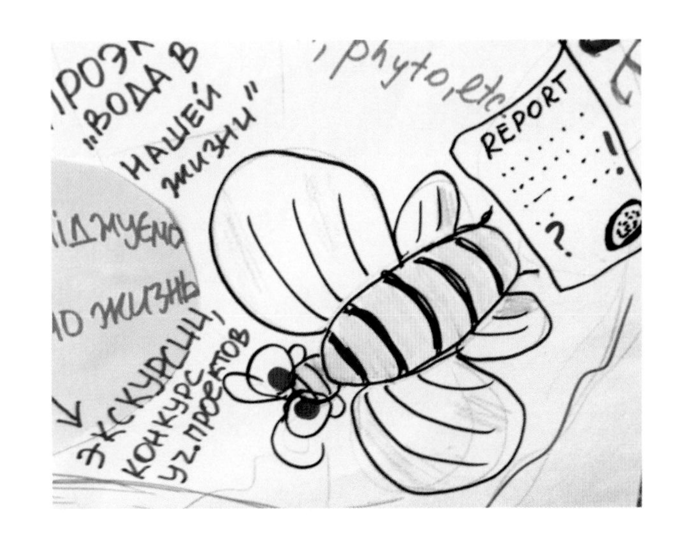

Activity 7: Values and action

The group might divide into subgroups each of which agrees to consider a particular value. They should write the value heading at the centre of a large sheet of paper, explore its meaning and consider what actions in the school adopting such a value encourages and discourages. They should write around the value heading the difference that absorbing the value deeply into the culture of the school would make to what happens in classrooms, staffrooms, around the school and in relationships. The results of these discussions could be shared in the group. They could consider the following questions.

- *How would activities in the school change if there were general agreement on a framework of inclusive values?*
- *To what extent could values dialogues between staff and with children promote changes in actions in the school?*

Activity 8: What is inclusion?

The co-ordinating group can share their views on inclusion and those of others in the school using indicator A.2.4 'Inclusion is viewed as increasing participation for all.' They might then look at Figure 4 on page 22. The ideas in Figure 4 summarise aspects of the approach to inclusion in the Index and each element could be discussed briefly, in turn. The first refers to the idea of inclusion as values into action as discussed in pages 24-33.

Conversations about inclusion often reveal strongly held views. It is unlikely that everyone will agree on every aspect of the view of inclusion in the Index. Yet we hope it makes sense to see it as concerned with all children and all adults, that it is about fundamental values and that it involves making changes to the cultures, policies and practices in the school. Beyond this broad consensus, deeper differences may be simply acknowledged or resolved over a longer period of time.

Develop a common language

It may be a good idea for the co-ordinating group to share their view of the *Index* concepts before they introduce them to others. Activities 8, 9 and 10 can work best after people have read the indicators and questions which draw on these concepts. People using the Index have found that they revise and develop their approach to inclusion, barriers, resources and support for diversity as they work through it.

Reviewing change and development in the school

The *Index* can provide an opportunity to review the way development planning takes place at the school. Schools differ in their approach to development planning. Some involve a wide group of people working together in a relatively systematic way. In other schools, a written document may be produced by very few people or mainly a single person. The Index can help anyone

Activity 9: Barriers and resources

The co-ordinating group might consider barriers to learning and participation and resources to support learning and participation after reading about them in Part 2 of the Index, pages 44–48. They might consider:

- *What barriers to learning and participation arise in the school?*
- *Who experiences barriers to learning and participation?*
- *What resources to support learning and participation exist within the adults, children and environments in and around the school?*
- *How can additional resources be mobilised to support learning and participation within the school?*

The idea of mobilising resources within adults, children and environments is emphasised throughout the Index and it may be worth members of the group considering how the idea permeates the indicators and questions. It is emphasised across the curriculum for example in the idea that all curriculum areas in section C1 should be linked locally and also globally, in the idea of everyone having a school job in indicator A1.7 'The school is a model of democratic citizenship', and in many other indicators.

Activity 10: What is support for diversity?

A broad notion of support is introduced on page 48, as: 'all activities which increase the capacity of a school to respond to diversity in ways that value everyone equally'. The co-ordinating group might consider:

- *What activities within the school count as support?*
- *What are the implications of the* Index *definition of support for the work of staff?*
- *What are the implications of the* Index *definition of support for its co-ordination?*

with thinking what to write in a school development plan. We hope that such engagement will encourage people to see benefits in widening and deepening the involvement of staff, children and young people and their families so that their knowledge and ideas can make a difference.

Most schools are involved in a variety of school development activities or programmes that do not appear in their school development plan. These may have been initiated from within the school or in response to a local or national initiative or inspection visit. The Index group might list these activities and consider how they can be made part of the formal plan and evaluate the extent to which they are linked to inclusive values.

Activity 11: Reviewing school development planning

The members of the group might review their current school development plan. They might discuss the process of development planning in the school by responding to the questions in Indicator B1.1: 'The school has a participatory development process'. They might reflect on the guidelines in Figure 28 and review planning using the following questions:

- *How has the school changed over the last year and why?*
- *What is the content of the plan and to what extent does it reflect the changes that have happened and are taking place?*
- *What development activities take place which are not in the plan?*
- *To what extent do the priorities in the plan help to put inclusive values into action?*
- *How is the plan implemented?*
- *How might the planning process and content and implementation of the plan be improved?*
- *How might the Index contribute to improving the plan?*
- *How could a plan be produced that is accessible to all adults and children connected to the school and lifts their spirits.*

Index Account 5 | Joining the *Index* to the school improvement plan

Turner Infant School put the Index at the centre of its approach to school improvement. They set up a new team to broaden consultation with governors, parents and children but after a child asked 'what do we do while the adults are talking' they revised their approach to including the views of these young children. Parents filled in questionnaires and were involved in focus groups. The views of parents and children on behaviour, bullying and playground use led to substantial change. An early action was to divide the playground into zones with different activities and to increase adult supervision. They built these consultations into annual routines with the focus groups with parents run by other parents which marked a significant point in the developing trust between teachers and parents in the school.

The school integrated the Index into what they needed to do to obtain the Rights Respecting Schools award. They talked with parents and governors when they were leaving the school at a point of openness and reflection to provide fresh insights on what they could improve. There was a move to use staff expertise more resourcefully after the head told his staff: 'you don't blow your own trumpets enough'. So staff invited others to come and see learning activities they felt to be particularly successful. One member of staff led on environmental issues; improving a community garden, recycling food waste from classrooms and kitchens prompted by the indicator on waste (B1.13) which also led to a discussion of package free lunches and many children adopting them.

After a mass of activities, the Index has now become integrated into the School Improvement Plan. There is a column in the plan for the contribution of the Index to meeting any particular priority so 'it forces people who are responsible for that area of the plan to actually look at the Index and use it'. The Index has helped to knit together the improvement of the school. As the head commented: 'It has to work because it shares our values'.

A plan for developing a school written under the headings of cultures, policies and practices by colleagues from Azerbaijan. The development dove has barriers weighing down its feet.

Figure 28 Guidelines for a value-led development plan

A plan might contain:

- Reference to the values guiding the development of the setting.
- Short, medium and longer term priorities selected after considering:
  - wide consultation with staff, parents, children and relevant others
  - existing knowledge, experience and self-reflection of school leaders
  - externally imposed requirements
  - reflection on links between appraisal and the development plan
  - opportunities that have presented themselves
  - the need to link cultures, policies and practices
- Reference to indicators/questions that will support implementation.
- Specifications for action, including as appropriate:
  - what needs to be done
  - who will take responsibility for the various tasks required
  - what resources can be mobilized in support
  - time scales

Review and revision of plan should:

- take place about every three months
- consider new priorities that have arisen
- check on evidence for development

Consider the integration of programmes and initiatives

Schools may be engaged in activities initiated for all sorts of reasons: because of the enthusiasm of staff and parents, the emergence of funding possibilities or pressures from government. Sometimes initiatives can fail to build on what is already being done by staff around a particular issue. For example, the promotion of 'learning outside the classroom'[49] may not integrate with the way staff have been using teaching and learning activities to respond to learning that takes place in children's homes – see Activity 12.

Explore the Planning Framework

There is a Planning Framework on page 179 which the group can photocopy and use to record their priorities for development. They might consider how developments may need to take place in each dimension and section of the Index if they are to be sustained. A priority might be framed in terms of an issue that can be linked to an indicator or group of indicators, a question or group of questions.

49 Department for Education and Skills (2006). *Learning outside the classroom*. London, DfES.

Activity 12: Economies of effort

The group might examine the initiatives and programmes that have taken place in the school in the previous year and are planned for the future both within and outside the school development plan. They might then look at lists of activities brought together under the heading of inclusive educational development in Figure 14 on page 41. They might consider the example of the way government concerns to increase the engagement of schools with global and sustainability issues overlap with each other, on page 42-43 and how both could be promoted by the single principled approach to development of the Index. Dialogues might happen around the following questions:

- *To what extent do interventions, initiatives and programmes in the school overlap?*
- *How could initiatives and programmes be better co-ordinated?*
- *How could initiatives and programmes be better integrated into the ordinary activities of the school?*
- *How might a framework of values help to draw interventions together and support their implementation?*

Activity 13: Supporting priorities and planning interventions

When a priority is selected from one dimension it may be clear that developments need to take place in other dimensions to support it. For example, if developing an anti-bullying policy is adopted as a priority for development work from dimension B, it should be related to the indicators on relationships in dimension A. The group might select a proposed priority for development, perhaps arising from their discussion of their earlier responses to the Indicators Questionnaire, place it within the Planning Framework and then consider the following:

- *What changes would have to take place in other sections to ensure that development is supported?*
- *How could the priority for development be implemented?*

Activity 14: How could the *Index* help with implementing actions currently in the plan?

The members of the group might look at planned actions in the school development plan and explore how working with the Index might improve the way they are implemented.

Address barriers to using the *Index*

After reviewing the materials, the group may may wish to share ideas about the best ways to introduce the Index to others in the school, the barriers they are likely to encounter, and the strategies for overcoming them.

Phase 2: Finding out together

Raising awareness

Before any specific planning decisions are made, the wider school community will need to be informed about the Index. This might happen in a staff development day as suggested below. An awareness-raising session might be led by one or several members of the planning team familiar with the Index materials who model collaboration. It could involve someone from outside the school, who participants trust with their openly expressed opinions such as someone from the Local Authority, not seen as having an inspectorial role, or a colleague from another school who has already worked with the Index. Staff may need to be reassured that they are not expected to change everything in the school at once. The Index helps in selecting priorities for the school development plan and in making inclusive and coherent change. Additions to the planning group might be made as a result of this occasion.

Make the *Index* materials available

Discussions about the Index work best when people have access to the materials. It may be easiest to negotiate one's way around a hard copy of the book, but when people have bought a copy of the book a pdf version is also made available so that a wider group have access to it. This allows people to use their desk computers, laptops and tablets to work with it and to make the materials available for parents or anyone connected to the school who does not have a hard copy. It is also possible to photocopy the questionnaires and other pages for discussion on a particular topic at a meeting.

A staff and governor development day

A staff development day, when staff and governors can work together, is one way to begin to broaden consultation. An outline of such an event is given in Figure 27. The day might involve more than one school working collaboratively. An aim for the end of the day might be to share priorities for development for the school which will be collated by the planning team. But the impetus created by the day may push development in unanticipated directions.

Before the day, activities will need to be selected and adapted. Decisions will have to be taken about whether and how to initiate dialogues about values and the development of a values framework; how to explore the indicators and whether copies of the Indicator questionnaire, planning framework and school development plan are needed. People may be offered the five minute introduction encouraged to arrive with a favourite question as in Activity 2 or the organisers of the day may select questions that they see as most pertinent to the issues of the school. Arrangements will need to be made to record views expressed by different groups.

The co-ordinating group will be able to judge from their own experience of working with the materials, how much time will be needed by others to complete tasks. They will need to keep people moving through the tasks, if all activities are to be completed.

The introduction to the *Index*, which could be a collaborative presentation, could start with the illustration on page 9, which summarises some of the ways that the Index contributes to the development of schools. It might discuss the framework of values, the way initiatives can be integrated, and the use of concepts of barriers, resources and support.

Figure 29 **A staff and governor development day: inclusive values into action**

9 – 9.30 am	An introduction to the *Index* (plenary)
9.30 – 10.30 am	Favourite questions (Activity 2)
	Using the indicators to identify concerns (Activity 3)
10.30 –11.00 am	Tea/coffee
11.00 – 11.30 am	Values into action (Activity 7)
11.30 am – 12.30 pm	Inclusion, barriers, resources and support (Activities 8, 9,10)
12.30 – 1.30 pm	Lunch
1.30 – 2.30 pm	Reviewing school development planning (Activities 11, 12, 13)
2.30 – 3.30 pm	Sharing ideas about priorities for development and further investigation (groups then plenary)
3.30 – 3.45 pm	Next steps in the process (led by the co-ordinating group)
3.45 pm	Tea

Provisional areas for development and further investigation

Generally, once people have engaged with the indicators and questions, they are able to identify specific areas where they think development should take place in the school as a whole but may also see things that they want to begin to change immediately either on their own or with colleagues. Some areas may be identified where further investigation is required before a decision can be made. However, some priorities will only emerge as the information from different groups is brought together and as the consultation is extended and completed.

Planning next steps

At the end of a development day the chair of the planning group could outline what will happen with the information gathered and the views expressed. The co-ordinating group needs to finish collecting information from staff and governors and collate it. Areas may be identified where more information is needed from children, parents/carers and other community members. The group will need to plan how to gather the views of those unable to attend the day.

Explore the ideas of children

Schools using the Index find that consultations with children and young people can reveal important areas for development including barriers to learning and resources to overcome them that they have not previously considered. Gathering information about the school from children can be integrated into the curriculum, for example in language work, in looking at evidence in science, or as part of the school becoming a model democracy. All children in the school should have an opportunity to contribute in some way, even if only some contribute through detailed dialogue.

Questionnaires can be useful in gathering information with children but may contribute most when used with a group to prompt dialogue. Two questionnaires about 'my school' are included in Part 5, one generally for older primary and secondary age children and another for the youngest children which schools can adapt. Children may need help in responding to statements on a questionnaire. With young children it may be best to read each question and offer help to those who have difficulty with the language or instructions or in writing their priorities at the end of the questionnaires. Children may need to be encouraged to give a considered and honest view rather than one said to please staff or other children. Questionnaires can be adapted, for example to a particular

Index Account 6 | Joining the *Index* to the school improvement plan

In Leander, an inner-city secondary school, almost all the children had a Bangladeshi heritage although within the area of the school a substantial minority of children were white. There were also many more boys than girls at the school, since some of the Muslim parents in the area preferred their daughters to attend single-sex schools. There was concern about membership by boys of local gangs and the way this created conflict in the school. Members of the local community attributed these problems, in part, to the lack of space in their flats and houses and the lack of amenities for young people in the area. There was a difference of opinion in the school about why so few children took Bengali at GCSE. The head of modern languages suggested that the children were not interested, whereas other staff with a Bangladeshi background felt it was because insufficient value was placed on the children's home language, Sylheti, a Bengali dialect. Parents complained too about the lack of modesty permitted by showering arrangements.

The following specific statements were added to the general questionnaire for schools:

- I wish there were an equal number of boys and girls at this school.
- I wish there were a greater mix of children from different backgrounds.
- I would like to study Bengali at GCSE.
- My family has a good understanding of what happens at school.
- The teachers have a good understanding of the communities around this school.
- Children should be able to chat in Sylheti during lessons.
- Children who are learning English get the help they need.
- I feel comfortable with the shower arrangements for PE.
- I feel uncomfortable in certain lessons because of my religious beliefs.
- I worry about getting into trouble with gangs.
- I can mix with children inside school who do not live in my area.
- I can mix with children outside school who do not come from my area.
- My family would disapprove of who I mix with in school.
- It is easier to mix with children of the opposite sex inside than outside school.
- There is a place for me to do my homework at home.

age group and to reflect the issues of a particular area as in Index Account 7.

In addition to using questionnaires, there are a number of ways teachers can engage children in expressing their likes and dislikes about the school and their assessment of barriers to, and resources for, learning. Careful attentive listening to what children say and don't say can be the most powerful guide to their concerns as it may be to the concerns of adults.

Photographs can also be taken of places to seek out or avoid in the school and the surrounding area and ideas about how to

Activity 15: Capturing images of barriers and resources

Digital or other cameras have been used with children as a powerful way of eliciting views about school. Children might take pictures in relation to the following questions:

- *What helps you to learn?*
- *What stops you learning?*
- *What makes you feel good about the school?*
- *What would you like to change?*

improve the school can be elicited using maps and drawings, children's own plays performed by children or puppets, and responses to stories, films and dramas. Everyone can be involved in observing, documenting and reporting on practice, in order to engage in shared review and suggestions for change. In both primary and secondary schools but particularly the latter, shadowing a group for a day can give an understanding of their experience of different teaching and learning activities, playgrounds, friendships, teachers and teaching assistants. A combination of views of children's experience can be put together into a mosaic.[50]

Explore the ideas of parents/ carers and members of local communities

Consultation with parents/carers and other community members may reveal further perspectives on the school from people who think deeply about children's education. A questionnaire for parents/carers, 'my child's school' is also provided in Part 5. Like other questionnaires, this might be used as an invitation to parents to more detailed dialogue about barriers and resources at the school.

Schools have tried a number of ways to encourage parents to complete questionnaires. In one school parents' views were gathered during the school's 'Annual Summer Fayre'. In another school questionnaires were given to parents during the school's consultation evening, which they completed while waiting for appointments with teachers. The following day questionnaires were sent by post to parents who had not come. Each questionnaire had a tear off slip for entry into a prize draw.

The planning group might have its own ideas about increasing the involvement of parents particularly where attendance at school meetings has previously been low. They might consider meeting parents away from the school if attendance is likely to be greater in a different setting. A variety of opportunities to contribute may need to be arranged. In one school a parent liaison worker employed in the school, and a member of the planning group, arranged for translation of questions for those parents/carers fluent in languages other than English and acted as interpreters in the discussion groups. Other schools have exchanged translations of questionnaires.

Meetings will be based on a wish to hear the views of parents/carers and might be set up as a collaboration between staff and parents/carers. The meeting might explore the following questions:

- What are the strengths of the school?
- What would help to improve the learning of your child/children in this school?
- What could be done to make your child/children happier in school?
- What would you most like to change about this school?

Parents might come to the meeting having filled in a questionnaire or this might be used as a follow up to it, or as a way of gathering information from those unable to attend. As well as working with parents/carers, it may be helpful to find out the views of others in the communities surrounding the school. The child population may not reflect the composition of the area, in terms of ethnicity, impairment or class. Finding out the views of community members may help the school in efforts to make the school more representative.

50 Clark, A. and Moss, P. (2005) *Spaces to Play, More listening to young children using the mosaic approach*, London, National Children's Bureau.

Index **Account 8**	**Daring to develop in Redlands High**

In Redlands High School the assistant head who was also a geography teacher, was concerned about the lack of parent involvement. She decided that they might like to experience what it was like to be a student at the school and so sent out an invitation for parents to come and sample a geography lesson. She had eighty positive responses and put on three separate lessons in the evening. She was a very confident teacher and this idea would not appeal to everyone, though others will have their own imaginative ways of increasing involvement with parents. She had mentioned her innovation during a discussion of the impact of using the Index in her school and it was pointed out that although there was much encouragement for schools to have close relationships with families this specific suggestion was not there. She responded: "Yes, you are right, but the Index helped me dare to do it."

Negotiate priorities for development

In order to draw up a plan, the co-ordinating group will need to collate and analyse the priorities for development selected by everyone who has been consulted. This might be best done immediately the information is collected. Information from children, parents/carers, staff and governors might be kept separate so that differences of perspective can be revealed and explored. It may be important to look at the views of sub-groups of staff such as teaching assistants or those in different departments.

A supporter from outside the school might have been chosen for their capacity to help with this process thought it is important to encourage involvement and ownership of development from all staff, parents/carers, children and governors and from members of the local community. As ownership is spread, new offers to share in development work may emerge.

Additional information may be needed before priorities can be finalised. During the consultations, issues will have been identified which can be clarified by gathering further information. For example, it might be necessary to analyse attendance records or the test results of children by gender and ethnicity. The need to gather of additional information may have emerged during the consultation process such as a need to ask new staff about the success of their induction. The gathering of further information can be built into development activity, for example, when teachers and teaching assistants help to improve teaching and learning by observing, recording and reflecting on each other's practice.

The co-ordinating group will need to make sure that the opinions of less powerful groups are not lost and that the voices of children and parents/carers in particular are reflected in the final plan so that they learn that their opinions really matter. Priorities may vary widely in the time and resources required to implement them.

Figure 30 provides some examples of priorities identified by schools. *Index* Account 6 reports on the results of consultation in one school.

Integrate consultations into everyday life

Encouraging wide involvement in planning is an aspect of the development of an inclusive community and should be sustained when an initial flurry of consultation is over. So expanding on the ways these groups routinely contribute their ideas is as important as a single wide consultation. The co-ordinating group can review the structures that are in place for listening to the voices of all staff, children, parents/carers and governors and seek ideas from these groups to expand them. They might share ideas with other schools or across a local authority. Children might research ways to increase participation as a project in language work or citizenship education. A parent room might be established, once a month the hall might be turned into a democratic forum. Participation is one of the values underlying the Index and the indicators and questions contain many suggestions for giving adults and children a greater say in their schools.

Figure 30 Examples of school priorities

- Introducing rituals for welcoming new children and staff and marking their departure.
- Establishing staff development activities to make lessons more responsive to diversity.
- Introducing career structures for teaching assistants.
- Linking work on growing vegetables within the school grounds, cooking in the school kitchen, composting, food production in local farms.
- Improving access in the school for disabled children and adults.
- Integrating all forms of support within the school.
- Introducing values literacy activities for adults and children, including 'values of the month'.
- Arranging joint training for teaching assistants and teachers.
- Developing collaborative learning for children.
- Researching bullying and revising the anti-bullying policy.
- Increasing the involvement of children in decision-making about school policies.
- Promoting positive views of ethnic diversity in teaching and displays.
- Improving communication between the school and parents/carers.

Phase 3: Producing a plan

Put priorities into the development plan

In order to increase the possibilities that new actions taken by the school will be sustained, the planning group may need to review and suggest modifications to the existing school development plan. This will require support from the head and other senior members of the school. It may be necessary compromise in recognition of the different interests within and beyond the school. This negotiation about the connections of school priorities to inclusive values, is amongst the most important tasks of the planning group.

For each new priority the group will need to consider time-scale, resources, allocations of responsibilities and professional development implications. Having short and medium term goals can help to sustain a focus on more ambitious priorities. Responsibility for checking the progress of each priority could be allocated to a member of the planning team but though progress implementing the plan the responsibility of everyone.

Criteria for evaluating implementation will need to be drawn up. Index questions can form the basis of these criteria where priorities have emerged from particular indicators. It may be useful to look at the inter-connections between indicators so that such questions can be drawn from a number of indicators.

Phase 4: Taking action

Put priorities into action

People do not need to wait for the emergence of a school plan to act on the development of shared values, for example in the way human resources are used or how leaning activities link closely to local and global environments and events. A record of work with the Index might try to capture such impacts. Some reports of work with the Index are presented in the accounts in this section, and have have been collected in print[51] and on the website indexforinclusion.org.

Maintain development

As priorities are put into action, commitment has to be maintained. Activities to create more inclusive cultures can sustain, and be sustained by, the active involvement of staff, governors, children and parents/carers. Where priorities challenge deeply held beliefs, considerable effort may be required to overcome resistance. The planning team can encourage dialogue about differences and may need to refine developments so that they are widely supported. *Index* Account 9 provides an example where work with the Index supported adults and children in a school to make widespread changes after difficult beginnings.

51 Rustemier, S. and Booth, T. (2005) *Learning about the Index in use, a study of the use of the Index in schools and LEAs in England*, Bristol, CSIE.

Index Account 9 Providing a new sense of direction

Before using the *Index*, Hind Primary School was in 'special measures', seen to have staffing and discipline problems. Relationships between staff and with governors and parents were poor. The head teacher acknowledged that staff 'assumed they knew' what parents wanted. Staff were 'asked to do things they didn't particularly believe in'. Teachers expressed disappointment with the performance of children but ignored their positive achievements. An Index co-ordinating group included governors, parents and staff and was steered by a critical friend, respected within the school and local authority. Consultations were broad, and the results were 'very challenging'. For example, parents/carers recorded their views of staff attitudes to their children: 'they don't care for them', 'they have favourites'.

The head's first concern was communication with parents, which needed particular attention. She started by making sure parents/carers and governors were better informed. The school brochure was rewritten in plain English, she set up times to talk about the curriculum and homework and opportunities for parents to join in activities with their children. She had assumed that staff felt involved in what was happening but found that she needed to set up regular staff meetings because they felt left out of her plans.

Joining and leaving the school became seen as significant 'rites of passage'. The induction morning for new children involved parents, teachers, the chair of governors and the chair of the parent-teacher association. It started with a joint assembly and ended with shared lunch. Parents were invited to the following assembly where the children were presented with a reading folder bearing the school logo. At the end of the year, there was a barbecue for school leavers with parents and governors invited and with live music.

Staff introduced further changes: pictures of all staff were placed at the entrance to the school with a two-way intercom and CCTV at the door to allay parents'/carers' security concerns; children accumulated a portfolio of their best work throughout the school; a weekly school newsletter was produced by the Year 6 ICT Club; the head became more accessible and visible at the beginning and end of the day; circle time included positive mentions of good behaviour and work; two teaching assistants were available to ease into the day children who were having difficulties at home.

Staff felt that the *Index* helped the school to put 'the child at the centre':

> "with everyone, the dining room supervisors, the teaching staff, the teaching assistants, the kitchen staff, the caretakers, cleaners, all in a circle around that child, all with their bit to say. It's about the child learning and having high expectations but it's about the child having a say too, not just being done to, but doing things as well."

A school council was planned and elected children were given assertiveness and conflict management training so that they could support children who were isolated or were bullied. The head felt that using the *Index* was 'pulling us all together in one common focus':

> "While I can see the benefits in all schools, I think for schools that have gone through periods of upheaval and disruption, like this one, it actually provides a good way forward."

Phase 5: Reviewing development

Review and celebrate progress

The person responsible for implementing a priority in the development plan will lead the checking and recording of progress and propose any required adjustments to the plan. A half-termly record of progress might be circulated in newsletters, assemblies, staff meetings, staff development days, registration/tutorials, circle time, children's councils, notice boards, websites and community organisations. Inclusive changes in the cultures of a school may go beyond any particular planned priority and will be revealed through sharing observations and stories about progress in putting inclusive values into action.

The team might invite other schools using the *Index* to join them in a celebration of what has been achieved in the past year. They might involve staff, parents/carers, children, governors and community members in creatively presenting their experience of the work, verbally or pictorially. A photograph of this display might form their year's inclusion award in the entrance hall.

Reflect on work with the *Index*

The planning team can review past work and decide how the materials can best be used to support school development in the future in relation to the questions in Figure 31 overleaf.

Next steps

The final phase of the process may coincide with the end of a year of working with the *Index*. In some schools, the majority of staff will be familiar with the Index at this point, but new staff might have the process explained to them as part of their induction programme into the cultures, policies and practices of the school. The revisiting of the indicators and questions as part of a review of progress may lead to new priorities for development in the development planning cycle blended with the continuing process of *putting inclusive values into action*.

Figure 31 Reviewing work with the *Index*

How and to what extent:

- Has the planning group been successful in its composition, equality of participation, sharing of tasks, consulting with others, and supporting inclusive development?
- Has he Index influenced changes in the school?
- Has there been a change in commitment towards more inclusive ways of working in the school?
- Has the Index influenced dialogues about values?
- Has the Index helped to draw together interventions, initiatives and programmes?
- Has the Index prompted increased attention to school cultures?
- Has the Index concepts (inclusion, barriers, resources and support for diversity) affected thinking about school policy and practice?
- Has the development process been inclusive and who else might contribute to it in future years?
- Have the indicators and questions helped to identify priorities that had been overlooked?
- Have the dimensions and sections of the Index been useful in structuring school development planning?
- Have developments been sustained and how might this process be improved?

4 Indicators with questions

Indicators with questions

Section 4 contains indicators with the questions that define their meaning and provide for a detailed review of a school.

A complete list of indicators was given in part 1 of the *Index* on pages 14-15. Just underneath most indicators in this section we have referred to a number of other indicators to show interconnections within and across Dimensions. The ones we have mentioned are notional, encouraging you to make your own connections when it comes to planning development within your school. Each dimension is colour coded at the edge of the page and a change of tint shows a change of section. For all the indicators in Dimension A and B and for section 2 in Dimension C we have stopped asking further questions when a page was filled. We have also avoided going beyond z in numbering and this has meant that some questions have been combined. Other important questions may occur to you which you want to include as part of the investigation of the cultures, policies and practices of your school and the lines at the end of each indicator suggest that you might want to do that.

Section 1 of Dimension C is an exception. It contains an outline for a curriculum, with each indicator containing unnumbered questions, fleshing out a curriculum area, grouped under a number of sub-headings, but always starting with 'Linking locally and globally' and always finishing with 'Linking present, past and future'. For ease of reference we have given the sub-headings a letter. Each area is given a minimum of two pages.

Dimension A: Creating inclusive cultures

A1: Building community

1 Everyone is welcomed.
2 Staff co-operate.
3 Children help each other.
4 Staff and children respect one another.
5 Staff and parents/carers collaborate.
6 Staff and governors work well together.
7 The school is a model of democratic citizenship.
8 The school encourages an understanding of the interconnections between people around the world.
9 Adults and children are responsive to a variety of ways of being a gender.
10 The school and local communities develop each other.
11 Staff link what happens in school to children's lives at home.

A2: Establishing inclusive values

1 The school develops shared inclusive values.
2 The school encourages respect for all human rights
3 The school encourages respect for the integrity of planet earth.
4 Inclusion is viewed as increasing participation for all.
5 Expectations are high for all children.
6 Children are valued equally.
7 The school counters all forms of discrimination.
8 The school promotes non-violent interactions and resolutions to disputes.
9 The school encourages children and adults to feel good about themselves.
10 The school contributes to the health of children and adults.

A1.1 Everyone is welcomed.

A2.9 The school encourages children and adults to feel good about themselves;
B1.6 The school seeks to admit all children from its locality.

a) Is the first contact that people have with the school welcoming?
b) Do staff, children and families create a sense of community at the school?
c) Is the school welcoming to all parents/carers and other members of its local communities?
d) Is the school welcoming to those who have recently arrived from elsewhere in the country or other countries?
e) Do staff, children and parents/carers greet each other in a polite and friendly way?
f) Do staff, children, parents and governors make an effort to learn each other's names?
g) Are people's spirits lifted by a visit to the school?
h) Is the quality of relationships seen to be more important for making people feel welcome than the quality of buildings and equipment?
i) Is the school welcoming to all children from its local communities, irrespective of financial circumstances, family arrangements, heritage and attainment?
j) Is the school concerned to welcome those who may have faced exclusion and discrimination such as travellers, refugees, asylum seekers and children with impairments?
k) Do documents, notices and displays demonstrate that the school welcomes people with heritages and identities not currently represented in the school?
l) Does information provided to parents/carers and job applicants make clear that having children and staff with diverse backgrounds and interests is important to the school?
m) Is school information made accessible to all, for example by being translated, Brailled, audio recorded, or in large print when necessary?
n) Are sign language and other first language interpreters available when necessary?
o) Does the entrance hall reflect all members of the school and its communities in signs and displays?
p) Do displays link the school to other parts of the country and the world?
q) Is the entrance designed for the enjoyment of adults and children connected to the school rather than to impress inspectors?
r) Do signs and displays avoid jargon and clichés?
s) Are there positive rituals for welcoming new children and staff and marking their leaving whenever this happens and whoever it involves?
t) Do children feel ownership of their classrooms or tutor room?
u) Do children, parents/carers, staff, governors and community members all feel ownership of the school?

v) ______________________________

w) ______________________________

x) ______________________________

A1.2 Staff co-operate.

C2.9 Staff plan, teach and review together;
C2.10 Staff develop shared resources to support learning.

a) Do staff create a culture of collaboration for everyone at the school?
b) Do staff uncover barriers to greater collaboration and attempt to resolve them?
c) Is teamwork between staff a model for the collaboration of children?
d) Are all staff good listeners?
e) Do staff get on well together?
f) Do staff take an interest in each other's lives and work?
g) Do all staff, both teaching and non-teaching, enjoy working together?
h) Do staff treat each other with respect whatever their roles and perceived status?
i) Do staff respect each other without regard to gender, sexual orientation, ethnicity or impairment?
j) Do all staff feel valued and supported?
k) Do staff engage in exploratory dialogue rather than competitive discussion?
l) Is it understood that staff from the local area make a particular contribution to developing school cultures?
m) Do staff who come from the area around the school feel that their local knowledge in valued?
n) Do all staff feel welcome at whole staff social events?
o) Do staff routinely share ideas about classroom and out of school activities?
p) Are significant events such as births, birthdays, deaths, weddings and civil partnerships given the same attention irrespective of the roles and perceived status of staff?
q) Are all staff invited to staff meetings, do they attend and do they contribute?
r) Do staff feel comfortable in voicing disagreement in meetings?
s) Are staff comfortable about asking each other for advice about teaching and learning?
t) Do staff feel at ease in discussing with colleagues difficulties they have in relationships with children?
u) Do staff notice when colleagues are stressed, or otherwise having difficulties, and offer support?
v) Can difficulties in collaboration between staff be discussed and resolved constructively?
w) Do staff in school consider how to overcome barriers to collaboration that arise when many staff leave or join the school?
x) Do staff stick up for each other if they are being bullied by other staff?
y) Are regular supply staff and other temporary staff encouraged to be actively involved in the life of the school?
z) Are staff unions encouraged to make a contribution to school life?

aa) ____

ab) ____

ac) ____

A1.3 Children help each other.

B1.7 All new children are helped to settle into the school;
C2.5 Children learn from each other.

a) Do children take an interest in each other's lives and what each other learns?
b) Do children and adults identify barriers to the greater collaboration of children?
c) Do children understand how accepting and valuing others helps them to feel good about themselves?
d) Are supportive friendships actively fostered?
e) Do children learn to share rather than compete for friends?
f) Do children invite others to join in their games when they see they have no-one to talk to or play with at break times and lunchtimes?
g) Do all staff encourage the building of relationships for children in break times and before and after school?
h) Do children understand how to see things from another's point of view?
i) Do children engage in activities together outside school that they were developing in school?
j) Do children seek help from each other?
k) Are children aware of the things they can do to help others and the ways others can help them?
l) Do children willingly share their knowledge and skills?
m) Do children offer help to each other when they think it is needed without expecting anything in return?
n) Do children refuse help politely when they do not need it?[52]
o) Do children take pleasure in each other's achievements?
p) Do displays celebrate collaborative work by children as well as individual achievements?
q) Do children appreciate the efforts of other children irrespective of their level of attainment?
r) Do children understand that different degrees of conformity to school rules may be expected from different children?
s) Do children tell a member of staff when they or someone else needs assistance?
t) Do children feel that disputes between them are dealt with fairly?
u) Do children learn how to resolve disputes that arise between them?
v) Do children learn to speak up for others who they feel have been treated unfairly by other children or adults?

w) ______________________________

x) ______________________________

y) ______________________________

52 This question came from Sapon-Shevin, M. (1999) Because we can change the world: a practical guide to building co-operative, inclusive classroom communities, Boston, Allyn and Bacon.

A1.4 Staff and children respect one another.

A2.9 The school encourages children and adults to feel good about themselves;
C2.8 Discipline is based on mutual respect.

a) Is everyone addressed respectfully, by the name they wish to be called, with the correct pronunciation?
b) Is everyone referred to with the gender pronoun they would prefer to be used for them?
c) Do staff view children as human beings like themselves rather than as lesser beings?
d) Do children view staff as human beings like themselves rather than as enemies or oppressors?
e) Do children and adults respect each other's needs for privacy?
f) Do children and adults respect each other's belongings?
g) Is every child known well by some members of staff?
h) Do children feel that they are liked by teachers and other staff?
i) Do children treat all staff with respect irrespective of their roles in the school?
j) Do children help staff when asked?
k) Do children offer help when they see it is needed?
l) Do staff and children look after the physical environment of the school?
m) Are basic facilities for children and adults such as toilets, showers and lockers, kept in good order?
n) Do children know who to see when they have a problem?
o) Are children confident that when they say they have a problem it is taken seriously?
p) Are children confident that they will get help if they experience difficulties?
q) Are all members of the school regarded as both learners and teachers?
r) Are significant events, such as births, marriages, civil partnerships, deaths and illnesses, divorce, dissolution, separation and illness acknowledged appropriately?
s) Is it recognised that everyone, not just members of 'ethnic minorities', has a culture or cultures?
t) Is it recognised that all cultures and religions encompass a range of views and degrees of observance?
u) Can children and adults be supported to acknowledge that they are hurt, depressed or angry on a particular day?
v) When staff feel cross or frustrated do they continue to speak to children with respect?
w) Is it accepted that negative personal feelings about others can be expressed in private as a way of overcoming them?
x) Do staff and children respect the confidentiality of private conversations unless this will result in harm to another?

y) ______________________________

z) ______________________________

aa) ______________________________

A1.5 Staff and parents/carers collaborate

B1.1 The school has a participatory development process;
Section C1 (Linking locally and globally).

a) Do parents/carers and staff respect each other whatever their perceived class or status?
b) Do all parents/carers feel that their children are valued by the school?
c) Do staff feel that parents/carers appreciate what they do?
d) Are parents/carers well informed about what goes on in school?
e) Are parents informed clearly and promptly when an issue of wide concern arises in the school?
f) Are there a variety of opportunities for parents/carers to be involved in the school?
g) Are the different contributions that parents/carers can make to the school equally appreciated?
h) Do staff use their own experience of being a parent to improve their relationships with the parent/carers of children in the school?
i) Do staff avoid blaming children's problems on their coming from 'a single parent family' or broken home'?
j) Do staff appreciate the support that children receive from parents/carers whether or not they live full-time with two parents in their house?
k) Do staff get to know about the variety of children's extended families?
l) Do staff and parents/carers negotiate how they prefer to be addressed?
m) Do staff avoid using a generic 'mum' or 'dad' to address or talk about parents?
n) Are parents/carers clear about whom to approach to discuss concerns?
o) Do parents/carers feel that their concerns are taken seriously?
p) Are all parents/carers invited to discussions and informed about children's education?
q) Are extended family members welcomed as contributors to children's education?
r) Do staff avoid only contacting parents/carers to complain about a child?
s) Are there regular exchanges of information between homes and schools?
t) Is there a place where parents/carers can meet, exchange ideas, and make a cup of tea/coffee or prepare a cold drink?
u) Do parents/carers encourage other parents/carers to participate in school activities so that no-one feels left out or marginalised?
v) Do meetings with parents share knowledge about children rather than only convey knowledge from staff to parents?
w) Are parents/carers clear about how they can support children's learning at home?
x) Do staff increase involvement with parents/carers by holding meetings at a variety of times and places?
y) Do staff address fears that parents/carers may have about visiting schools and teachers?
z) Do staff avoid feeling threatened by parents/carers they see as of higher status or more knowledgeable than themselves?
aa) ______________________________
ab) ______________________________
ac) ______________________________

A1.6 Staff and governors work well together.

A1.2 Staff co-operate;
A1.5 Staff and parents/carers collaborate.

a) Do staff meet and get to know the governors?
b) Are pictures of the governors and their interests displayed in the school?
c) Are governors given the information they need to understand their role and do their job?
d) Do governors understand the way the school is organised?
e) Do staff and governors know, and agree about, their respective contributions and powers?
f) Are new governors introduced to the school and how it operates by children and all categories of staff ?
g) Do governors reflect the composition of the school communities?
h) Do governors endeavour to set aside any perceived status differences between them?
i) Is the contribution of all governors equally valued?
j) Are governors meetings well-chaired with agreed timings for items, including any other business and an agreed finishing time?
k) Are governors meetings enjoyable?
l) Do governors tell others about the satisfactions of being a governor so that the number of people who seek to be a governor is increased?
m) Are members encouraged to bring up issues of concern, for which adequate time is given, even if they have not previously been included on the agenda?
n) Are governors meetings made enjoyable with food and drink available for those who come to them hungry and thirsty?
o) Do governors meetings encourage participation from all their members?
p) Do governors who are staff of the school feel free to express an independent voice?
q) Are decisions taken where appropriate by secret ballot?
r) Do governors have an established way of visiting the school and contributing to school life?
s) Do governors make an effort to get to know children at the school?
t) Are the skills and knowledge of governors known and valued?
u) Do all governors feel involved in drawing up and reviewing school policies?
v) Are governors invited to share professional development opportunities with staff?
w) Do staff and governors share an approach to how the school should respond to the difficulties experienced by children and how support should be provided?
x) Do staff and governors aim to minimise the categorisation of children as 'having special educational needs'?
y) Do staff and governors challenge each other if they display discriminatory attitudes?

z) ____________________

aa) ____________________

ab) ____________________

A1.7 The school is a model of democratic citizenship.

B1.1 The school has a participatory development process;
C1.13 Children learn about ethics, power and government.

a) Does everyone learn to get on well and to be good citizens by being at the school?
b) Do staff, children and families deliberately create a culture of participation and collaboration?
c) Do children learn to be active citizens from each other as well as adults?
d) Do all staff welcome the active participation of children and adults in the school?
e) Is the active participation of children and adults evident in classrooms, staffrooms, the school grounds, before and after school, in displays and school events?
f) Do children and adults share meanings of democracy?
g) Do children and adults consider the extent to which their school encourages democratic participation?
h) Does the school have public forums where adults and children regularly share their ideas?
i) Does the school celebrate progress in the recognition of rights and democracy including key developments in its own history?
j) Are there regular times when classes and the whole school engage in voting about issues of importance for the school?
k) Do all children have an opportunity to be involved in a School Council or Children's Parliament?
l) Do all children engage in jobs which contribute to the development of the school?

Jobs might include:

Community visiting
Composting
Cooking, serving, clearing food
Creating art
Curating school's collection of treasures
Developing/tidying school grounds
Documenting animal and bird visitors to the site
Documenting school histories
Increasing biodiversity
Instructing in sport
Job interviewing
Language ambassadors
Looking after the library
Looking after school animals
Looking after school pond
Monitoring energy use
Network technicians
Organising school post
Play leading
Producing and teaching art
Producing/writing for a school newspaper
Providing community entertainment
Reading to others
Recycling
Resolving conflicts
Returning lost property
School gardening
School guides
Stage managing
Staging plays
Teaching chess
Tree planting
Waste reduction e.g. waste-free lunches
Welcoming new staff/ receiving visitors
Writing poetry, school chronicle
Etc, etc, etc...

m) ____________________

n) ____________________

A1.8 The school encourages an understanding of the interconnections between people around the world.

Section C1 (Linking locally and globally);
C2.6 Lessons develop an understanding of the similarities and differences between people.

a) Are the links of adults and children in the school with others around the world used as a starting point for expanding an understanding of global connections?
b) Is the location of the school in its region, the country and connections with the world viewed from a variety of historical and geographical perspectives and evident in displays?
c) Do children gain an idea of the way global interconnections between people change over time?
d) Are children aware of how the lives of people in one part of the world affect those in another?
e) Do children explore global influences on what they learn, the words they speak, the art they look at, the music they hear, the energy they consume, the food they eat, the newspapers and books they read, the sports and games they play and watch?
f) Do adults and children show how being a global citizen involves everyday actions?
g) Are children good neighbours to people who arrive in their country from another part of the world?
h) Do children explore the nature of constructive and oppressive relationships between countries?
i) Are children helped to understand the meaning of racism and xenophobia and how it affects attitudes between peoples and countries?
j) Do children learn about the way countries are connected through trade?
k) Do adults and children explore the possibilities for making their purchases ethical?
l) Does the school have a commitment to Fair Trade in its purchasing and banking activities?
m) Do children learn what happens to loans and aid given to economically poor countries?
n) Do children learn the extent to which relationships between countries are based on a commitment to values of equality, participation and non-violence?
o) Do children learn about the significance of the arms trade in their country?
p) Do children have an understanding of the way the activities of corporations and banks as well as governments can affect the lives of people around the world positively and negatively?
q) Is the school linked to a school in an economically poor country?
r) Does the school ensure that relationships with adults and children in any link school are based on equality, respect and the development of dialogue rather than charity?
s) Is the school linked to a school in a different location within its own country, either urban or rural?

t) ______________________________

u) ______________________________

v) ______________________________

A1.9 Adults and children are responsive to a variety of ways of interpreting gender.

A2.9 The school encourages children and adults to feel good about themselves;
C1.6 Children learn about health and relationships.

a) Do adults and children recognise that not everyone thinks of themselves as male or female?
b) Do staff reflect on the complexity of their own identities as gendered beings?
c) Do staff feel able to allow children the freedom to develop their genders in the ways that help children to feel most at ease?
d) Do children learn that one can have a strong sense of one's gender as male, female or transgender without this fixing one's ways of behaving, expressing feelings, interests and attitudes to achievements?
e) Do adults discuss the extent to which they hold stereotypic views of gender roles and how expressing such attitudes can narrow the ways in which children express their gender?
f) Do adults and children avoid pinning down other people to a particular style of being a boy or a girl by labelling them, for example as a tomboy?
g) Are adults and children involved in finding ways to reduce any over-representation of boys in those seen to be 'naughty' or to experience difficulties in learning?
h) Do adults and children have a language to talk about gender, gender ambiguity and fluidity, masculinity and femininity?
i) Do staff have an alphabetical list of children in registers rather than separate lists of boys and girls?
j) Do children have the opportunity to engage in gender mixed sport and P.E.?
k) Do adults and children challenge ideas that men and women should have different roles in the school, in other work, in looking after children or doing chores in the home?
l) Is the work that adults and children do as carers appreciated, irrespective of their gender?
m) Do staff educate all genders to recognise that being the parent/carer of young children is frequently among the most important and satisfying activities people do in their lives?
n) Is it understood that gender is a more important aspect of the identity of some people than others, and that this may change over time, like the significance of a religion or ethnicity?
o) Do pre-schools, primary schools as well as secondary schools, actively encourage the appointment of men to a variety of roles?
p) Does the school avoid encouraging gender stereotypic styles of dress in school uniforms?
q) Do staff and children discuss the cultural pressures on men and women to cover up or uncover parts of their bodies?
r) Are all children encouraged to come to school in clothes and shoes that allows them to move freely?
s) Are children discouraged from seeing one gender or form of masculinity or femininity as more important than another?

t) ______________________________

u) ______________________________

v) ______________________________

A1.10 The school and local communities develop each other.

Section C1 (Linking locally and globally);
C2.14 Resources in the locality of the school are known and used.

a) Does the school engage in activities to involve its surrounding communities including elderly people, disabled people, local shops and businesses and the range of local ethnicities?
b) Does the school draw on the varied experience of local people in supporting curriculum activities in school?
c) Does a school newspaper highlight local people, events, and businesses?
d) Does the school have a calendar of celebrations and special interest days or a week which are shared with local communities?
e) Do local communities participate equally in the school, irrespective of their class, religion or ethnicity?
f) Do people in the local communities feel that the school belongs to them even if they do not have children at the school?
g) Does the school provide musical, drama, dance events and art exhibitions for people in surrounding communities?
h) Does the school arrange classes, such as in art, language, literacy and numeracy that parents and community members want?
i) Does the school make a contribution to events put on by its local communities?
j) Is the school aware of existing community development plans to which it can contribute?
k) Does the school consult local people including councillors, community and youth workers, police, and local charities, in planning its community involvements?
l) Does the school collaborate over the provision of health and social work services to local people?
m) Do members of local communities share facilities with staff and children such as the library, hall and cafeteria?
n) Do school meals draw on local growers and providers of fruit and vegetables?
o) Are all sections of local communities seen as a resource for the school?
p) Is there a positive view of the school within the local communities?
q) Is there a positive view of local communities within the school?
r) Does the school encourage applications for work in the school from local people?
s) Does the school support projects to improve and conserve the local environment, for example, in streams, rivers and canals?
t) Does the school work with others to keep an area in their locality free of litter and dumped objects?
u) Does the school encourage the planting of trees?
v) Does the school help with the development of local green areas by planting trees, sowing seeds?

w) ______________________________

x) ______________________________

y) ______________________________

A1.11 Staff link what happens in school to children's lives at home

A1.5 Staff and parents/carers collaborate; B1.7 All new children are helped to settle into the school; Section C1 (Linking locally and globally); C2.4 Children are actively involved in their own learning.

a) Are staff aware of the variety of children's home cultures and family circumstances?
b) Do staff recognise that some children may feel more at home in school than others?
c) Do adults and children acknowledge that people can experience severe discomfort when their cultures and identities are not respected?
d) Do adults ensure that all children see themselves and their backgrounds reflected in the school, in materials and displays and in the links made with their home knowledge in learning activities?
e) Do schools recognise that for some children schools may feel a safe haven compared to home?
f) Do adults recognise that children may display skills and interests at home that they do not show in school, such as talking, joking, caring, managing, cooking, reading, counting, designing, making, collecting, plant growing?
g) Do adults endeavour to enable children to draw on all their knowledge and skills that they display at home in learning and relationships in school?
h) Do adults and children recognise that getting to know another person requires an interest in entering into dialogue with them rather than detailed prior knowledge of their cultural or specific home situation?
i) Do staff question any tendency to make learning activities most appropriate for children who they see as similar in background to themselves?
j) Do staff from outside an area understand that they may be seen as visitors to the community by adults and children from the local area?
k) Do staff avoid making assumptions about the activities and beliefs of a particular child based on their heritage?
l) Do adults and children recognise the possible discomfort of anyone who has moved away from family and/or friends?
m) Do adults and children recognise the feelings of cultural dislocation that may be felt by people who have joined the school, such as refugees and asylum seekers?
n) Do the cultures of the school reflect the mix of genders, classes, ethnicities, heritages, family relationships, sexual orientations amongst children, parents/carers and staff?
o) Are significant events in children's lives marked in ways that respect their cultures?
p) Are cultural norms and personal preferences respected about modesty in arrangements for showers and swimming?
q) Do staff encourage children to have access to clubs and events local to their homes, even if the school is not in their home area?

r) ______________________________

s) ______________________________

t) ______________________________

A2.1 The school develops shared inclusive values.

Connected to all other indicators

a) Do staff, governors, parents/carers and children give time to talking about values, their implications for action, the nature of their own values and how they differ between people?
b) Are values understood as revealed through actions rather than words?
c) Is everyone in the school committed to the equality of value of all people and to the participation of all?
d) Do adults and children explore the values behind their ways of working and acting in the school?
e) Do adults and children avoid assuming that everyone in a community shares the same values?
f) Is it understood that it involves practice and trust to honestly express the values that inform one's own actions?
g) Is it understood that agreement about values is usually partial, since differences of view, for example about participation and equality, may be revealed as conversations deepen?
h) Do staff, children, parents/carers and governors broadly agree upon a framework of values that can be drawn on in shaping actions within the school?
i) Is an agreed framework of values used to resist pressures from outside the school to act according to different values?
j) Do staff review their practices in the light of their agreed values and propose changes where practices are informed by values that they reject?
k) Is it understood that applying shared values may involve steering between competing interests, for example, when one child's participation interferes with that of another?
l) Do adults and children draw attention to actions inside and outside the school that are inconsistent with an agreed framework of values?
m) Are changes in the school made in accordance with an agreed framework of values?
n) Do discussions go beyond headings for values to the complexity of their meanings?
o) Do staff and children link any summary statement of school values to more detailed understandings?
p) Are the limitations of ideas of national, global or Western values explored?
q) Does the school publicise its values and encourage others to engage with staff and children on the basis of the values agreed within the school?
r) Does an agreed framework of values apply equally to adults and children?
s) Is it recognised that we all have to work hard to act in accordance with our values?
t) Is it understood that a strong framework of values may be held by people with no religion as well as a variety of religions?
u) Is it understood that having a religion or a particular political position does not ensure inclusive values?
v) Do people connect the ways they act outside school with the way they act inside it?
w) Is it understood that the implications of some values, such as caring equally for all and encouraging hope in the future, are aspects of the professional duties of staff?
x) ______________________________
y) ______________________________

A2.2 The school encourages respect for all human rights.

A2.3 The school encourages respect for the integrity of planet earth.

a) Does the school encourage a belief that everyone has rights and they have them equally?
b) Is respect for rights encouraged in the way adults and children treat each other?
c) Is it understood that the notion of rights presupposes a common set of values to do with equality, compassion and respect for diversity?
d) Is it recognised that a person's rights can only be limited when exercising them directly infringes the rights of another?
e) Is it considered that limiting the rights of someone whose actions we disapprove of (for example in relation to a prisoner's right to vote) reduces respect for rights for everyone?
f) Do children and adults see a commitment to rights as a way of valuing everyone equally irrespective of their backgrounds, opinions and identities?
g) Are basic rights understood as a right to food, clothing, shelter, care, education, safety, free expression of views, paid work, involvement in decisions and respect for one's identity and dignity?
h) Do children learn about the history of slavery and the extent of its continued presence in their own country and around the world?
i) Do children learn about present and past campaigns for human rights in the UK and elsewhere?
j) Do children learn how they can contribute to campaigns for human rights?
k) Does the school link national and global justice with the idea of rights?
l) Do children learn how the world would change if there was less injustice?
m) Is the notion of rights connected to the idea of global citizenship?
n) Is it understood that inequalities in society deprive people of the capacity to exercise their rights?
o) Is it understood that rights commonly go unrecognised?
p) Is the extent of preventable hunger and disease explored within the school?
q) Do children learn about human rights documents such as the Universal Declaration of Human Rights and the Convention on the Rights of the Child (see list on page 188)?
r) Do adults and children consider the extent to which the content of human rights documents can be improved?
s) Do adults and children consider how support for human rights is included within national laws?
t) Are children aware of the abuse of human rights in their own and other countries even where human rights documents are signed and apparently agreed by governments?
u) Is it understood that all children have a right to attend their local school or one of their local schools?
v) Do children and adults speak up for others who are unjustly treated inside the school?
w) Do children and adults find ways to speak up for those who are unjustly treated nationally and internationally?
x) Is the importance of rights used to challenge inequalities and prejudice such as sexism, classism, racism, Islamophobia, disablism, homophobia and transphobia?
y) Does the school council help to promote the Convention on the Rights of the Child?

A2.3 The school encourages respect for the integrity of planet earth.

A2.2 The school encourages respect for all human rights; C1.7 Children investigate the earth, the solar system and the universe; C1.8 Children study life on earth.

a) Do adults and children recognise rights of non-human nature, both living and non-living?
b) Do adults and children explore the meaning of environmental sustainability, in terms of the continuity and lack of disturbance of species, ecosystems and landscapes?
c) Do adults and children reflect on the Universal Declaration of The Rights of Mother Earth (see extract on page 190)?
d) Do adults and children consider how dependent they are on the well-being of the planet?
e) Do adults and children adopt a duty of care towards the seas and land of the planet?
f) Do adults and children reflect on the view that the earth is there to be tamed, exploited and conquered by people?
g) Do adults and children reflect on the view that people should live in harmony with the earth among other species and the planet's natural formations?
h) Do adults and children come to their own view of their relationship to the earth?
i) Do adults and children discuss the view that economies and profits should only be developed to the extent that they maintain the health of the planet?
j) Do adults and children consider that if everyone consumed at the rate of the richest nations then humans would require several earths to survive?
k) Do adults and children consider that while some resources of the planet are finite, education, culture, music, games, information, friendship and love are not?
l) Do adults and children consider the view that conduct which pollutes, over-develops and places the survival of life at risk should be classed as an international crime?
m) Do adults and children consider the possibility that polluting land and water should be a crime irrespective of whether it can be proven that it harms people?
n) Do adults and children consider who can own land, seas, rivers and lakes on the earth?
o) Do adults and children consider the historical rights to the use of land of indigenous people who did not have formal contracts of ownership?
p) Do adults and children consider the consequences of the loss of access to common land shared between citizens in their own and other countries?
q) Do adults and children consider who owns and who claims to own air and water?
r) Do adults and children consider how people can challenge environmental pollution and what happens when they do?
s) Do adults and children consider the implications of a commitment by each generation to pass on a thriving planet to future generations?
t) Are crimes considered against future generations which imperil their health, survival and safety,severely damage the environment, deplete resources, cut down forests and threaten the survival of other species and ecosystems?
u) Do adults and children consider the ecological debt to the planet and future generations owed by present generations which they need to pay back?
v) Do adults and children recognise that a greater debt to the planet is owed by those who have consumed the most?
w) Do adults and children consider how a small additional pollution of land, seas and air can have disproportionate effects, like a final grain of sand on a sand pyramid or a slightly harder crack on a coconut, a tiny fire in a forest, or one more story circulating the internet of a head beaten by the police of an oppressive regime?

A2.4 Inclusion is viewed as increasing participation for all.

A2.1 The school develops shared inclusive values.

a) Is inclusion understood as a never-ending process of increasing participation of all?
b) Is participation understood as going beyond access to living and learning co-operatively and valuing each other's identities?
c) Is inclusion understood as a principled approach to the development of all aspects of a school, as well as education and society more widely?
d) Is inclusion seen to be concerned as much with how schools, families, environments and the wider society can be developed to foster and sustain participation as with encouraging the participation of individuals?
e) Is inclusion seen to be concerned with the participation of adults as well as children?
f) Is inclusion about everyone, not just children with impairments or those seen as 'having special educational needs'?
g) Do staff avoid seeing barriers to learning and participation as caused by deficiencies or impairments in children?
h) Is it understood that anyone can experience barriers to learning and participation?
i) Is it understood that who experiences barriers to learning and participation varies with context?
j) Are barriers to learning and participation seen to arise potentially in interactions with all aspects of a school: its cultures, policies, buildings, curricula and approaches to teaching and learning?
k) Are barriers to learning and participation seen to arise from national policies, local and national cultures and values and other pressures from outside the school?
l) Are attitudes about the limits to mainstream community membership challenged, such as a view that children with severe or multiple impairments cannot be part of the mainstream?
m) Is an 'inclusive school' understood as 'moving towards inclusion' rather than as at a destination?
n) Is it understood that increasing inclusion involves counteracting exclusion and discrimination?
o) Is exclusion understood as a process that may start in classrooms, playgrounds and staffrooms and end with a child or adult leaving the school?
p) Are excluding pressures recognised as always present and always needing to be counteracted?
q) Is there an emphasis on the appreciation of difference rather than conformity to a single 'normality'?
r) Is diversity valued and seen as a resource for learning rather than as a problem?
s) Is there a shared resolve to minimise inequalities of opportunity in the school?

t) ______________________________

u) ______________________________

v) ______________________________

A2.5 Expectations are high for all children

C2.2 Learning activities encourage the participation of all children;
C2.7 Assessments encourage the achievements of all children;
C2.12 Homework is set so that it contributes toevery child's learning.

a) Does every adult and child feel that the highest achievements are possible in their school?
b) Do all children and adults understand that there is no limit to what they can achieve?
c) Do staff recognise efforts that must be made to counter any low expectations for children, including those living in poverty, children in public care, Travellers, those learning English as an additional language and children categorised as 'having special educational needs'?
d) Do staff avoid relegating the teaching of children experiencing the greatest barriers to learning and participation to the least qualified and experienced staff?
e) Do adults and children understand how much more they achieve when they feel valued for what they do and who they are?
f) Do adults and children take pride in their achievements?
g) Do staff avoid conveying a sense of failure in children and their families by perceiving children as not keeping up with 'normal development'?
h) Are the achievements of children valued in themselves rather than in comparison with others?
i) Do staff recognise that when children see themselves as 'no good' at an area of the curriculum this can take a lifetime to undo?
j) Do staff avoid making comparisons between the achievement of a child and a brother or sister or neighbour?
k) Do staff and children attempt to counter negative views of children who find lessons difficult?
l) Do staff avoid labelling children as of greater or lesser ability based on their current achievements?
m) Do staff and children avoid the use of derogatory labels of low achievement?
n) Do staff and children counter negative views and use of derogatory labels for children who are keen, enthusiastic or attain highly in lessons?
o) Do staff avoid creating a layer of children seen to have 'special educational needs' and to be of limited 'potential'?
p) Do staff avoid creating a layer of children seen as 'gifted and talented' and to have greater potential' than others?
q) Do staff encourage a view that everyone has gifts and talents?
r) Are children entered for public examinations when they are ready rather than at a particular age?
s) Is there an attempt to address some children's fear of failure?

t) ______________________________

u) ______________________________

v) ______________________________

A2.6 Children are valued equally.

B1.8 Teaching and learning groups are arranged fairly to support all children's learning.

a) Does the variety of backgrounds of adults and children make a positive contribution to school and community?
b) Are national and regional accents and dialects seen to enrich the school and society?
c) Is a commitment to valuing all children's languages reflected in learning activities and the clubs and examinations offered?
d) Do adults avoid having favourites and set aside any feelings of dislike for particular children?
e) Is the learning of quiet children as encouraged as those who make a louder contribution?
f) Do adults avoid demonising particular children in stories about their negative exploits?
g) Are staff sensitive about all children's family arrangements in talking of events such as Mother's or Father's Day?
h) Do all children have the opportunity to appear in school assemblies and music, drama and dance productions?
i) Are differences in family structure acknowledged and appreciated?
j) Do staff avoid seeing middle class children as more valuable to the school than working class children?
k) Do staff avoid using curriculum levels or achievements in public examinations as a way of making some children feel more valuable and others less so?
l) Are gay, lesbian, bisexual, transgender and intersex people valued within the school and represented within the curriculum?
m) Do staff avoid representing one religion as more important than others or no religion?
n) Are children, staff and parents/carers with impairments as welcomed into the school as those without impairments?
o) Are there as many occasions for appreciating the efforts of lower as higher attaining children including those who do well in examinations?
p) Does the reporting of achievements within and beyond the school include all children?
q) Is the work of all children displayed within the school and classrooms?
r) Do all children leave secondary school with a recognised accreditation?
s) Are the achievements of children given equal support and prominence irrespective of gender?
t) Do staff avoid creating hierarchies of children by contrasting mainstream with 'special needs' or even 'included' children?

t) ______________________________

u) ______________________________

v) ______________________________

A2.7 The school counters all forms of discrimination.

A1.8 The school encourages an understanding of the interconnections between people around the world; A1.9 Adults and children are responsive to a variety of ways of being a gender; A2.4 Inclusion is viewed as increasing participation for all; A2.2 The school encourages respect for all human rights; B2.9 Bullying is minimised; C2.6 Lessons develop an understanding of the similarities and differences between people.

a) Is it recognised that everyone absorbs prejudices against others which take effort to identify and reduce?
b) Do adults consider their own attitudes to diversity and identify their prejudices so as to better support children to identify and reduce theirs?
c) Do adults and children identify areas of discrimination which need to be addressed?
d) Is all discrimination understood to involve intolerance to difference and abuse of power?
e) Is attention paid to the way a general intolerance to difference may be felt personally as classism, sexism, disablism, racism, homophobia, transphobia, Islamophobia etc?
f) Is it recognised that institutional discrimination can stem from cultures and policies which devalue the identities of, or otherwise discriminate against, some groups of people?
g) Is it recognised that a culture in which respect for diversity becomes widely shared as a value is the best way to prevent and reduce discrimination?
h) Are legal requirements to reduce 'inequalities' in relation to ethnicity, disability, gender, sexual orientation, sexual identity, religion, belief and age part of comprehensive plans to counter all forms of discrimination?
i) Is the devaluing of people because of their weight identified as discrimination and countered?
j) Do staff avoid suggesting that there is a single national identity or way of being in the school?
k) Do staff avoid stereotyped roles for children in school productions, for example, according to colour of hair, skin colour or gender?
l) Is there recognition that knowledge about their impairments makes only a limited contribution to planning education for children?
m) Do staff counter stereotyped attitudes towards people with impairments when they are described, for example, as objects of pity or heroic battlers against adversity?
n) Is it understood that disabilities may arise in interactions between people with impairments and their environments but may also be wholly produced by discriminatory attitudes and institutional barriers?
o) Is any exclusion of children with severe impairments from the school understood to reflect limitations of culture, attitude and policy more than practical difficulties?
p) Do children avoid racist, sexist, homophobic, disablist and other forms of discriminatory name calling?
q) Does the school avoid filtering systems which unfairly restrict access to websites, for example those relevant to the experience of lesbian, gay, bisexual, transgender and intersex people?

r) ____

s) ____

A2.8 The school promotes non-violent interactions and resolutions to disputes.

A1.9 Adults and children are responsive to a variety of ways of being a gender;
B2.9 Bullying is minimised.

a) Is non-violence understood as non-coercive interaction as well as absence of physical conflict?
b) Are disputes in the school resolved through dialogue rather than coercion based on differences in perceived status and physical strength?
c) Do adults model non-coercive interaction?
d) Do people learn to respond to challenges to their ideas so that they prompt reflection on what should be thought and done differently?
e) Does everyone learn skills of negotiation, conflict resolution and the mediation of disputes?
f) Are abuse, discrimination, harassment and bullying understood as forms of violence?
g) Is it understood that collaboration is easier when people feel secure in their identities?
h) Are discussions chaired so that they are not dominated by any individual, group or gender?
i) Are those who are often excessively angry helped to find other ways to express themselves?
j) Are children directed to martial arts activities and clubs as a way of developing confidence and assertiveness without aggression?
k) Do people help each other to make contributions that respect the contributions of others?
l) Do people reflect on how their feelings about others affect interactions with them?
m) Do children draw on poetry, literature, music, drama, puppetry to understand feelings?
n) Do children learn about the consequences of seeking revenge for perpetuating individual and international conflicts?
o) Do children and adults discuss the limits to the acceptable portrayal of violence, including degrading relationships between genders, in films and computer games?
p) Does the school emphasise its human rather than its business priorities?
q) Does the school avoid treating children as examination fodder?
r) Are children taught about the origins of conflicts over territories, identities, resources and intolerance to difference, and how they can be reduced through peaceful means?
s) Do children learn to question the need for any gender to dominate another?
t) Do children consider violence between genders and how such patterns of violence can be interrupted?
u) Is it explored how some male identities encourage violence towards males and females?
v) Is it understood how men and women may contribute to forming aggressive masculinities in children?
w) Do children explore what they gain and lose from joining gangs and how violence between gangs can be avoided inside and outside school?
x) Are children supported to find activities outside school which reduce any involvement in violence between gangs?
y) Are children helped to avoid carrying knives or other weapons?
z) Is it considered that violence, directed internally, can produce depression and self-harm?

A2.9 The school encourages children and adults to feel good about themselves.

A1.4 Staff and children respect one another; A2.10 The school contributes to the health of children and adults; B2.9 Bullying is minimised; C1.6 Children learn about health and relationships.

a) Does the school encourage adults and children to experience pleasure in learning and relationships?
b) Does the school help children and adults to escape the tyranny of ideas of normality?
c) Do children learn that it is common and alright to feel different from others?
d) Do adults and children avoid overvaluing thinness?
e) Do adults and children help to counter stereotypes of beauty in the media and in its own cultures?
f) Do adults and children feel enriched by the range of identities, backgrounds, ethnicities, genders and ways of viewing the world at the school?
g) Do adults and children feel that it is fine to express differences of identity and views?
h) Does the school encourage a view of personal well-being which is linked to the positive wellbeing of others in the school, its communities and globally?
i) Does the school encourage a view of personal well-being which is linked to environmental improvement and the integrity of the planet?
j) Is an effort made to ensure that everyone at the school can have friends?
k) Do children learn about good relationships from the way people treat each other in the school?
l) Does the school try to raise the self-esteem of children and adults who experience difficulties?
m) Do adults and children recognise that loss of self-esteem can reduce achievements and increase bullying?
n) Do adults and children understand that a person's appearance or the way they are referred to may not reflect the gender that they feel?
o) Are staff aware that using gendered facilities such as toilets or changing rooms may be a source of distress to some children who are transgender or intersex?
p) Are adults and children sensitive to the stresses that growing up and puberty can place on some people's view of their gender?
q) Are there ample, clean, safe places for adults and children to look after themselves when they are menstruating?
r) Are children and adults sensitive to the stresses that menstruation can place on some people?
s) Are long journeys avoided for children with impairments to and from school by encouraging a view that children and young people have a right to attend their local school?
t) Is care directed to boys as well as girls involved in creating school-age pregnancy?
u) Do schools avoid stigmatising girls who become pregnant or have children?
v) Do staff and children sensitively discuss issues of bereavement so that they know how to support each other if a child or adult in the school dies?
w) Is it recognised that death of a friend, family member or otherwise significant person may affect someone for many years and more at particular times, such as anniversaries?

A2.10 The school contributes to the health of children and adults.

A2.9 The school encourages children and adults to feel good about themselves;
C1.1 Children explore cycles of food production and consumption;
C1.6 Children learn about health and relationships.

a) Do adults and children consider the contributions to health of a healthy environment, play, pleasurable activity, friendships, absence of stress, a good diet and physical fitness?
b) Do adults and children avoid viewing people as unhealthy or having a medical condition because they appear different from themselves?
c) Are barriers to health identified within the school, its communities and surrounding environment?
d) Are there clear procedures for distributing and monitoring children's use of medicines?
e) Do adults and children have training in first aid and know how to respond to health crises, for example in relation to diabetes or epilepsy?
f) Is a quiet private space available for children and adults when pressures feel too great and someone to talk to if needed?
g) Are stress and anger seen to arise from the difficult circumstances of some children?
h) Are children given opportunities to meditate and learn about meditation?
i) Is counselling available for those who experience prolonged distress or are regularly angry?
j) Is a room available for medical attention, care support or regular physiotherapy?
k) Is there accessible and ample drinking water?
l) Do staff, children and families develop health promoting diets at school and at home?
m) Are there opportunities for people to share their health concerns such as comfort eating?
n) Are children helped to resist pressures from manufacturers to consume in ways that contribute to ill-health?
o) Are physical activities promoted for the pleasures as well as health benefits they bring?
p) Do children regularly take part in learning activities outside the classroom including open-air activities?
q) Do games and PE lessons encourage sport and fitness for all and involve sports, dance, aerobics, martial arts, Tai Chi and yoga?
r) Are children and adults encouraged to engage in physical activity each day and to take pleasure in walking or cycling to school?
s) Do children feel safe in all areas of the school?
t) Is there a balance between safety concerns and encouraging children's experience?
u) Are hazards assessed and addressed in journeys to and from school?
v) Do parents park well away from the school when delivering and collecting children?
w) Is the safety of school vehicles regularly checked?
x) Are lessons provided in safe cycle use?
y) Do adults and children wear a helmet when cycling to school?
z) Do children learn how to avoid the dangers of online networking and other internet sites?

aa) ______________________________

ab) ______________________________

Dimension B: Producing inclusive policies

B1: Developing the school for all

1. The school has a participatory development process.
2. The school has an inclusive approach to leadership.
3. Appointments and promotions are fair.
4. Staff expertise is known and used.
5. All new staff are helped to settle into the school.
6. The school seeks to admit all children from its locality.
7. All new children are helped to settle into the school.
8. Teaching and learning groups are arranged fairly to support all children's learning.
9. Children are well prepared for moving on to other settings.
10. The school is made physically accessible to all people.
11. The buildings and grounds are developed to support the participation of all.
12. The school reduces its carbon footprint and use of water.
13. The school contributes to the reduction of waste.

B2: Organising support for diversity

1. All forms of support are co-ordinated.
2. Professional development activities help staff respond to diversity.
3. English as an additional language support is a resource for the whole school.
4. The school supports continuity in the education of children in public care.
5. The school ensures that policies about 'special educational needs' support inclusion.
6. The behaviour policy is linked to learning and curriculum development.
7. Pressures for disciplinary exclusion are decreased.
8. Barriers to attendance are reduced.
9. Bullying is minimised.

B1.1 The school has a participatory development process.

A1.4 Staff and children respect one another; A1.5 Staff and parents/carers collaborate; A1.6 Staff and governors work well together; A1.10 The school and local communities develop each other; A2.4 Inclusion is viewed as increasing participation for all; Section C (Linking locally and globally).

a) Is there a 'development plan' for the school and its surroundings that is widely known and agreed by staff, governors, parents and children?
b) Are the opinions of children, parents/carers and governors sought about the nature of barriers to learning and participation and how the school might be improved?
c) Are the views of community members sought on how the school and its communities can contribute to each other's development?
d) Do the opinions of staff, children, parents, governors and communities make a difference to what happens in school?
e) Do parents/carers, children, governors feel that consultation with them is an ordinary part of their involvement in the school?
f) Is the implementation of the school development plan active and reviewed regularly with modifications introduced when necessary?
g) Do members of the school reflect on the changes that have happened in the previous twelve months and the reasons for them?
h) Do staff consider which changes happened as a result of the development plan and which happened for other reasons?
i) Do staff consider that change becomes development when it reflects desired values?
j) Do adults and children increase their influence over the development of their school by basing it on a shared framework of inclusive values?
k) Is it understood that connecting values to actions on the cultures, policies and practices of the school can contribute to continuous, sustained school development?
l) Do staff recognise that barriers to learning and participation experienced by children can be reduced by improving teaching and learning activities and approaches to teaching and learning?
m) Do school members reflect on the way cultures of the school can impede and promote inclusive development?
n) Are policies produced with the intention of improving the cultures and practices of the school, rather than satisfying inspectors?
o) Are all policies linked to clear implementation strategies?
p) Are the effects of school policies on the cultures and practices of the school monitored and changed as necessary?
q) Do adults and children share ideas with, and visit, partner schools (perhaps in another country) in order to assist the development of each others' schools and environments?

r) ______________________________

s) ______________________________

t) ______________________________

B1.2 The school has an inclusive approach to leadership.

A1.2 Staff co-operate;
B1.4 Staff expertise is known and used;
C2.9 Staff plan, teach and review together.

a) Is it understood that strong leaders can be collaborative rather than autocratic?
b) Does the school avoid the restrictions on relationships and learning that can arise from a rigid hierarchy of senior management, middle management, non-management (workers) and children?
c) Is important knowledge about the school shared amongst staff so that disruption is minimised if a senior person is away or leaves the school?
d) Does the school avoid pressures towards unthinking compliance either with school management or government directives?
e) Does the head teacher avoid passing on directives from outside the school as if they cannot be adapted to school cultures, policies and practices?
f) Do senior staff help to reduce the amount of time staff spend on paperwork?
g) Do staff resist pressures to do things which are in conflict with their values?
h) Are people who are promoted careful to avoid behaving as if an increase in status automatically confers greater knowledge?
i) Are senior staff careful to avoid favouring some staff over others?
j) Do people who are promoted continue to show a willingness to acknowledge when they have made mistakes?
k) Are decisions made on the basis of the arguments put forward rather than the exercise of power?
l) When people have put in extensive work on particular issues is this respected in making decisions?
m) Are the relevant knowledge and skills of staff respected in making decisions?
n) Do a variety of staff chair meetings and ensure that everyone can contribute?
o) Are senior teachers there to support and advise rather than inspect or manage the detail of other people's work?
p) Are all adults and children expected to be, or become, self-managing?
q) Is authority seen to reside in knowledge, wisdom, and skills rather than in a particular job position?
r) Are the head teacher and other senior staff selected in part because of their skills in helping other staff to encourage learning in diverse groups?
s) Do the head teacher and other senior staff have expertise in encouraging dialogue?
t) Do staff listen carefully to each other's arguments and seek clarification before disagreeing?
u) Are there non-coercive ways of resolving disagreements?
v) Is there an open and equitable distribution of resources in the school?

w) ____________________

x) ____________________

y) ____________________

B1.3 Appointments and promotions are fair.

A1.2 Staff co-operate;
B1.2 There is an inclusive approach to leadership.

a) Are opportunities for appointments open to all who are eligible, inside and outside the school?
b) Do staff avoid trying to gain advantage by excessive self-promotion of their knowledge and experience?
c) Are staff discouraged from seeking advantage by spending excessive hours at the school which staff with different home commitments or priorities could not match?
d) Does the school make clear and widely known its commitment to appointments free of bias in gender, ethnicity, disability, age, sexual orientation or any other irrelevant respect?
e) Does the school avoid discriminating in appointments on the basis of age, for example, in order to avoid higher salaries earned by older staff?
f) Does the composition of teaching and non-teaching staff reflect the communities in the school's locality?
g) Are people encouraged and mentored to put themselves forward for promotion irrespective of gender, home circumstances, ethnic background or any other irrelevant respect?
h) Do staff, particularly in primary schools and pre-schools see it as natural for men to take a caring role with young children?
i) Are all those who think they might like to apply for a post encouraged to do so?
j) Do the head teacher and other staff avoid giving particular encouragement to close friends or allies to seek promotion?
k) Is the governing body creative in encouraging parents and teachers to see the pleasure and relevance of work as a governor so that a number of people put themselves forward?
l) Do promoted posts reflect the balance of genders and backgrounds of staff in the school?
m) Are posts of higher status reflective of all sections of the school's communities?
n) Is there representation on appointments committees from across school staff, governors and the children's school council?
o) Where the school has an attachment to a particular faith is discrimination minimised in appointments on the basis of faith?
p) Do appointments panels have a mix of genders, ethnicities and backgrounds which reflect the communities of the school?
q) Are staff unions involved in helping to draw up guidelines for appointments and promotions?
r) Are applicants for jobs asked to present an aspect of their work to staff, governors, parents/carers and children?
s) Is there a strategy for removing barriers to the appointment of staff with impairments?
t) Is the valuing of diversity an essential criterion for the appointment of staff?
u) Are temporary replacements found for absent support staff as well as classroom and subject teachers?

v) ______________________________

w) ______________________________

B1.4 Staff expertise is known and used.

B1.2 The school has an inclusive approach to leadership.

a) Are staff genuinely interested in each other's knowledge and expertise?
b) Are all the skills, knowledge and interests of teacher and non-teacher staff widely known, not just those implied by their job title or given in their job description?
c) Are staff consulted on how best to use their skills and knowledge for the benefit of the school and its communities?
d) Are teachers and teaching assistants encouraged to draw on all their skills and knowledge to support learning of children and young people?
e) Are staff encouraged to develop new expertise and interests?
f) Are staff encouraged to share their new knowledge, interests and expertise?
g) Do members of staff readily offer to share their knowledge and skills?
h) Are staff careful not to overlook the knowledge and skills of colleagues, such as Art and Physical Education teachers, in working with diverse groups of children?
i) Do staff decide what additional expertise they wish to draw on from outside the school?
j) Do the variety of languages spoken by staff contribute to the development of a language learning school?
k) Is it recognised that it is alright for different people to have different personal and professional strengths?
l) Do staff meet to pool their ideas and expertise in order to improve each other's teaching and resolve each other's teaching difficulties?
m) Do staff listen to each other and offer alternative perspectives on concerns about children without negative judgement?
n) Are the differences in culture and background of staff drawn upon in developing curricula and learning activities?
o) Do staff learn from instructive practices and experience in other schools?
p) Are local special school staff invited to share expertise with mainstream staff about teaching and learning with diverse groups?
q) Are observations about the school sought when staff are about to leave or have left the school, for the fresh insights they may be willing to share?
r) Is it recognised that younger staff may make a particular contribution to school life which differs from that of older staff?
s) Is it recognised that what people offer a school may change as they get older and that this may be to the advantage of colleagues?

t) ______________________________

u) ______________________________

v) ______________________________

B1.5 All new staff are helped to settle into the school.

A1.2 Staff co-operate;
C2.9 Staff plan, teach and review together.

a) Is there an agreed induction policy for staff, governors and parent helpers?
b) Does the induction policy lift the spirits of new staff?
c) Are new staff provided with all the information they need about the school including school policies and the school and environment development plan?
d) Are new staff asked what additional information they need, and is it provided?
e) Are all newly appointed staff invited to visit the school before their official start date?
f) Are new members of staff allocated a mentor to help them settle into the school and meet with them on their first day and regularly after that?
g) Is the mentor regularly available in person or by phone in the first weeks to answer questions?
h) Does the head teacher meet with new staff as close as possible to their first day?
i) Are all new staff formally welcomed by governor and parent representatives?
j) Are all new staff formally welcomed by representatives of the children?
k) Are new staff supported to make contributions to staff meetings?
l) Do staff already in post recognise the difficulties that new staff may have in settling into a new job in what may be a new country or locality?
m) Do longer serving staff invite new staff, especially those new to the area or the country, into their homes and to meet socially outside school?
n) Do longer serving staff avoid making new staff feel that they are outsiders, for example by the use of a 'we' or an 'us' which excludes them?
o) Do existing staff take a genuine interest in who new staff are and what they can offer to the school?
p) Are new staff encouraged to know that their presence and contribution will make a difference to the cultures of the school?
q) Are newly qualified teachers helped to make good use of their additional professional development time?
r) Are all new teachers and support staff linked into established structures for mutual support, observation of practice and discussion of possibilities for development of teaching, learning and support activities?
s) Do permanent staff treat temporary staff, student teachers and teaching assistants on placement as full colleagues?
t) Are the observations about the school of new staff and students on practical placement, sought and valued for the fresh insights and opportunities for action that they may provide?

u) ______________________________

v) ______________________________

w) ______________________________

B1.6 The school seeks to admit all children from its locality.

A2.6 Children are valued equally.

a) Is the wish to include all children from the locality publicised as school policy?
b) Is the comprehensive and community nature of the school reflected in its name?
c) Are all children from the locality encouraged to attend the school irrespective of attainment, impairment or background?
d) Are Traveller children who visit the area actively welcomed to the school?
e) Does the school seek to overcome barriers to participation for the variety of ethnic groups in the locality?
f) Are children of asylum seekers and refugees encouraged to attend the school?
g) Are children of families temporarily resident in the area encouraged to join the school?
h) Are families from the locality with children currently in special schools encouraged to send these children to the school?
i) Do staff advocate for the rights of children with impairments to attend their local school?
j) When a child who has had difficulties at another school joins the school do staff avoid suggesting that membership of the school is only provisional?
k) Does the school discharge its legal duty to ensure that children in public care are given first priority to attend the school?
l) Does the school make known its interest in welcoming 'looked-after children' to the school?
m) Does the school comply with the law requiring them not to hold interviews or use information from conversations with parents, siblings or comments from anyone who knows a prospective entrant?
n) Does the school avoid asking for donations from families before a child can join the school?
o) Where the faith status of a school creates a balance of ethnicities unrepresentative of the surrounding communities does the school make strong relationships and work with other schools in the area?
p) Where a school has an attachment to a particular faith does proximity to the school take precedence for admission over the religious attachment of a child's family?
q) Do schools with an allegiance to a particular faith avoid restrictions on the appointment of staff of a particular faith group?
r) Does a school with a faith attachment minimise religious division, for example, by not favouring a particular branch of Christianity or Islam?
s) Is there an increase in the proportion of children from the locality included within the school?
t) Is there an increase in the diversity of children from the locality included in the school?

u) ______________________________

v) ______________________________

w) ______________________________

B1.7 All new children are helped to settle into the school.

A1.3 Children help each other; A1.4 Staff and children respect one another;
A2.6 Children are valued equally;
C2.5 Children learn from each other.

a) Are there opportunities for children to visit the school before they join?
b) Is there an agreed programme for helping children to settle?
c) Do all staff greet children in a friendly way?
d) Is there a single induction policy for children whenever they join and wherever they arrive from?
e) Does the induction programme work equally well for children and their families whether they join at the start of the school year or some other time?
f) Do staff and children address the difficulties of building a community when there is a large number of children leaving and joining the school each year?
g) Are new children buddied with more experienced children when they first enter the school?
h) Are all children helped to feel at home?
i) Is it recognised that some children may find it more difficult to feel at home than others?
j) Are children encouraged to feel that their contributions make a difference from the time they first join the school?
k) Is information available for parents/carers on the national and local school and education systems as well as about the school?
l) Does the induction programme take into account differences in attainment and home language?
m) Are adults and children, already known to new children, involved in welcoming these children when they first join?
n) Are steps taken, after a few weeks, to find out how settled new children feel in the school?
o) Is there support for children who have difficulty memorising the building layout, particularly when they first join the school?
p) Are there child-friendly maps of the school available for children?
q) Are new children clear about who to see if they experience difficulties?
r) Are new children made to feel that their work and views are important from the first day that they join the school?
s) Are children given opportunities to contribute to improvements in a 'settling in' policy?
t) Do adults and other children go out of their way to find out the names of people who have just joined the school?
u) Are children introduced to the school values and how people are expected to treat one another when they first join?
v) Is the experience of joining a new setting integrated into classroom activities?

w) ______________________________

x) ______________________________

z) ______________________________

B1.8 Teaching and learning groups are arranged fairly to support all children's learning.

A2.6 Children are valued equally.

a) Are teaching groups treated fairly in the use of facilities, location of teaching rooms, allocation of teaching staff and staff cover?
b) Does the school avoid consistently allocating lower quality spaces, for example mobile classrooms, to children perceived as having low status in the school because of age, attainment or impairment?
c) Are staff aware of the messages about identity and self-esteem that are provided in any unequal use of spaces in the school?
d) Do staff establish opportunities for children to learn from, and teach, each other in diverse groups?
e) In planning learning groups, is attention paid to children's wishes, friendships and the presence of others who speak the same languages?
f) Is the organisation of teaching groups according to levels of attainment or impairment, minimised?
g) Do schools avoid making non-teaching staff responsible for the progress of children with the lowest attainments or who experience the greatest barriers to learning and participation?
h) Do schools avoid identifying and grouping a disproportionate number of boys as low attaining or as requiring an alternative curriculum?
i) Do staff avoid grouping children on the basis of their challenging behaviour where this limits the children's capacity to support each other?
j) Where setting occurs, are there plans to prevent negative effects, such as disaffection in lower sets?
k) Where setting occurs, do all children have regular opportunities to move between sets?
l) Do schools avoid restricting the curriculum (such as omitting a foreign language) for children who are given additional literacy support or are in a lower set for English?
m) Are seating arrangements within classes changed as necessary to discourage the creation of conflict between groups for example in relation to gender or ethnicity?
n) Are seating arrangements within classes changed as necessary so that children do not discourage each other's learning?
o) Are schools mindful of their obligation to educate together children who do and do not experience difficulties in learning?
p) Where there is an imbalance of girls and boys in a group do children understand the importance of mutual respect and encourage everyone's contribution?
q) Where there is a large imbalance of girls and boys in a particular year's intake, do schools consider establishing some single-sex classes?
r) Where there are option choices, are all children allowed to make real choices?

s) ______________________________

t) ______________________________

u) ______________________________

B1.9 Children are well prepared for moving on to other settings.

C1.12 Children learn about work and link it to the development of their interests.

a) Do staff respect the contributions to children's learning of those who have worked with the children they teach in previous years in the same school or a different school?
b) Do staff collaborate over a transfer file so that it is valued and used by receiving teachers?
c) Do staff take the opportunity of their involvement in transfers to see education from a different point of view?
d) Do staff recognise that children may need help to re-engage with the pleasures of learning after examinations at the end of primary school or after GCSEs?
e) Are clearly written, jargon free, accessible booklets and web pages available about schools, with contributions from children?
f) Are children introduced to the routines of a new setting before transfer?
g) Are parents provided with accurate information about possible schools?
h) Do transfers of children between schools inform the curriculum of receiving and sending schools, such as in the creation of virtual tours, maps, weekly planners and creative drama about movement of people between places?
i) Are there dialogues between staff and children from receiving and sending schools about the extent to which their values are shared?
j) Do staff engage in bridging activities before transfer?
k) Can curriculum activities started in one school, such as modern foreign languages, continue through extra-curricular activities if necessary?
l) Do schools put on activity days before transfer so that children can meet staff and children from the receiving school?
m) Do children who have moved on to another setting, return to advise children who are about to transfer?
n) Are concerns about friendships and bullying allayed by staff and children from the receiving school?
o) Do schools encourage relationships across years so that children do not feel vulnerable by being the youngest and smallest in a school?
p) Do the early years of secondary schools incorporate elements of primary schools by reducing movement of children and staff?
q) Is there co-ordination of support for children moving between schools?
r) Is care taken over the transfer of confidential information?
s) Are parents of children with statements of 'special educational needs' supported to find a welcoming local mainstream setting when they leave the school?
t) Is it recognised that children who have had many moves may find it harder to move to a new situation?
u) Do children continue interests and activities across schools and when they leave school?
v) Are all children encouraged to consider a variety of trajectories in continuing education and employment?
w) Are children helped to be independent when they leave school by learning about budgeting, cooking, cleaning, health, relationships, clothes washing, leisure and work?

B1.10 The school is made physically accessible to all people.

A1.1 Everyone is welcomed;
B1.6 The school seeks to admit all children from its locality;
B1.11 The buildings and grounds are developed to support the participation of all.

a) Is there an accessibility plan to increase ease of physical access to the school?
b) Does the school pay attention to the requirements of legislation to make progress each year on the accessibility of the school?
c) Is disabled access part of the building improvement plan which is integrated into the school development plan?
d) Is the accessibility plan part of a concerted effort to ensure that staff and children with impairments wish to come to the school?
e) Is the accessibility plan part of a concerted effort to support people with impairments to enjoy visiting and using the school premises?
f) Are the needs of deaf and partially hearing, blind and partially sighted people, parents with young children, including double buggies, the elderly as well as people with physical impairments, considered in making the buildings accessible?
g) Are disabled people of a variety of ages, including those within children's families and local communities, consulted about the accessibility of the school?
h) Does the school recognise that people with similar impairments including staff and children in the school may have quite different views of how the environment can be made accessible for them?
i) Is disability access audited each year in order to make improvements to the building improvement plan?
j) Is equipment adjustable so that it can be easily and safely used by people of differing heights and those in wheelchairs?
k) Are all aspects of the school made accessible including entrances and exits, classrooms, corridors, toilets, gardens, playgrounds, canteen, signs and displays?
l) Are pathways around the school made easily negotiable for people with impairments, for example through lighting, colour schemes and floor strips?
m) Is particular attention paid to maintaining the dignity of children and adults in accessible facilities?
n) Is particular attention paid to the nature of alarms, safety and evacuation procedures?
o) Is the school designed so that use of spaces is as comfortable for people with impairments as for those without impairments?
p) Is accessibility seen as about disabled staff, governors, parents/carers, visitors to the schooland other members of the community, as well as children?
q) Are projects concerned with improving the accessibility of the school buildings, facilities and grounds, integrated into the school curriculum?

r) ______________________________

s) ______________________________

t) ______________________________

B1.11 The buildings and grounds are developed to support the participation of all.

A1.10 The school contributes to the health of children and adults;
A2.4 Inclusion is viewed as increasing participation for all;
B1.10 The school is made physically accessible to all people.

a) Is the building development plan designed to increase participation of adults and children in the school, reflecting contributions from staff, children and parents/carers?
b) Are there efforts to make all parts of the school look attractive to adults and children, for example, through collaborative art projects and planting of flowers and shrubs?
c) Do school staff and governors have a long-term plan that reflects environmental as well as financial concerns?
d) Does the development of spaces in the school and its grounds respect the range of interests of children, rather than favouring any one group?
e) Do children share responsibility for ensuring that plants flourish in the buildings and surrounds of the school?
f) Are adults and children encouraged to go on visits to find out how to improve staffrooms, classrooms and school grounds?
g) Are adults and children encouraged to make suggestions about how the school buildings and grounds can be improved?
h) Does the school encourage art exhibitions and displays from its own children and adults and from its communities including other schools and colleges?
i) Does the playground have equipment for a variety of active and more contemplative pursuits such as music making?
j) Is the staffroom a welcoming space for all staff?
k) Do staff feel that they all have good working conditions?
l) Do building plans include a space for parents/carers to meet?
m) Is there a school garden with a variety of plants grown for food and for their attractiveness?
n) Does the school have its own allotment or share one if it does not have sufficient land to grow food?
o) Do the school grounds have a variety of areas to encourage a diversity of wild plants, animals and insects?
p) Are the school and classrooms filled with displays, plants and objects that stimulate curiosity, discussion and learning?
q) Are people able to raise concerns over the use of space and have their concerns resolved fairly?
r) Is the school made secure in a way that maintains the attractiveness of the site?
s) Are the buildings and grounds available for use by the community?
t) Is there a plan to support increased security of the setting through community ownership?

u) ______________________________

v) ______________________________

w) ______________________________

B1.12 The school reduces its carbon footprint and use of water.

B1.13 The school contributes to the reduction of waste;
C1.2 Children investigate the importance of water; C1.7 Children investigate the earth, the solar system and the universe; C1.8 Children study life on earth;
C1.9 Children investigate sources of energy.

a) Is the carbon footprint of the school understood as its annual greenhouse gas emissions?
b) Do staff and children consider that reducing activities involving greenhouse gas emissions is more important than precise measurement of carbon footprints?
c) Do adults and children draw up success indicators in reducing greenhouse gas emissions in school, in their lives outside school and by influencing other community members?
d) Are there adult and child co-ordinators for reducing the school's carbon footprint?
e) Do staff and children plan to reduce their carbon footprint at school and at home by controlling fuel and non-renewable electricity use in buildings, energy conservation, pupil and staff travel, waste management and the consumption of goods and services?
f) Is it considered that the best way of reducing energy use is through reduced production and consumption of goods?
g) Does the school make links with local energy efficiency experts?
h) Does the school produce its own electricity and/or heat through wind turbines, solar panels or heat pumps?
i) Does the school use a supplier that distributes electricity from renewable sources?
j) Is fuel consumption reduced by choice of heating boiler and other appliances, lagging pipes, loft and wall insulation, double glazing, and developing a green roof?
k) Does any new building meet the highest standards for energy conservation?
l) Is the heating system responsive to changes in temperature and adjusted downwards as people get used to wearing additional clothing?
m) Does the school use low energy light sources and install light sensors where lighting is required regularly but not constantly?
n) Does the school lobby for the producers of gas and electricity to limit energy production?
o) Are the demands on fuel use of information and computer technology (ICT) resources monitored and minimised by switching off when not in use?
p) Is the use of car travel reduced by car share, public transport, safe cycling and walking?
q) Does the school have comfortable showers to encourage cycling to school?
r) Does the school insist on criteria for purchasing which involve buying locally produced seasonally appropriate food and otherwise reducing food and product miles?
s) Do children investigate the dependence of organic and non-organic food on fossil fuels?
t) Is the school part of a local network that uses its shared buying power?
u) Does the school monitor its use of water and plan a reduction in its use per person?
v) Does the school collect rainwater in water butts for use in the school garden?
w) Does the school install a system for the purification of grey water (water used for washing) for its reuse in toilets and the school garden?
x) Is water use reduced in cisterns and urinals, by detecting and reporting leaks and by installing self-closing taps?

B1.13 The school contributes to the reduction of waste.

B1.12 The school reduces its carbon footprint and use of water; C1.1 Children explore cycles of food production and consumption; C1.2 Children investigate the importance of water; C1.7 Children investigate the earth, the solar system and the universe; C1.8 Children study life on earth.

a) Are adults and children encouraged to reduce waste production inside and outside the school by repair, reuse, composting and recycling?
b) Does the school encourage reduced consumption as the best way to reduce waste?
c) Do children research what waste is biodegradable, recyclable or neither?
d) Does the waste reduction policy emphasise reducing waste that goes to landfill?
e) Are there co-ordinators among adults and children for auditing waste composition and collecting, sorting, reducing and recycling waste?
f) Do children learn what happens to waste if it is and is not recycled?
g) Does the school consider joining a local school waste action club (SWAC)?
h) Do children learn about campaigns for reducing waste?
i) Do children learn about waste reduction through links with other schools?
j) Do children explore what gets recycled in different parts of the world?
k) Does the school buy products in returnable containers?
l) Does the school maximise its purchase of items made from recycled resources including renovated furniture?
m) Does the school encourage the purchase and use of food which has minimum packaging?
n) Are children and their families supported to design waste free packed lunches?
o) Does the school encourage the use of reusable plates and utensils?
p) Is food waste reduced by negotiations with children and families over meals and portion sizes?
q) Are there accessible collection points for food and other waste in strategic positions around the school?
r) Does the school serve as a recycling point for paper, cardboard, books, clothes, glass, plastics (including those not taken in home recycling schemes), electronic equipment, printer cartridges, light bulbs, mobile phones, batteries and CDs/DVDs?
s) Does the school have its own swap scheme and encourage the use of other schemes such as freecycle' and giving of unwanted items to charity?
t) Does the school collaborate with families and community groups to teach skills of repairing, renovating, sewing and altering clothes, within the curriculum and in clubs?
u) Is paper use reduced by two sided printing and labels for envelopes and folders?
v) Are there screens available where documents can be easily read online, and for parents and children to learn what is going on in the school, with help if necessary?
w) Is email used where possible to communicate with parents/carers?
x) Is the re-use of printer cartridges encouraged?
y) Are there easily accessible and clean sources of drinking water?
z) Does the school discourage the buying of manufactured bottled water by encouraging the filling of bottles from the drinking tap?

B2.1 All forms of support are co-ordinated.

C2.5 Children learn from each other;
C2.9 Staff, plan, teach and review together;
C2.10 Staff develop shared resources to support learning.

a) Is support understood as all activities which increase the capacity of the school to respond to the diversity of children in ways that value them equally?
b) Are all forms of support co-ordinated and adapted so that they contribute to the inclusive development of the school?
c) Is support understood to involve the mobilising of resources from within and outside the school?
d) Is it understood that developing inclusive learning activities and collaborative school and classroom cultures are forms of support?
e) Is it understood that developing a collaborative culture and the responsiveness to diversity of learning activities may mean that individual support is not required?
f) Is the development of peer support arising from a collaborating school culture given priority over providing adult support to individuals?
g) Does the school minimise the need for individual support from an adult to support the learning of children?
h) Is support understood to involve the removal of barriers to play, learning and participation?
i) Is support seen to include the development of curricula which engage the interests of children and draw on their experience?
j) Is support from education, health and social services integrated for children and families?
k) Are all support activities co-ordinated in a single support policy?
l) Is the support policy negotiated and agreed with parents?
m) Is the support policy made clear to those from outside the school who support learning and participation within it?
n) Is co-ordination of support led by a senior member of staff?
o) Are staff aware of all the human resources in adults and children which can be mobilised to support the development of learning and participation?
p) Are adult mentors and volunteers, including first language users and adults with impairments, drawn upon as resources for the school?
q) Does the school reduce barriers in communication between professionals with different backgrounds?
r) Do staff raise concerns if they feel that the actions of others are guided more by the maintenance of professional territories than what is best for children?
s) Are those who offer support from outside the school asked to co-ordinate their efforts with other overlapping interventions before they can be integrated into the school?

t) ______________________________

u) ______________________________

v) ______________________________

B2.2 Professional development activities help staff respond to diversity.

C2.9 Staff plan, teach and review together; C2.10 Staff develop shared resources to support learning.

a) Do professional development activities help staff to work with diverse groups?
b) Do staff develop their practice in recognising and countering discrimination and bullying, including classism, ageism, disablism, racism, sexism, homophobia, transphobia and discrimination in relation to religion and belief?
c) Do staff explore the extent of their own discriminatory beliefs and actions?
d) Do curriculum development activities always address the participation and learning of children differing in background, experience, gender, attainment and impairment?
e) Are staff and governors involved in planning their own professional development?
f) Do curriculum development activities address the reduction of barriers to learning and participation?
g) Do staff develop the use of outside spaces to build learning from the shared experiences of children?
h) Do staff develop ways to build learning from objects and artefacts of importance and interest to children?
i) Do professional development activities involve connecting values with actions to develop learning and participation?
j) Do professional development activities help to make full use of opportunities for learning outside the classroom?
k) Does professional development help in initiating lessons from children's shared experiences?
l) Do staff develop their expertise in establishing collaborative learning classrooms where activities involve both individual and group work?
m) Do teachers and teaching assistants learn together in order to increase their collaboration?
n) Do teachers and teaching assistants share opportunities to consider how to reduce the disaffection and disruption of children?
o) Are there opportunities for staff and children to learn about peer tutoring?
p) Do staff plan how to counter any over-representation of groups of children seen to experience barriers to learning and participation, for example, according to gender, ethnicity or class?
q) Are there opportunities for staff and children to learn about peer mediation of conflicts and disputes?
r) Do teaching and support staff increase their knowledge about using technology to work with diverse groups, such as white boards, cameras, television, DVDs, projectors, voice recorders and computers/internet?
s) Do staff learn how to help children to develop social networks that can support them within and beyond school, including Circles of Friends?
t) Do staff establish reading groups and informal seminars where they can learn together and share their expertise.

B2.3 English as an additional language support is a resource for the whole school.

a) Do adults and children share responsibility for helping children learning English as an additional language to acquire their new language?

b) Do staff acquaint themselves with the learning resources within the communities of those who have recently arrived in the country such as in religious and cultural institutions?

c) Does the school provide, or have links with, English language and literacy classes for parents/carers and older relatives, in settings that are attractive as places to learn for adults, irrespective of background and gender?

d) Does the school value the multi-lingual skills of those learning English as an additional language?

e) Do adults and children take an interest in the languages spoken by others and make efforts to learn some words in these languages?

f) Are the home languages of children integrated into classroom activities and homework?

g) Do schools ensure that children have an opportunity to reflect their language skills in their public examination options?

h) Does the school value such cultural gifts as the food, music and songs that children and their families bring with them from another country?

i) Does support for those learning English as an additional language address barriers to learning in all aspects of teaching, curricula and school organisation?

j) Are modifications to classroom language and learning activities which increase the involvement of children learning English as an additional language used to reduce barriers to learning and participation for other children?

k) Does support focus on identifying and overcoming the barriers to learning and participation of children rather than distinguishing between 'having a difficulty in an additional language' and having a learning difficulty'?

l) Are interpreters for Sign Language and other first languages, available to support those who need them?

m) Is the effect of moving country and culture recognised as a possible barrier to learning and participation?

n) Is the trauma of the experience of young people seeking asylum recognised as contributing to the difficulties they may experience in schools?

o) Do staff help children to understand that an interest in communicating with and listening to others can help to overcome barriers to communication with children with different languages and cultures?

p) Is teaching and support drawn upon, where available, from someone who shares a cultural background with children?

q) ______________________________

r) ______________________________

s) ______________________________

B2.4 The school supports continuity in the education of children in public care.

A2.1 The school develops shared inclusive values; A2.7 The school counters all forms of discrimination; B2.8 Barriers to attendance are reduced.

a) Are staff careful about intruding into the lives of vulnerable children without invitation?
b) Are staff aware of the poor record of their country in helping children in public care to avoid a troubled future as adults?
c) Do staff attempt to avoid a negative learning and employment trajectory for children and young people in public care?
d) Does the school avoid stereotyping children in public care as uniformly challenging?
e) Do staff help vulnerable children to contribute to decisions about their education and their lives more widely?
f) Does the school avoid blaming children in care and other vulnerable children for discriminatory behaviour towards them?
g) Does the school ensure that there are key people who act as links for children who need continuity of contact through their time in school and after leaving the school?
h) Do key members of staff for children in public care ensure that they overcome any barriersto good relationships when working with these children with colleagues with a different professional background?
i) Do all those working with children in public care agree on the benefits to children of educational achievements?
j) Do all staff take responsibility for helping vulnerable children to feel good about themselves?
k) Do staff reflect on the consequences of rejecting vulnerable children, including children who are in public care, or subjecting them to disciplinary exclusion?
l) Is particular attention given to overcoming barriers to involvement in extra-curricular activities?
m) Are special efforts made to build strong links with parents/carers?
n) Does support for children in public care encourage continuity in learning and minimise changes of school?
o) Is support in place to help those who have missed school to catch up without disrupting the building of friendships?
p) Does the school provide space at the end of the school day where children who need it can carry out school work?
q) Does the school provide a quiet space where children who need one can retreat at playtimes, and before and after school?
r) Are secondary schools and colleges mindful of the limited support that young people in public care may have after they reach eighteen years unless they ensure that such support continues?

s) ______________________________

t) ______________________________

u) ______________________________

B2.5 The school ensures that policies about 'special educational needs' support inclusion.

A2.4 Inclusion is viewed as increasing participation for all.

a) Where staff talk of a 'child with special educational needs' do they use it to mean 'a child with unmet needs', implying a lack in the environment rather than a deficit in a child?
b) Do staff reflect on their own experiences of learning to understand when and why children find learning difficult?
c) Are staff careful to avoid calling some children normal learners and implying that others with 'special educational needs' are less than normal?
d) Do staff consider replacing the notion of a child as 'having special educational needs' with a child who 'experiences barriers to learning and participation'?
e) Is it understood that using terms for impairment such as 'physical impairment', 'blind' and 'deaf' is compatible with avoiding the wider term 'special educational needs'?
f) Do staff resist an increasing tendency to label children as 'autistic', 'having Asperger's Syndrome', 'having attention deficit hyperactivity disorder', and other similar terms?
g) Do staff question the extent of drug use to control the behaviour of children?
h) Are barriers to learning and participation seen to arise in relationships, teaching approaches and learning activities, as well as social and material circumstances?
i) Do staff avoid using 'barriers' to imply deficits in children as in 'a child with barriers'?
j) Do staff respond to requirements to identify children as 'having special educational needs' without adopting the term in their own dialogues with children and each other?
k) Are resources to support students categorised as 'having special educational needs' used to increase the capacity of the school to respond to diversity?
l) Is a co-ordinator of support called 'a learning support', 'learning development' or 'inclusion coordinator', rather than a 'special educational needs co-ordinator'?
m) Does the co-ordinator of support work to increase the capacity of the school to respond to diversity in ways that value children equally?
n) Are children who experience barriers to learning and participation viewed as individuals with differing interests, knowledge and skills rather than as part of a homogeneous group?
o) Are attempts to remove barriers to learning and participation of one child used to provide ideas for improving the experiences of all children?
p) Is additional adult support seen as an entitlement for children when they need it rather than as requiring categorisation or formal assessment?
q) Are the details of an entitlement to support made public to children and parents/carers?
r) Is the withdrawal of children for support outside mainstream lessons minimised?
s) Is the idea that children in the same class might be doing different things in different spaces seen as an ordinary part of every child's experience?
t) Are Individual Education Plans about learning with others?
u) Is the preparation of Individual Education Plans for some children used as an opportunity to improve the teaching and learning arrangements for all children?
v) Do statements of 'special educational needs' address how barriers to learning and participation can be overcome through supportive teaching and learning arrangements?

w) ____

B2.6 The behaviour policy is linked to learning and curriculum development.

A1.4 Staff and children respect one another; A1.5 Staff and parents/carers collaborate; A1.9 Adults and children are responsive to a variety of ways of being a gender; B2.7 Pressures for disciplinary exclusion are decreased; B2.9 Bullying is minimised.

a) Is the behaviour policy clearly written and produced following wide consultation and agreement with children, parents and staff and their unions?
b) Does the code of conduct for the school apply to both adults and children?
c) Is the behaviour policy linked to the building of collaborating communities in the school and the sharing of values?
d) Are engagement with learning and improvements in relationships always the aim of interventions about behaviour?
e) Does the school seek to increase engagement in learning by improvements in learning activities?
f) Do concerns about how to increase engagement for some children involve reflection on ways to improve teaching and learning for all children?
g) Does the behaviour policy focus on preventing disaffection and difficulties with behaviour?
h) Do adults and children identify the circumstances when difficulties with behaviour arise so that the policy can address them?
i) Are policies to reduce difficulties with behaviour related to strategies for improving experiences of children before and after school and in playgrounds?
j) Does the behaviour policy address barriers to learning and participation in school policies and cultures as well as practices?
k) Is it understood that responsibility for improving relationships in the school is shared by all children and adults?
l) Does the policy encourage adults to share their difficulties and support each other to develop strategies that prevent conflict with and between children?
m) Does the behaviour policy address the well-being of children who are quietly troubled?
n) Does the school attempt to raise the feelings of self-worth of those with low self-esteem?
o) Do troubled children know that they can get support and attention before they exhibit disaffection?
p) Does the school draw on the support of social workers and youth workers in reducing conflict between groups of children with a history of conflict outside school?
q) Does the school use supply and substitute teaching in ways that minimise difficulties with behaviour, for example by drawing on the same people regularly and building in routine ways to support them?
r) Does the school explore links between disaffection in boys and attitudes to masculinity inside and outside school?

s) ______________________________

t) ______________________________

u) ______________________________

B2.7 Pressures for disciplinary exclusion are decreased.

A1.2 Staff co-operate; A1.4 Staff and children respect one another; A1.7 The school is a model of democratic citizenship; B2.6 The behaviour policy is linked to learning and curriculum development; C2.8 Discipline is based on mutual respect.

a) Is disciplinary exclusion seen as a process involving a gradual breakdown in relationships as well as the event of separation from a classroom or the school?
b) Does the behaviour policy attempt to minimise all forms of disciplinary exclusion whether temporary or permanent, formal or informal?
c) Is it understood that disciplinary exclusion can be interrupted by support and intervention in teaching and learning arrangements and relationships?
d) Do school policies help to minimise disciplinary exclusion from lessons?
e) Is the knowledge of children and parents/carers used to reduce disaffection and disruption?
f) Are there meetings, involving staff, children, parents/carers and others, that attempt to deal with problems flexibly before they escalate?
g) Are the connections recognised between devaluation of children, and disaffection, disruption and disciplinary exclusion?
h) Does the school avoid creating pools of disaffection in devalued teaching groups?
i) Does the school address feelings of devaluation when they arise in children, for example in ethnic minority or social class groups?
j) Does the school attempt to reduce conflict between ethnic or social class groups?
k) Are responses to concerns about the behaviour of children always to do with education and rehabilitation rather than retribution?
l) Are children, or others who are seen to have offended against the school community, treated with forgiveness?
m) Is it well understood as part of the school culture that people can apologise and make amends without ‘losing face’?
n) Is regular anger in children treated as a reason to find help rather than punishment?
o) Do staff retain their responsibilities to care for all children equally even when responding to difficulties with behaviour?
p) Are there clear, positive plans for re-introducing children who are not attending school for disciplinary reasons?
q) Do staff take responsibility for what happens to children when they are subject to disciplinary exclusion and are not in school?
r) Are there plans for managing and reducing the dependence of children and young people on nicotine and/or other drugs?
s) Are regular reports on disciplinary exclusion produced for staff, parents, governors and children?
t) Do staff monitor a reduction in temporary, permanent, formal and informal disciplinary exclusions?

u) ______________________________

v) ______________________________

B2.8 Barriers to attendance are reduced.

A2.9 The school encourages children and adults to feel good about themselves;
B2.9 Bullying is minimised.

a) Are all barriers to attendance explored within the cultures, policies and practices of the school as well as in children and young people's attitudes and homes?
b) Do staff investigate why children are regularly late and offer appropriate support?
c) Does the school know for how many children school is a positive and less than positive experience?
d) Are children encouraged to constructively express how their experience at school can be made more positive?
e) Do staff develop non-confrontational approaches to collaboration with parents/carers over unauthorised absence?
f) Does the school avoid using unauthorised absence as a reason for disciplinary exclusion?
g) Does the school avoid encouraging absence as an informal form of exclusion or in order to gain good examination or inspection reports?
h) Are children who have been absent given a genuinely warm greeting on their return to school?
i) Is the unauthorised absence of children treated equitably irrespective of gender or background?
j) Is the relationship recognised between absence and vulnerability, such as a lack of supportive friendships or insecurity over gender or sexual identity?
k) Is the relationship recognised between bullying and absence from school?
l) Does the school respond to child pregnancy in a way that is supportive and non-discriminatory towards girls?
m) Does the school actively support the return to school and participation of children who have had a bereavement, a chronic illness or other long-term absence?
n) Is there clear advice on extended leave to visit a 'home' country that has been negotiated with the school's communities?
o) Are staff encouraged to integrate into learning activities the experiences gained by those who have been away for extended periods?
p) Is there a co-ordinated strategy over school absence of children between the school and other agencies involved with them?
q) Is there an efficient system for reporting and recording absence and finding and understanding the reasons for it?
r) Is a record kept of absences from individual lessons?
s) Are connections made between absence from lessons and addictions to smoking and/or other drugs?
t) Are absences from particular lessons seen as a reason for exploring relationships with teachers and what is taught?
u) Is the unauthorised absence of children reducing?
v) ______________________________
w) ______________________________

B2.9 Bullying is minimised.

A2.8 The school promotes non-violent interactions and resolutions to disputes;
C2.6 Lessons develop an understanding of the similarities and differences between people.

a) Do adults and children negotiate a shared view of what counts as bullying?
b) Is there a statement about bullying, known and understood by everyone, which sets out what behaviours are acceptable and unacceptable, including cyber-bullying?
c) Is bullying seen as a potential part of all power relationships and as an abuse of power?
d) Is bullying seen in all forms of harassment and discrimination directed towards adults and children?
e) Are staff vigilant in stopping physical abuse 'games' such as grabbing, hitting or kicking children on their genitals?
f) Is bullying seen as concerned with verbal and emotional hurt as well as physical assault?
g) Is the threat of the withdrawal of friendship understood as a source of bullying?
h) Is bullying seen to occur when someone is made to feel vulnerable about their identity?
i) Are racist, sexist, classist, disablist, homophobic and transphobic comments and behaviour seen as aspects of bullying?
j) Are negative comments on personal characteristics such as hair colour or weight or the wearing of glasses seen as bullying?
k) Do staff and children challenge the use of the term 'gay' to mean that something is 'rubbish'?
l) Do staff avoid making assumptions about the reasons for bullying, for example that a child with an impairment is bullied because of a disablist attitude?
m) Do adults and children feel safe to identify themselves as other than heterosexual or neither male nor female?
n) Are a variety of organisations consulted in drawing up anti-bullying guidelines, for example concerned with Travellers, lesbian, gay, bisexual and transgender people, disabled people, asylum seekers and refugees?
o) Do children feel able to express different ways of being a boy, girl, neither or both without being teased or bullied?
p) Does the school distinguish between supportive and bullying styles of management?
q) Is bullying seen as a signal that the perpetrator may be vulnerable themselves and need support?
r) Does the school management hide, or avoid exploring, the extent of bullying in order to maintain a positive image of the school?
s) Can children who are bullied choose who to assist them from a number of staff with a mix of genders?
t) Are there people, in addition to Unions, who staff can turn to if they are bullied?
u) Are children trained to mediate in bullying incidents as part of their involvement in preventing and minimising bullying?
v) Are clear records kept about bullying incidents?
w) Is bullying being reduced?

v) ______________________________

Dimension C: Evolving inclusive practices

C1: Constructing curricula for all

1 Children explore cycles of food production and consumption.
2 Children investigate the importance of water.
3 Children study clothing and decoration of the body.
4 Children find out about housing and the built environment.
5 Children consider how and why people move around their locality and the world.
6 Children learn about health and relationships.
7 Children investigate the earth, the solar system and the universe.
8 Children study life on earth.
9 Children investigate sources of energy.
10 Children learn about communication and communication technology.
11 Children engage with, and create, literature, arts and music.
12 Children learn about work and link it to the development of their interests.
13 Children learn about ethics, power and government.

C2: Orchestrating learning

1 Learning activities are planned with all children in mind.
2 Learning activities encourage the participation of all children.
3 Children are encouraged to be confident critical thinkers.
4 Children are actively involved in their own learning.
5 Children learn from each other.
6 Lessons develop an understanding of similarities and differences between people.
7 Assessments encourage the achievements of all children.
8 Discipline is based on mutual respect.
9 Staff plan, teach and review together.
10 Staff develop shared resources to support learning.
11 Teaching assistants support the learning and participation of all children.
12 Homework is set so that it contributes to every child's learning.
13 Activities outside school lessons involve all children.
14 Resources in the locality of the school are known and used.

C1: Constructing curricula for all

Constructing Curricula for All (Section C1) offers an approach to curricula that takes inclusive values seriously. It encourages learning to be active, critical and reflective. It suggests learning activities linked to experience that promote an understanding of the interdependence of environments and peoples around the earth. Like other sections, it structures thinking around questions. We want them to be used to initiate a mass of investigations in and outside classrooms as children and adults look behind the indicators which form our subject headings. The active nature of learning is assumed whether we use the words, 'learn about', 'investigate', 'examine', 'study' or 'consider' in any particular question.

The task of structuring an approach to knowledge is huge. Because of the nature of the material, there are more questions for each indicator here than elsewhere in the *Index*. In this section, we have divided questions up with headings and sub-headings. We hope our questions will prompt the development of further questions to support the curiosity of children and adults. Many of the questions we ask in this section provide examples of what might be included in an answer. We hesitated to do this for we believe that learning activities should be much more open ended. But the content is here to show how these indicators can structure a curriculum which has depth as well as breadth, for children and adults of all ages; that it provides a viable alternative to traditional curricular structures.

This section is work in progress. But then all curricula suggestions might be seen in that way. They should be an invitation to adults and children in schools to draw on them to construct their own curricula together as they relate them to their own particular circumstances. Some of our suggestions are developed in more detail than others. We would like to add to this work in collaboration with those who engage with it, in England, other countries in the UK, and elsewhere in the world. As suggested in Part 2, we hope that people will contribute their responses and ideas for how these curricula suggestions can be further developed, by sending them to info@indexforinclusion.org. We will gather them together and make them available on the website indexforinclusion.org.

C1.1 Children explore cycles of food production and consumption.

A2.9 The school encourages children and adults to feel good about themselves; C1.6 Children learn about health and relationships; C1.7 Children investigate the earth, the solar system and the universe; C1.8 Children study life on earth.

Linking locally and globally

- Is there a school garden or allotment where children learn about growing plants for food?
- Is the school linked to a local farm?
- Do children consider where their favourite foods and drinks come from?
- Do children explore food preferences and diets in their own and other countries?
- Do families and communities encourage children to learn about the growing of food?
- Do children learn about food through school meals and use of the cafeteria?
- Do children study animal welfare from the school's dairy, egg and meat buying policies?
- Does the school buy food from local farmers and farmers' markets?
- Do people who buy, grow and prepare food in farms, homes and restaurants contribute to lessons?
- Do children identify global influences on what they eat, where it comes from and how it iscooked?
- Do children make a list of the places food comes from that appears in local food shops and supermarkets and estimate food miles involving all the journeys the food has made?
- Do children learn about local, national and global differences in what people eat?
- Do children examine how street traders supply cooked food locally and internationally?

Food cycles

- Do children learn how a food cycle involves soil preparation, planting, growing, picking, storing/preserving, processing, distributing/transporting, marketing, buying, storing, cooking, eating, treating waste, composting and fertilising?
- Do children learn how food cycles are linked to nitrogen, carbon and water cycles?

Food webs (See understanding life support systems, page 142)

- Do children create food webs which contain the sun, plant producers, animal consumers, scavengers and fungal and bacterial decomposers?

Growing and land use

- Do children learn about soils and how their composition affects what grows well in them?
- Do children learn about the role of bacteria in the development of fertile soils?
- Do children learn about the causes and consequences of soil erosion?
- Do children consider the consequence of using land for single and rotating crops?
- Do children consider why land is used to produce tea, coffee, sugar, alcoholic drinks, tobacco and illegal addictive drugs rather than food?
- Do children investigate who owns the land on which food is grown?
- Do children learn about the conversion of forest land to agricultural land and the effect this has on greenhouse gases?
- Do children learn the extent to which agriculture is mechanised in different countries?

Food seasons and weather

- Do children explore the relationship between food growing and seasons?
- Do children learn about the effects of climate on food growing?
- Do children consider how global warming and more extreme weather patterns are affecting food production and will affect it in the future?

Pests and weeds

- Do children learn how pests can be controlled naturally and artificially?
- Do children learn how weeds can be controlled naturally and artificially?

Animals for food

- Do children learn how farm animals are grown for food?
- Do children study fish for food from seas, rivers and fish farms?
- Do children explore the depletion of fish stocks, the effects of fishing quotas and the possibilities of the regeneration of stocks?
- Do children learn about the use of industrial methods for rearing animals for food?
- Do children investigate milk production from cows, sheep and other animals?
- Do children learn about egg production?
- Do children learn about bee-keeping for honey?
- Do children learn about animal diseases (such as foot and mouth and BSE) and the consequences of the spread of disease in their country and other countries?
- Do children study the use of pesticides and antibiotics in controlling disease in animals?
- Do children explore the use of hormones in promoting growth in animals?
- Do children consider how much land is needed for the same food value in growing vegetables and animals for food?
- Do children learn how cattle produce large quantities of greenhouse gas (methane)?

Transporting

- Do children learn how food travels globally and nationally from producers to consumers?
- Do children learn how animals are transported nationally and internationally for meat production and to be slaughtered?

Preparing and eating

- Do children learn to prepare and cook food in school?
- Do children consider the pleasures in cooking as well as eating?
- Do children learn about who prepares and cooks food and why some people do not?
- Do children learn about the extent to which people read about cooking, watch TV cookery programmes and cook themselves?
- Do children investigate the time different people have to cook?
- Do children learn about the extent to which pre-prepared foods are used because of the short time people have to cook?
- Do children consider how eating together sustains relationships between people?

Flavouring

- Do children learn about developments in the use of condiments and spices?
- Do children learn about the development of and uses of salt?
- Do children learn about the way salt and spices became valuable commodities in trade?
- Do children consider benefits and drawbacks of additives to food?
- Do children explore the way spices are used within different cultures and food traditions?

Preserving/processing

- Do children explore food preservation by refrigeration, canning, bottling, smoking, and salting?

Waste disposal, composting and fertilising.

- Do children learn about sewage systems and waste treatment?
- Do children learn about the use of manure for improving soil?
- Do children learn about approaches to composting, using compost bins and wormeries?

Nutrition, health and disease

- Do children explore who gets sufficient and insufficient nutritious food?
- Do children explore the importance of staple foods to many people around the world?
- Do children compare the food people need for health and what they eat?
- Do children distinguish between health promoting and unhealthy fast foods?
- Do children learn how contaminated food and water can be a source of disease?
- Do children learn how disease from food can be minimised through preservation, freshness, cleanliness and cooking?
- Do children explore the consumption of alcoholic drinks and how they contribute to health and ill health?

Food costs

- Do children learn about the costs of food and how this relates to income in different households?
- Do children learn how costs affect food choices?
- Do children consider the chain of effects of demands for cheap food on: animal welfare; pay and conditions for producers; degrading of land, use of fertilisers, herbicides and pesticides; loss of forests, biodiversity, soil fertility and land for local food; use of energy for storage, air, road transport and travel to out of city supermarkets leading to loss of small local businesses?

Food trade and business

- Do children learn how people make a livelihood in producing, marketing, processing, distributing, cooking and selling food?
- Do children learn how profits from the growing of food are increased through processing, incanning or cooking and freezing, and who benefits from them?
- Do children explore the extent to which food business is carried out by large and small producers, and large and small wholesalers and retailers?
- Do children learn how trade agreements and trade barriers can make it difficult for farmers in economically poor countries to compete with cheap imports from rich countries and to sell to those countries?
- Do children explore the rise and fall in food prices and how this affects people differently in their country and in other countries?
- Do children explore the way food prices vary with the cost of oil and the use of land for biomass fuels?
- Do children examine the way farmers can earn less while food prices increase?

Food ethics and politics

- Do children and adults discuss their responsibility to know about the conditions under which their food is produced, the welfare of people who produce it, and to act if these conflict with their values?
- Do children investigate why hunger arises in economically poor countries alongside food abundance for rich countries?

- Do children explore the concern of governments in economically rich countries about levels of obesity and what they do to reduce it?
- Do children explore the possibility that the majority of food and drink advertising on television is about foods which in large quantities contribute to ill-health?
- Do children explore the influence of corporations on the price and quality of food, its production and distribution and research to develop new sources and farming methods?
- Do children consider the principles of food sovereignty: that food is a right; producers should be respected; production should be local; local people should control the resources of its production; local skills should be developed; and food production should conserve nature? [39]
- Do children explore the environmental and health effects of eating meat, fish, dairy products, vegetarianism and veganism?
- Do children understand the principles behind Fair Trade and the arguments for and against expanding it?
- Do children learn the advantages and disadvantages of producing food organically or with the use of artificial pesticides and herbicides?
- Do children consider how pesticides, such as DDT, long banned in economically rich countries, are allowed for use in economically poor countries?
- Do children investigate why pesticides kill large numbers of people in economically poor areas in the world and why many more commit suicide by deliberately taking pesticides?
- Do children learn about the dangers of the use of pesticides and herbicides for growers and for consumers, for example in the way DDT becomes concentrated in breast milk?
- Do children learn how mothers with little access to clean water may be encouraged by corporations to use milk powder instead of naturally sterile breast milk?

Genetically modified crops

- Does the school encourage discussion of the benefits and problems of natural and artificial genetic modification?
- Do children investigate how seeds can be genetically modified to increase resistance to drought, pests, pesticides and herbicides and to make them infertile?
- Do children consider that the advantages and disadvantages of genetic modification may vary with the nature and purpose of the modification and its effects on people, other plants and animals?
- Do children discuss the benefits and drawbacks of genetically modified crops for suppliers of seeds, farmers and consumers?
- Do children explore the effects of resistance to pests on genetically modified crops on surrounding plants?

Linking past, present and future

- Do children explore how the production and consumption of food has changed over time in their own locality, country and around the world?
- Do children explore the effects that changing food choices have on health and the environment?
- Do children investigate the way diets have changed?
- Do children consider what food will be produced and consumed in the future in their country and around the world?
- Do children examine movements for urban farming?

39 The pillars of food sovereignty, in Millstone, E. and Lang, T. (2008) The Atlas of Food, who eats what, where and why, Brighton, Earthscan p.101

C1.2 Children investigate the importance of water.

B1.12 The school reduces its carbon footprint and use of water;
C1.5 Children consider how and why people move around their locality and the world;
C1.8 Children study life on earth.

Linking locally and globally

- Does the school adopt a local river or stream that can be investigated and conserved and through which children can understand ecosystems and water cycles?
- Does the school adopt a river in another part of the world and understand its importance to the lives of people there?
- Do people who sell water, supply water for homes, factories and farms and look after local waterways contribute to the curriculum?
- Is the school involved in the conservation of local rivers and waterways?

Using a finite resource

- Do children learn how water is essential for the life of plants, animals and people?
- Do children understand the significance to life of rivers, lakes and reservoirs?
- Do children understand that freshwater is a small part (2.5%) of the water on the earth and that only a third of this is available for use by living things?
- Do children learn how sea ice flows are mainly made of fresh water?
- Do children learn about the human uses of water for drinking, sanitation, personal hygiene and washing food, washing dishes and clothes, gardening, agricultural and animal farming including fisheries, industrial production and energy production?
- Do children explore the role of water in recreation?

A resource under pressure

- Do children explore the increasing demand on water from population growth, increased food production and other manufacture, affluent lifestyles and consumption?
- Do children consider the extent to which 'industrial lifestyles are as much supported by water as oil'?[40]
- Do children explore the pressures on water supplies from increased urbanisation, changes in river flows from dams and climate change?
- Do children consider the extent to which water is contaminated by human and animal waste and industrial processes?
- Do children learn about the consequences of drought in their own and other countries?
- Do children learn about the effects of water shortage on the movement of animals and humans?
- Do children learn about the relationship between water needs and water consumption?

Water as a habitat

- Do children investigate how first life forms developed in water?
- Do children learn about the creatures and plants that inhabit salt and fresh water?
- Do children learn about the consequences for water animals and plants of the diversion

Storing and delivering

- Do children learn how water is delivered to buildings, including their homes?
- Do children learn the extent to which farms are dependent on stored water?
- Do children learn how water is stored naturally and in human built tanks and reservoirs?
- Do children learn about the water table (aquifer) and the use of wells?
- Do children learn about systems of irrigation?
- Do children learn to consider the advantages and disadvantages of building desalination plants to provide fresh water?

40 Black, M. and King, J. (2009) The Atlas of Water, Brighton, Earthscan and this page is informed by a reading of that book.

Properties of water

- Do children investigate the movement of water in rivers and tides?
- Do children learn about the importance for maintenance of underwater life of the expansion of water as it freezes to ice?
- Do children investigate the way water can be transformed between solid, liquid and gaseous forms?
- Do children investigate the significance of the surface tension properties of water for the formation of rain drops and waves, the functioning of cells, upward movement of water in trees and other plants and circulation of blood in animals?
- Do children investigate the stabilising effect on climate of the slowness of temperature change of water compared to land?
- Do children investigate the use of water as a solvent?
- Do children investigate the use of water in producing hydrogen as a fuel?
- Do children investigate the use of water as a coolant in engines and power stations?
- Do children explore the changes of water to steam and the uses of steam?
- Do children learn about the power in moving water, and how this can be controlled for generating electricity from rivers and the sea?
- Do children learn about the effects of uncontrolled movement of water from glaciers, avalanches, floods and tsunamis?

Water and climate

- Do children study the water cycle involving evaporation, condensation, precipitation?
- Do children learn about clouds?
- Do children learn how rain falls in relation to hills and valleys?
- Do children consider variations in rain and snow fall, droughts and floods?
- Do children learn about mudslides and avalanches?
- Do children consider the formation of fogs and mists, dew and frosts?
- Do children investigate patterns of snowfall in their own and other countries?
- Do children consider the consequences of rising sea levels due to global warming?

Water and health

- Do children learn about the importance of water for hygiene?
- Do children learn about the development of the flushing toilet, its advantages and disadvantages and the extent of its use around the world?
- Do children learn about the extent of water pollution and the consequences this has for living things?
- Do children consider how water is made safe for drinking?
- Do children learn about the role of water in spreading disease in their own and other countries?

Ethics, ownership and conflict

- Do children learn about the extent to which people have access to clean drinking water?
- Do children learn about the advantages and disadvantages of the public or private ownership of a nation's water?
- Do children learn how fresh water shortages and the control of water lead to conflicts around the world?

Linking past, present and future

- Do children explore the changing patterns of rainfall over time?
- Do children investigate changing sea levels?
- Do children explore changing demands for fresh water?
- Do children consider how water shortages can be avoided in the future?

C1.3 Children study clothing and decoration of the body.

Linking locally and globally

- Does the school invite local clothes shops, laundries, designers, makers and repairers, jewellers, hairdressers and tattooists to explain their work?
- Do children learn about the spread of clothing styles from one country to another?
- Do children explore the global diversity of clothing conventions?
- Do children learn about the connection between clothing, seasons, temperature and weather in their own and other countries?
- Do schools connect their choice of clothing in cold weather to the need for heating in homes and other buildings?
- Do children explore the spread of particular 'western' styles of dress such as business suits, ties and jeans?
- Do children explore the way traditional styles of dress are retained by particular groups and genders?
- Do children learn how diversity of clothing styles in the world is being reduced?

Clothing cycle

- Do children study a clothing cycle from the production of raw materials, marketing and fashion, manufacture, purchase, use, repair, exchange, recycling, discarding and disposal?

Production

- Do children learn how shoes and clothing are made from plants, animal wool/fur and skins, silk and oil-based sources?
- Do children learn the proportions of shoes and clothing made from different sources?
- Do children develop an understanding of the variety of ways in which clothes and shoes are manufactured?
- Do children learn about the extraction of precious metals and stones for jewellery?

Fashion and marketing

- Do children learn about the design of hats, clothes, shoes and jewellery?
- Do children learn about the way clothes and jewellery are marketed and sold?
- Do children learn how branding affects the desirability, value and price of clothes, shoes, bags?
- Do children learn about the way the promotion of fashion and style is connected to pressures for the consumption of clothes and shoes?

Clothing choice

- Do children explore the pressures which determine the clothes and shoes that they wear?
- Do children learn to make active choices in the clothes and ornamentation that they wear?
- Do children learn why people wear clothes in public and private?
- Does the school explore the way groups and cultures encourage and require men and women to cover or display the face and body?
- Do children explore how and why conventions arise for particular clothing to be worn for particular groups in particular contexts, such as school, work and evening clothes?
- Do children explore the reasons that clothing choices may differ according to gender in their own and other countries?

- Do children consider how clothing may display membership of a group or sub-culture?
- Do children learn how and why people change clothing styles with age?

Jewellery and body decoration

- Do children explore the extraction of minerals for jewellery?
- Do children explore the production and use of jewellery?
- Do children explore body ornamentation, such as painting, tattooing, piercing, scarring?
- Do children learn about fashions in hair-styles?
- Do children consider the reasons why people dye, grow and remove their hair?

Maintaining clothes

- Do children learn about different approaches to washing and drying clothes?
- Do children learn techniques for repairing clothes?

Recycling and disposing of clothes

- Do children learn what happens to clothes when they are not wanted or are worn out?

Clothing and body decoration ethics

- Do children learn about the hidden costs of cheap clothing in low pay, child labour and poor working conditions?
- Do children consider the extent of pollution from the use of pesticides in cotton growing?
- Do children trace the price paid for, and profits made from, producing raw materials, making cloth and other materials and the manufacture, distribution and retail selling of clothes, shoes and jewellery?
- Do children investigate the extent to which the desire to control mining of precious stones and metals has contributed to wars?
- Do children learn about fair trade in clothing?
- Do children explore the idea of ethical clothing and what this might mean for clothing choices they make and clothing recommended by the school?

Linking past, present and future

- Do children learn how clothing fashions vary from one period to another?
- Do children investigate the extent to which campaigns have halted the fur trade?
- Do children learn how body ornamentation fashions vary from one period to another?
- Do children consider the future availability of clothing materials?
- Do children consider the future costs of clothing?

C1.4 Children find out about housing and the built environment.

B1.12 The school reduces its carbon footprint and use of water.

Linking locally and globally

- Do children examine the variety of buildings in their locality?
- Do children consider what buildings in their locality they like and why?
- Do children explore what buildings are allowed to be built in their area?
- Do children learn the extent to which building in their city or neighbourhood is planned?
- Do builders, machine operators, electricians, plumbers, carpenters, painters and decorators, roofers, tilers, plasterers, stone masons, architects, demolition workers and town planners contribute to the curriculum in the school?
- Do children learn about the variety and properties of building materials, such as brick, mud, metal, wood, plastic, straw bales, felt, canvas, in their own and other countries?
- Do children learn about the variety of homes, such as boats, tents, caravans, brick and stone buildings, homes from found materials and stilt houses?

Rural and urban homes and buildings

- Do children learn about the origin of cities and how they change over time?
- Do children learn about the distribution of people between cities and rural areas and the differences in their experience of the built environment?
- Do children learn the different purposes for building, such as for factories, offices, prisons, civic buildings, churches, barns, homes, restaurants and cafés?
- Do children consider the changes in buildings in rural areas arising, for example, from changing rural populations and farming methods?
- Do children learn about the reasons for the location of homes?
- Do children explore how water, electricity and gas are delivered to homes?
- Do children learn how waste is removed from homes and other buildings?
- Do children learn how and why buildings are demolished?

Forms of building and building materials

- Do children learn about the construction of homes in buildings of different sizes and numbers of storeys from bungalows to tower blocks?
- Do children survey homes built for single people, adults with and without children and extended families?
- Do children learn about the way foundations for homes are made and how these depend on ground conditions and expectations of storms and earthquakes?
- Do children learn how buildings are made waterproof?
- Do children learn how glass was developed for use in windows?
- Do children consider the extent to which the materials in buildings reflect local sourcing?

Building design and planning

- Do children learn about the way homes and other buildings are designed?
- Do children explore possibilities for energy efficient building design?
- Do children consider how homes are decorated?
- Do children explore why houses get built on flood plains?

Home occupation

- Do children learn about how homes are owned, mortgaged, rented and squatted?
- Do children investigate the cost of building, buying and renting homes?
- Do children learn about the possessions that people have in their homes and how and why these differ?

Building machines

- Do children examine the large machines used in building, for digging, shifting, hoisting, drilling and mixing cement and concrete?
- Do children learn about the small machines, power and hand tools used in building?
- Do children learn about past and present approaches to scaffolding?

Home safety

- Do children learn about the safety of homes in storms, fires, floods and earthquakes?
- Do children learn how electrical appliances, sockets and electrical wiring can be used safely in homes?
- Do children learn why water is kept separated from electrical wiring and appliances?
- Do children learn about the prevention of fire hazards from electrical and gas appliances and the use of smoke alarms?
- Do children learn about house insurance and covering of risk?

Heating and cooling

- Do children learn how buildings are heated and cooled?
- Do children learn how buildings can be made more energy efficient through, for example, choice of building materials, insulation and draught reduction?

Building business

- Do children learn how people enter occupations to do with building, architecture and planning?
- Do children explore what it means to be self-employed or work for small or large building organisations?
- Do children learn the extent to which builders specialise or acquire several skills?

Ethics and politics of building

- Do children learn about reasons for homelessness and who it affects?
- Do children consider what makes a more and less desired neighbourhood?
- Do children explore the choices and economic circumstances affecting where people live?
- Do children explore why some people have much more space to live in than others?
- Do children learn how people's homes are affected by wars and their aftermath?

Linking past, present and future

- Do children learn how buildings have changed over time?
- Do children consider how and why cities have grown?
- Do children investigate the changing population of rural areas?
- Do children consider how the amount of rural land has reduced?
- Do children consider future approaches to building?

C1.5 Children consider how and why people move around their locality and the world.

C1.13 Children learn about ethics, power and government

Linking locally and globally

- Do children consider keeping a record for a week or a month of the journeys they make from home to other places within or outside the area where they live?
- Do people contribute to the curriculum who run local travel businesses, drive taxis, buses, trains, work with engines, sell and service cars and bicycles and make local transport decisions?
- Do people contribute to the curriculum whose families have stayed in an area for a long time?
- Do people contribute to the curriculum who have arrived from other countries or whose parents or grandparents or more distant ancestors arrived from other countries?
- Do children consider forms of transport used in different parts of the world?

Attachment to place

- Do children learn about the importance of a place of origin to many people?
- Do children consider what makes a place good to live and stay in?

Why people move

- Do children investigate how people move around to fulfil basic needs for food, water, fuel for cooking, warmth and transport, shelter, safety, education and work?
- Do children investigate how people choose to move for tourism, exploration, sport and relationships?
- Do children learn how the tourism industry promotes travel?
- Do children learn about travelling lifestyles in their own and other countries?
- Do children learn how people are displaced by change of land use, such as hydro-electric projects?
- Do children learn how people are displaced by conflict?
- Do children learn how people are displaced by environmental degradation?
- Do children explore why people become refugees and seek asylum?
- Do children consider the reasons for space exploration?

Trade

- Do children learn about the role of local and distant trade in promoting travel?
- Do children learn about the role of exchange in trade?
- Do children learn how people move to obtain raw materials?
- Do children learn about how profits are made in trade?
- Do children learn about the advantages and disadvantages of restricted and unrestricted trade for economically rich and poor countries?
- Do children learn about the power of international organisations and agreements to regulate trade?

Conflict, invasion and occupation

- Do children learn about the reasons people go to war?
- Do children learn how countries occupy the countries of others to control resources?
- Do children learn why some parts of the world have strategic importance?

Modes of transport and forms of propulsion

- Do children consider how people move around by walking, running, swimming, cycling, in wheelchairs, on animals, in lorries, cars, trams, trains, boats, sailing ships, steam and diesel ships, hot air and helium balloons, helicopters, hovercrafts, aeroplanes and rockets?
- Do children learn about the creation of road and rail networks?
- Do children learn about the development of wheels and engines, jet and rocket propulsion?

Transport and the environment

- Do children consider the extent to which travel depends on the availability of fossil and other nonrenewable fuels?
- Do children learn about the effects on the environment of moving goods using different forms of transport over different distances?
- Do children consider how use of environmentally friendly transport such as walking and cycling can be increased?
- Do children explore how car use is popularised by advertising, TV programmes and sport?
- Do children learn how choice of car and air transport become part of people's identities?

Navigation and maps

- Do children learn about the development of maps?
- Do children learn about the development of navigation at sea using stars, clocks and maps, and global positioning systems?

Controlling movementt

- Do children consider who owns and uses a passport?
- Do children consider how visas are granted and refused?
- Do children learn about the restriction placed on movement by land ownership, natural boundaries and national borders?

Movement and ethics

- Do children explore the hidden costs of car and air travel in environmental damage?
- Do children learn about the way people who seek asylum are treated when they come to this country?
- Do children explore the effects of attracting skilled people from economically poor to economically rich countries on the economies and services in their countries of origin?
- Do children learn about the views people take about how free they should be to travel to the countries of others and how free others should be to travel to their country?
- Do children learn about the particular responsibility for displaced a nd vulnerable people in countries with which the UK is, or has been, at war?
- Do children discuss the nature of an ethical immigration policy?

Linking past, present and future

- Do children investigate how modes of transport have changed?
- Do children examine how the use of private cars has increased?
- Do children study how patterns of migration have changed?
- Do children learn how the rise and fall of empires affects movement and migration?
- Do children consider how and why transport may change in the future?
- Do children consider possible future movements and controls on movement of people around the world?

C1.6 Children learn about health and relationships.

A2.9 The school encourages children and adults to feel good about themselves;
A2.10 The school contributes to the health of children and adults;
C1.1 Children explore cycles of food production and consumption;
C1.2 Children investigate the importance of water.

Linking locally and globally

- Do children learn from their own and other people's experiences of health and ill-health?
- Do local people contribute to the curriculum who promote physical, mental and environmental health and/or treat ill-health?
- Do children learn about the differences in patterns of disease between countries?
- Do children learn about the relationships between poverty, disease and food and water shortage and quality?

Meanings of health

- Do children consider what they mean by being healthy?
- Do children explore what being healthy means to different people?
- Do children consider whether a good healthy life is one that lasts as long as possible?

Health and bodies

- Do children learn about the anatomy and physiology of human bodies?
- Do children learn about the role of genes and DNA in development?
- Do children learn about the dependence of development on the nature of the environment?
- Do children consider how bodies change as they age?

Health and disease

- Do children explore the extent to which ill-health may be reduced and prevented by changes in environment and nutrition, increasing amounts of exercise, reducing stress and medical and paramedical interventions?
- Do children consider developments and breakthroughs in the treatment of ill-health?
- Do children learn how diseases are spread by people, other animals including birds and insects, air and water?
- Do children learn about the role of bacteria, viruses and prions in producing disease?
- Do children learn about the role of bacteria in maintaining health?
- Do children learn about the development of antibiotics?
- Do children explore the extent to which over-prescription of antibiotics has contributed to resistance to them?
- Do children study the prevalence of 'superbugs' in hospitals?
- Do children learn about cancer and how treatments have been developed?
- Do children investigate how and why life-expectancies differ between individuals and groups?
- Do children learn how the pharmaceutical industry promotes health and notions of illness?
- Do children learn about the importance of use of medicines in improving the lives of some people?
- Do children learn about the role of treatment of disease in prolonging lives?
- Do children explore the different reasons for cosmetic surgery?
- Do children explore the value of different ways of treating illness?

Mental health

- Do children examine the effect of people's circumstances on how good they feel about themselves?
- Do children learn how some people have persistent mental states that prevent them doing what they want to do?
- Do children consider how some people's persistent states of mind interfere with what others want to do?
- Do children explore the extent to which people are seen as having a mental illness?
- Do children investigate the variety of ways in which people are helped to overcome mental illness and increase their mental health?
- Do children learn about the extent to which drugs are prescribed because of people's anxiety, depression or other mental problems?
- Do children explore the effects of drugs to reduce mental problems on bodies and minds?
- Do children consider the relationship between fulfilling activity and mental health?

Relationships

- Do children discuss the nature of friendships and how they can be deepened, maintained and lost?
- Do children consider the different forms of relationships with acquaintances, friends and family?
- Is the knowledge of children of the variety and complexity of relationships drawn on in the curriculum?
- Are the human situations that are shared from television and other media used in lessons?
- Do children learn about the different meanings of love?
- Do children reflect on the ways feelings push them to act in positive and negative ways towards others and themselves?
- Do children learn about trust in relationships?
- Do children learn about the varieties of ways of being in a family?
- Do children learn about the ways people can make families out of groups of friends who care for each other?

Caring for children

- Do children learn about the satisfactions of a variety of futures with and without having children?
- Do children explore the patterns of caring for children within their own and other communities nationally and internationally?
- Do children learn about the responsibilities and potential difficulties of caring for young children and as they grow up and the joys that may last throughout life?

Sexual relationships and sex education

- Do staff avoid attributing particular sexual feelings to those who may not have them?
- Is the focus in sex education on relationships and pleasure as well as pregnancy and sexually transmitted diseases?
- Are children given full information about the changing incidence, risks of acquiring, and treatment for sexually transmitted diseases?
- Is sex education linked to the choices that people can make about their lives and bodies?
- Do children discuss the possibilities for deep friendships between sexual partners and how people may feel if friendship is absent?
- Do children discuss feelings of jealousy and how they affect sexual and other relationships with friends and in the family?

- Do children explore the different ways girls/women and boys/men are affected when they have created a pregnancy?
- Do children consider the common responsibility of boys/men and girls/women for actions that created a pregnancy?
- Do staff avoid presenting long-term monogamy as the way everybody would prefer to organise their lives?
- Does sex and relationship education concern boys, girls, transgender, transsexual and intersex people, whether they see themselves as heterosexual, lesbian, gay or bisexual?

Health and drugs

- Do children learn about the extent of the use of legal and illegal mind-altering drugs?
- Do children learn about the social and health consequences of the use of illegal and legal drugs?
- Do children explore the use of, and addiction to, prescription, legal and illegal drugs and how this affects minds, bodies and lives?
- Do children learn about the differing extents to which people consume alcohol?
- Do children learn about the pressures to use legal and illegal drugs from advertising, from shops and pubs and within child and adult cultures?

Health and food

- Do children explore what makes foods health-giving or harmful?
- Are discussions of healthy eating linked to an understanding of family budgets?

Health and ethics

- Do children explore the arguments for and against legalising the production and distribution of illegal drugs?
- Are different views discussed of the contribution to health of vegetarianism, veganism and fish and meat eating?
- Do people consider the extent to which cosmetic surgery for reasons not directly related to health involve surgeons and nurses in unethical behaviour?
- Do children explore the interests of food manufacturers in promoting healthy and unhealthy foods?
- Do children explore the differing extents to which life-saving and life-prolonging drugs and medical treatment are available to wealthy and poor people nationally and globally?
- Do children learn about the way finite national health budgets involve priority decisions about who can be treated and at what expense?

Linking past, present and future

- Do children investigate how patterns of disease have changed?
- Do children learn how life expectancy has changed and how it might change in the future?
- Do children explore how changes in life-expectancy affect the potential for long relationships?
- Do children learn how care and hygiene at childbirth has changed and has affected life-expectancy for women?
- Do children consider how patterns of disease might change with increasing resistance to antibiotics and changing climate?

C1.7 Children investigate the earth, the solar system and the universe

A2.3 The school encourages respect for the integrity of planet earth; B1.12 The school reduces its carbon footprint and use of water; B1.13 The school contributes to the reduction of waste; C1.2 Children investigate the importance of water; C1.5 Children consider how and why people move around their locality and the world; C1.8 Children study life on earth; C1.9 Children investigate sources of energy.

Linking locally and globally

- Do children consider how they would tell their address to someone who lives nearby, in Africa or Asia, another planet, another solar system or galaxy and how this might differ from how they learn to write their address?
- Do children take photographs of their local environment, landscapes, skyscapes, cloudscapes and weather variations and exchange them with people in other parts of the country, other parts of the world?
- Do children photograph, paint or draw those details of their local environment they like and dislike and comment on their choices?
- Do adults and children share an understanding of the way environments in one part of the world affect people in other parts of the world through the use of fossil fuels, loss of forests, earthquakes, nuclear accidents, volcanic eruptions?
- Do children consider how their local landscape has changed over time?
- Do schools ask local amateur or professional astronomers; physicists; chemists; miners; users of metal detectors; clockmakers; geographers; cartographers; meteorologists; soil scientists; landscape photographers, designers and artists; writers; and friends to share their understanding of their planet and appreciation of landscapes and skyscapes?
- Do children keep a record of the accuracy of local weather forecasts?

The solar system, the galaxy and the universe

- Do children learn about their star, the sun, as one amongst many stars?
- Do children consider the sun as the source of the earth?
- Do children consider the sun as the source of the energy on the earth?
- Do children consider the life-cycle of stars?
- Do children investigate the earth as one of the planets that moves around the sun?
- Do children study the orbit of the earth and how knowledge about it emerged?
- Do children learn about their galaxy, the Milky Way, and other galaxies?
- Do children investigate the way stars look at different times and from different places?
- Do children consider the universe as all galaxies and all matter?
- Do children learn how the vast majority of the universe is made up of hydrogen and helium?
- Do children learn how all stars, planets and life on earth, including their bodies, has emerged from the matter in the universe?
- Do children study how light is produced by, and travels from, the sun and stars?
- Do children study how interstellar distances are measured in light years?
- Do children understand that it is the past of the universe that is studied because of the time it takes for light to reach the earth?
- Do children explore the development of astronomy and use of telescopes to investigate the universe?

Gravity

- Do children learn how gravity holds them and the atmosphere onto the earth?
- Do children learn how gravity has sculpted the universe?
- Do children learn how gravity holds the sun and the planets and moons in their orbits?

The earth's magnetism

- Do children learn about the magnetic field of the earth and the magnetic poles it produces?
- Do children learn how the magnetic field of the earth has changed and the magnetic poles have reversed?
- Do children explore the role of the earth's magnetic field in protecting the atmosphere by diverting charged particles from solar wind?

Time, clocks and calendars

- Do children learn about time and its measurement?
- Do children learn about the year as time the earth takes to orbit the sun?
- Do children understand the way the spin of the earth produces day and night?
- Do children investigate how the tilt of the earth produces seasons?
- Do children consider the orbit of the moon round the earth as a measure of months?
- Do children learn about longitude and latitude and the way time is set from longitude zero at Greenwich?
- Do children examine geological time periods in the history of the earth?
- Do children investigate different ways of making calendars and how they have changed?

The earth and its moon

- Do children consider the origins of the moon as a chunk of the earth split off by impact from another planet?
- Do children study the composition of the moon and the implications of the discovery of water on it?
- Do children research the size and distance from the earth to the moon and how these allow for total eclipses of the sun?
- Do children consider how the moon creates tides?
- Do children consider how tides would be affected if the moon were closer to the earth?
- Do children investigate how the spin and stability of the earth will be affected by the increasing distance of the moon from the earth?

The oceans

- Do children learn about the extent of the oceans and how they affect and are affected by the weather?
- Do children learn about the transmission of energy in waves?
- Do children learn about the effects of waves and tides on changing coastal landscapes?
- Do children investigate the way sand is produced and beaches are formed?
- Do children learn about the causes and effects of tidal waves or tsunamis?

The land

- Do children investigate how the earth's surface moves along fault lines on tectonic plates?
- Do children consider continents and their continued movement?
- Do children consider the formation of mountains, valleys, rivers and lakes and other landscapes?
- Do children learn about the structure of rock on the surface of the planet and how and when rocks were formed?
- Do children learn about the formation of soils?

Inside the earth

- Do children learn about the internal structure of the earth?
- Do children study how the inside of the earth is revealed in earthquakes and volcanoes, geysers and hot springs?

The earth's materials

- Do children learn about the composition of the earth, its naturally occurring elements and molecules?
- Do children learn about the way elements and molecules exist naturally as gases, liquids, but mainly solids?
- Do children learn how atoms and molecules can be rearranged to form gases, liquids and solids?
- Do children learn how the elements of the earth were formed during the life-cycle of stars?
- Do children study the internal structure of atoms?

Resources from the earth

- Do children learn how some of the materials of the earth, such as diamonds and gold, have been given special financial value by people?
- Do children learn how the resources of the earth are, and have been, exploited for personal gain and human benefit in drilling, mining and quarrying?

The atmosphere and its structure

- Do children learn about the composition of the atmosphere, how it was formed, its significance for sustaining life and how and why it changes?
- Do children consider how the atmosphere is kept in place?
- Do children consider the thinness of the atmosphere in relation to the diameter of the earth?
- Do children learn about the insulating properties of the atmosphere?
- Do children learn how the matter of the atmosphere is more concentrated closer to the earth?
- Do children learn how the temperature of the atmosphere is warmer closer to the earth?
- Do children consider the importance of the ozone layer in absorbing radiation?
- Do children learn about the different effects of land and sea on air temperature?
- Do children learn how the temperature of the atmosphere changes its pressure?

Climate and weather (see C1.2 Children investigate the importance of water: Water and climate p127)

- Do children consider the variations in climate around the world and how this is a consequence of the earth's relationship to the sun?
- Do children consider how climate varies in relation to seas and mountains?
- Do children consider how winds are produced?
- Do children study how winds move from high to low atmospheric pressure?
- Do children learn about the formation of storms, thunderstorms, hurricanes, typhoons, tornados, sandstorms?
- Do children consider the effects of regular winds such as monsoons and trade winds on how people plan their lives and movements?
- Do children learn about ocean currents and weather systems: the Gulf Stream, El Niño and El Niña?
- Do children learn about jet streams and how this affects flying times for aeroplanes?

Understanding climate change

- Do children consider the nature of greenhouse gases, their sources and the length of time they last in the atmosphere?
- Do children understand water vapour as a greenhouse gas that contributes a multiplier effect as temperatures rise?

- Do children explore the effects of industrialisation on the use of fossil fuels and production of greenhouse gasses?
- Do children learn how the greenhouse effect operates and how global warming accelerates?
- Do children consider the contribution of human activity to the production of greenhouse gases and climate change through use fossil fuels, destruction of forests and increased consumption of meat and manufactured goods?
- Do children consider how global warming produces: changes in animal and plant behaviour, forest loss, changing patterns of disease, extreme weather, faster monsoon rains, rising sea levels, floods, mudslides, loss of Arctic and Antarctic ice, receding glaciers, loss of reflection from snow of heat radiation, threats to water supply and food security?
- Do children consider how increased levels of carbon dioxide in the atmosphere acidify the seas with consequences for corals and other marine life?
- Do children learn about the loss of permafrost – permanently frozen soil water – affecting a quarter of northern hemisphere land, and how this leads to collapse of trees and buildings and release of methane and carbon dioxide from dead organic matter?

Combating climate change

- Do children investigate how global warming can be slowed and reduced by energy efficiency, reduced consumption, reduced dependency on fossil fuels and increasing use of renewable energy sources?
- Do children learn about the arguments for and against nuclear energy as a way of reducing dependence on fossil fuels?
- Do children consider the arguments for and against the use of land for biofuels?
- Do children consider the arguments for and against companies and governments offsetting their emission of greenhouse gasses by planting trees or buying credits to pollute from low consumers of energy?
- Do children learn about international agreements to combat climate change and what their supporters and critics say about them?
- Do children investigate the way people have adapted to changing climates?
- Do children learn about attempts to adapt to a life of reduced consumption, local organic food growing, and reduced use of fossil fuels in such movements as Transitions?

The planet and ethics (See A2.3 The school encourages respect for the integrity of planet earth.)

- Do children explore how the conservation of resources is an imperative for human and animal welfare?
- Do children consider how reduced ice cover in the Arctic and Antarctic may encourage some to further exploit the earth's resources?
- Do children learn how human action can reduce the environmental deterioration of the planet?
- Do children explore how environmental degradation and global warming affect some people more than others, according to poverty, gender and power?
- Do children consider the way poverty and wealth can both lead to the lack of the conservation of finite resources?

Linking past, present and future

- Do children learn how climates have changed in the past and may change in the future?
- Do children learn how time became regulated around the world?
- Do children learn about the way environments have deteriorated and been improved locally and globally?
- Do children consider possible future pressures on the environment from growth in populations and their consumption?

C1.8 Children study life on earth.

A2.3 The school encourages respect for the integrity of planet earth; B1.12 The school reduces its carbon footprint and use of water; B1.13 The school contributes to the reduction of waste; C1.2 Children investigate the importance of water;
C1.5 Children consider how and why people move around their locality and the world;
C1.7 Children investigate the earth, the solar system and the universe;
C1.9 Children investigate sources of energy.

Linking locally and globally

- Are children encouraged to record, through writing, drawing, video, audio and photography, the variety of animal and plant life within the buildings, grounds and surroundings of the school?
- Do children engage in projects to restore streams, rivers, endangered plants and wildlife?
- Is the school linked to national and international organisations which can provide opportunities for exploring plant and animal diversity?
- Does the school draw on the support of local gardening societies, beekeepers, plant nurseries, animal welfare organisations, conservationists, environmental campaigners?
- Are lessons responsive to changes in seasons, the growth of trees and other plants, and the migration of birds and other animals?
- Do children consider the effects of their pet cats on birds and small mammals?
- Does the school have a pond for studying pond creatures and water plants?
- Are plants grown in the school grounds that are attractive to butterflies and other insects?
- Does the school contribute to the development of local bird populations, through feeding, nesting boxes and campaigning for the preservation of habitats?
- Does the school encourage the provision of habitats for creatures vulnerable to environmental decline, such as bees and frogs?
- Are plants grown in the school grounds which are adapted to local climate conditions?
- Do children learn about the way animals and plants are adapted to the conditions in different parts of the world?
- Do children contribute a daily species to a class or school corner of world species, indicating where it is found and in what numbers?

Ecological principles

- Are ecological principles considered as a way to link the running of a school to the principles that sustain life? [41]
- Is interdependence as well as competition and dominance seen as an underlying principle of living systems and used as a guiding metaphor for the school?
- Are living things seen to exist in mutually interdependent webs or networks? [42]
- Is life seen to be supported in nested systems, each dependent on its relationship to a wider system and ultimately the planet and the universe?
- Are the interactions within eco-systems seen to be controlled by cycles of water and other nutrients?
- Is life seen to depend on flows of energy that start from the energy of the sun?
- Are all environments seen to be in a constant state of development?
- Are healthy eco-systems (biological communities in distinctive physical environments) seen to be self-regulating, in a state of dynamic balance?
- Do children understand that the balance of eco-systems can be so disrupted that they cease to be self-regulating?

41 An example, initiated by a 15 year-old student, is given in Stone, M. (2009) *Smart by Nature: Schooling for sustainability*, pp174-183, Healdsburg, Watershed Media.

42 The six notions in italics here are from Fritjof Capra (2005), Speaking nature's language in Stone M. and Barlow Z. eds. *Ecological Literacy: Educating our children for a sustainable world.* San Francisco, Sierra Club Books.

Attitudes to other living things

- Do children explore their feelings about the natural world of plants, animals and microbes?
- Do children explore the attitudes of themselves and other people to the conservation of animals and plants?
- Do adults and children understand the way they share eco-systems with other living things?
- Do children learn that they are made out of the same few elements as other living things?
- Do children consider whether they need other species more than other species need them?
- Do children consider the beauty and value of animals and plants that they may dislike, such as spiders, slugs, wasps, snakes, nettles and thistles?

Understanding biodiversity

- Do children study the variety of living things including animals, plants, fungi, bacteria and other single celled organisms?
- Do children explore the idea that the vast majority of living organisms are single celled microorganisms?
- Do children learn that the vast majority of animals are insects?
- Is biodiversity seen to involve eco-systems, the variety of species and genetic variation within a species?
- Do children learn about the variety of eco-systems on land, in water and in the margins between them?
- Do children understand the importance of chemicals, rocks, soil, shelter, food, oxygen and water within eco-systems?
- Do children learn how plants, animals, micro-organisms and their environment interact to form self-maintaining eco-systems?
- Are children aware how they depend for their welfare on the health of other species, such as bees for pollination and bacteria for digestion, fixing nitrogen and composting?
- Do children explore the way that species diversity varies with climate, altitude, predators, and the success with which particular species colonise an ecosystem?
- Do children explore the extent to which new species are discovered and lost, even before they are discovered?

Understanding evolution

- Do children investigate the way fossil records show biodiversity in different geological periods?
- Do children consider how fossils contribute to an understanding of evolution?
- Do children learn about the nature of species and how they have evolved?
- Do children learn the reasons why species survive, spread or become extinct?

Classifying living things and eco-systems

- Do children explore the different ways in which living things can be grouped, such as by appearance, those that can mate to produce fertile offspring, usefulness for food or medicine and size?
- Do children explore ways of dividing living things hierarchically from domains to species?
- Do children learn how the different eco-systems can be grouped in biomes in relation to climate, latitude, altitude and fresh water and oceans?

Understanding life support systems

- Do children explore food chains and food webs?
- Do children consider how food webs involve the sun, plant producers, animal consumers, scavengers and fungal and bacterial decomposers?
- Do children learn about the nitrogen cycle and how its contribution to ecological balance can be disrupted by overuse of fertilisers?

- Do children learn about the carbon cycle and how its contribution to ecological balance can be disrupted by loss of forest and use of carbon based fuels?
- Do children learn about the water cycle and how the availability of water for living things can be disrupted by pollution and river damming and diversion?

The structure of living things

- Do children learn about the internal structures of plants and animals?
- Do children learn about the variety of different cells in plants and animals?
- Do children learn how all the different cells in animals are formed from common cells in the embryo?
- Do children learn about genes and chromosomes?
- Do children learn about the unique genomes of each species?
- Do children investigate the common ancestry revealed in genomes of different plants and animals?
- Do children learn how genes can be naturally and artificially modified?
- Do children learn how living things are constructed from molecules?
- Do children learn how the molecules from which living things are constructed, draw on a small number of the total number of chemical elements (59% Hydrogen, 24% Oxygen, 11% Carbon, 4% Nitrogen, 2% others)?
- Do children learn how the interactions of molecules of living things are explored in biochemistry?
- Do children investigate the composition of skeletons, shells and corals?

Threats to biodiversity

- Do children learn about the accelerating rate of loss of species of animals and plants, globally?
- Do children consider causes of mass extinctions of species in the past and the threat from humans in the present 'Holocene extinction'?

Human population growth and consumption

- Do children consider the effects of an increase in human population (from 2.5 billion in 1950 to 7 billion estimated for 2012) on habitats of plants and animals?
- Do children consider how slowly human populations respond to reductions in human fertility rates?
- Do children explore the way population growth reduces with reductions in poverty?
- Do children explore how the effects of human population growth depend on the quantity of finite resources that are consumed?

Hunting

- Do children explore the threat to species from legal and illegal hunting and fishing?
- Do children explore the international trade in endangered species?

Loss of habitat

- Do children document the reducing extent of forests in their own and other countries and the implication for maintaining species of animals and plants?
- Do children consider the implications of having half of all species diversity within tropical rain forests?
- Do children consider habitat loss from increased urbanisation and road networks?
- Do children consider habitat fragmentation from roads and agriculture?
- Do children consider losses of habitats from drainage of wetlands?

Pollution and disease

- Do children learn about the particular pressures on fresh water habitats from pollution?
- Do children consider the effects on biodiversity of use of herbicides and insecticides?
- Do children investigate the increasing amounts of industrial waste and untreated sewage in rivers and seas?
- Do children consider the threat to biodiversity from plant and animal disease?

Introducing and losing species

- Do children consider the potential negative effects on local plants of introducing plants from other eco-systems better able to compete for nutrients, water and light?
- Do children consider the effects of introducing animals better able to compete for food and water from another eco-system?
- Do children learn about the way the loss of a plant or animal from an eco-system affects the survival of other plants and animals?

Farming and fishing methods

- Do children consider the threat to species by over-exploitation of land and seas?
- Do children explore the great reduction in strains of crops being used as a result of industrial farming methods in their own and other countries compared to the wide variety of crops in countries using less mechanised methods?
- Do children learn how fishing methods and intensity affect marine species?
- Do children learn how the reduction of genetic diversity (through selective breeding) can make plants more vulnerable to disease?
- Do children consider the threats to genetic diversity from the introduction of genetically modified crops?

Climate change (See C1.7 Children investigate the earth, the solar system and the universe.)

- Do children explore the effects on biodiversity of human produced climate change?

Improving biodiversity

- Do children investigate the conservation efforts for animals and plants in their country and around the world?
- Does the school draw up a plan for increasing biodiversity within its surroundings?
- Do adults and children learn about ways of encouraging wildlife in the countryside alongside the cultivation of land for the growing of food?
- Do children investigate the way fishing and animal stocks can be restored by restrictions on fishing and hunting?
- Do children examine the extent to which zoos can contribute to the conservation of species?
- Do children explore the extent to which the loss of habitats for animals and plants are reversed?
- Do children consider how farming methods can be changed so as to reverse reduction of biodiversity?
- Do children learn about the reintroduction of native species into habitats that they previously occupied?
- Do adults and children learn how degraded land can be recovered, such as in the Loess plateau in China?

Biodiversity and ethics

- Do children consider how poverty can lead to the neglect of the environment?
- Are children encouraged to appreciate beauty in the diversity of living things living in their natural habitats?
- Do children consider the arguments for and against the maintenance of a diversity of plants and animals?
- Are children aware of the medicinal properties of plants and the small number of plants that have been investigated for these properties?
- Do children explore the way variation in species of plants can provide new strains for food when crops have become vulnerable to insects or disease?
- Do adults and children consider the effects on conserving biodiversity of the international Convention on Biological Diversity and the National Biodiversity Strategies and Action Plans (NBSAP) that flow from it?
- Do adults and children consider the extent to which international targets to reduce species loss by 2010 were missed?
- Do adults and children consider the way international corporations regulate themselves, and can be regulated, to reverse pollution, over-exploitation and the reduction of habitats?
- Does the school consider the value of linking itself to the UN decade of biodiversity 2011-2020?

Linking past, present and future

- Do children consider the way the landscape has changed in their area through, for example, the presence of shrubs and trees, cultivation, road construction, building and the effect on animals and plants?
- Do children explore the different ways in which living things have been grouped historically in their country and by different peoples around the world?
- Do children consider the way animals and plants have changed in their country and in other countries?
- Do children consider the future if present rates of species loss are maintained?
- Do children consider the future if species loss is slowed and stopped and how this might be achieved?

C1.9 Children investigate sources of energy.

B1.12 The school reduces its carbon footprint and use of water;
C1.7 Children investigate the earth, the solar system and the universe;
C1.8 Children study life on earth.

Linking locally and globally

(See B1.12 for activities linking fuel use to the school and local area)

- Do children investigate the variety of ways electricity is produced in their locality?
- Do children trace the supply of electricity from production to their schools and homes?
- Do children trace the supply of gas, oil, petrol and diesel from extraction to use at home and school?
- Do local suppliers of fuel and users of solar panels, wind turbines, and thermal heat pumps contribute to the curriculum?
- Do children learn how fuels are used in different parts of the world?
- Do children learn how much fuel is consumed by different groups of people in their own and other countries?

Understanding energy

- Do staff discuss 'energy' in a way that helps children to understand their changing world whilst avoiding conflict with its use in physics?
- Is energy understood as a capacity to make something move; to do work?
- Are people and animals understood as sources of energy that can work machines and carry loads?
- Do children consider where the energy in their bodies comes from?
- Do children learn how sources of energy are needed for cooking, heating, cooling, lighting, home and industrial machines and transport?
- Do children consider the extent to which the sun is the source of energy on the earth?
- Do children learn how the energy from the sun contributes to the creation of carbon based fuels and other energy sources such as winds and waves?
- Do children understand the way plants convert energy from the sun into food and fuel?
- Do children consider the origin of energy that comes from the earth's core, from tides and nuclear fission?
- Do children consider how the sun's energy originated following the formation of the Universe involving gravitational collapse of matter and nuclear fusion?
- Do children reflect on whether the sum total of energy and matter in a universe in which energy is conserved is zero if the universe started from zero matter and energy?
- Do children explore how energy from the earth's interior has resulted in continental drift, mountain ranges, erupting volcanoes and earthquakes?
- Do children understand that energy has different forms (magnetic, kinetic, heat/thermal, light/radiant, sound, chemical, electrical, gravitational, elastic, nuclear)?

Renewable and non-renewable energy sources

- Do children learn about renewable energy from the sun, wind, rivers, plants or biomass, waves, heat pumps and geothermal sources?
- Do children consider how hydrogen can be produced as a renewable fuel that can be made by using other energy sources, both renewable and non-renewable?
- Do children learn how wood is used as a renewable and non-renewable source of fuel in different parts of the world?

- Do children explore how wind has been used as a direct source of energy in windmills?
- Do children learn how coal, oil, gas and uranium are non-renewable sources?
- Do children investigate how non-renewable sources of energy are extracted from the earth and seas?
- Do children learn how oil is refined for use in petrol, diesel and jet engines?

Producing electricity

- Do children learn how electricity is produced by converting renewable and non-renewable sources of energy?
- Do children learn how electricity can be produced using renewable sources in hydro-electric power from rivers, waves and tides, wind turbines, geothermal sources, heat pumps using temperature differences and solar power?
- Do children learn how electricity can be produced from non-renewable sources of energy in coal, gas-fired and nuclear power stations?
- Do children learn about the use of steam in electricity generation?
- Do children learn about turbo-alternators and the role of magnetism within them?
- Do children learn how responsive electricity generation is to the reduction of electricity use in homes and schools?

Energy supply and storage

- Do children learn how fuels are transported?
- Do children learn how fuels are stored?
- Do children learn how gases can be stored as liquids?
- Do children learn how electricity is delivered to homes and buildings in the national grid?
- Do children learn how locally produced electricity can contribute to the national grid?
- Do children learn how electricity can be stored in batteries?

Fuel business

- Do children learn who earns money from extracting and distributing fuels, generating and distributing electricity?
- Do children consider the relevant costs of producing electricity using renewable and nonrenewable sources?
- Do children explore how financial conditions can be changed to favour energy production from renewable or non-renewable sources?
- Do children consider the extent to which it is in the interests of producers of energy to encourage consumption rather than conservation?

Reducing use of carbon-based fuels

- Do children consider the amount of electricity generated by non-renewable fossil-based fuels (90%), the implications for greenhouse gas emissions and how this can be reduced?
- Do children consider how demand for electricity can be reduced by using it more efficiently?
- Do children consider how the use of carbon-based fuels can be reduced by cutting down the consumption of goods which depend on them?
- Do children consider how they can challenge the pressures to consume from governments, advertising, shops and corporations?
- Do children consider how wanting to consume becomes part of our identities so that consuming makes us feel good?
- Do children explore the extent to which we need to change ourselves if we want to consume less?

Fuel ethics

- Do children learn about the human and environmental hazards in extracting oil, gas, coal and fissionable uranium from the earth and seas?
- Do children investigate the extent to which the citizens of a fuel producing country benefit from the extraction of oil or other fuels from their land?
- Do children learn about changing availability of wood for fuel and the environmental consequences of using it?
- Do children consider the arguments for and against the national ownership of fuel extraction and electricity production?
- Do children learn the risks to the environment posed by extracting less accessible sources of oil under the sea or below ice caps?
- Do children consider how countries go to war to secure their supplies of oil and gas?
- Do children learn the consequences of the large scale production of biomass (fuel oil from plants) for the destruction of animal and plant habitats and the reduced availability of land for growing food?
- Do children learn the effects of biomass fuel production on the price of food?
- Do children compare the human costs and dangers of different forms of energy production?
- Do children consider the consequences for the way societies are organised if people have to ensure the safety of the nuclear waste over hundreds of years?
- Do children learn about the interconnection between nuclear fuels and weapons industries?
- Do children learn how energy suppliers differ in their commitment to using renewable sources and how this might affect the choices made by families and schools?

Linking past, present and future

- Do children learn about peak oil and how people will adapt as availability of oil declines?
- Do children investigate how the availability of oil affected the development of petrol, diesel and jet engines?
- Do children learn how people lit and heated their homes and cooked at various times in the past?
- Do children explore the changing use for fuel of wood, peat, coal, gas and oil?
- Do children learn how and why fuel consumption in different parts of the world is changing?
- Do children consider how people will heat their homes, travel and make things in the future?

C1.10 Children learn about communication and communication technology.

A1.8 The school encourages an understanding of the interconnections between people around the world; C1.11 Children engage with, and create, literature, arts and music.

Linking locally and globally

- Do local newspaper journalists and owners, website designers, hardware and software producers, non-fiction writers and phone businesses contribute to the curriculum?
- Do children explore who in the world speaks the languages spoken by children in school?
- Do children communicate with others locally and at a distance on paper, by online communication including email and by telephone?
- Do children learn the extent to which people communicate in similar and different ways around the world, for example through speaking and writing and the use of technology?
- Is the school linked to other schools locally and nationally and in another country?

Means of communication

- Do children investigate communication through speech, writing, newspapers and books, radio, television, internet, assistive technology, mobile phones, landlines, emails and social networking?
- Do children investigate the role of the media in influencing attitudes, beliefs and knowledge?
- Do children consider how they and others are influenced by advertising?
- Do children learn about the development of the internet and how it is used?
- Do children learn the extent to which computers are used in practice to gain knowledge, social networking and for playing games?

Languages and dialects

- Do children learn about the languages spoken and signed in the world, their geographical spread and interconnection?
- Do children explore reasons for learning additional languages such as for work, pleasure in communication with those from another country and to aid tourism and exploration?
- Are all children and adults in the school encouraged to learn additional spoken or signed languages?
- Are children helped to become fluent speakers, readers and writers or fluent signers of their first language?
- Do children learn how linguistic diversity in the world is being reduced?
- Do children investigate how and why English has become the dominant world language?
- Do children explore the effects of English becoming a world language on the education of children in other countries?
- Do children investigate the effect of the internet on the way people communicate around the world?

Overcoming barriers to communication

- Do children understand how communication can be obscured through the use of codes, and through the use of jargon understood within particular groups?
- Do children consider how dialogue depends on equalising power between speakers and listeners?
- Are children taught to listen, read, write and reflect carefully as aids to communication?
- Are children taught to develop precision in spoken and written communication?

- Do children explore what can impede and help communication across commuities and cultures, within and between countries?
- Do children explore what can impede and help communication between generations?
- Do children learn the differing roles that gesture and facial expression play in communication?

Communication and communication technology business

- Do children explore phone, television, newspapers, radio, advertising, computer hardware, software, website and computer game businesses and industries?
- Do children explore the way computer software has changed the interaction between businesses, such as banks, and their customers?
- Do children explore the way business software has changed universities and schools?
- Do children explore how people make money from selling on the internet?
- Do children consider how those who create search engines and social networks make money?
- Do children explore the work of teachers, translators and interpreters?

Communication and communication technology and ethics

- Do children learn about differences between homes in access to communication technology?
- Do children learn how sourcing the minerals for mobile phones may fuel conflicts in economically poor countries?
- Do children explore the benefits and hazards of the internet?
- Do children consider how dialects, accents and choice of vocabulary are valued and devalued in England and may be associated with a perceived class position?

Linking past, present and future

- Do children learn about the past from oral and written histories?
- Do children learn how the nature of the past is communicated through a geological and fossil record, by buildings and other artefacts, symbols and documents?
- Do children learn how forms of communication have changed and are changing, for example with disappearing languages, the increasing status and spread of English and phone and computer use?
- Do children consider how other languages may become more dominant than English as the economic power of countries changes?
- Do children investigate the development of means of communication including horseback, fire and smoke, telegraph, telephone, mobile phone, and multimedia phone?
- Do children learn about the development of radio and television as means of distant communication?
- Do children learn how changes in communication media have altered the way people spend their time?

C1.11 Children engage with and create literature, arts and music

Linking locally and globally

- Does the school encourage local artists, photographers, composers, musicians, and other performers, poets and writers to exhibit and perform in the school and share their skills?
- Does the school have a festival where children and adults from the school and surrounding communities can perform?
- Are children and their families encouraged to visit local art and craft studios?
- Do children consider differences from each other in what they like to watch, read, and listen to?
- Do children investigate how their favourite books, television programmes, films are produced?
- Do children consider the differences in the art, music, plays and poetry that are produced in different parts of the world?
- Do children consider how art, music, drama from one country is taken up in another?
- Do children understand that all countries have contemporary writers, artists, dancers, musicians, and that looking only at traditional forms in countries of the Global South can lead to stereotyping?
- Do children learn that all art forms involve a fusion of influences?

Developing interests

- Is everyone seen as a creative writer, storyteller, poet, film maker, photographer, singer, dancer, musician, actor, painter, sculptor, ceramicist, quilt maker?
- Are students encouraged to develop interests in the creative arts that prompt activities outside school?
- Are there a variety of opportunities to hear singing, music, stories, poetry and see photographs, films, drama, dance and visual arts?
- Are children encouraged to discover and pursue the art, dance, drama, music that they most appreciate?

Music

- Are children encouraged to engage with a range of forms of music?
- Are all children given opportunities to learn and play a variety of bought and/or homemade stringed, brass, woodwind and percussion instruments?
- Do children learn about composition and how to convey feeling and meaning?
- Are there opportunities to join in a variety of choirs?
- Does the school develop its repertoire of songs, that everyone knows?
- Is the repertoire of songs linked to those known and liked by children?
- Are there opportunities for singing songs of a variety of styles?
- Is the repertoire of songs linked to the ones children bring with them from previous schools?
- Does the school learn from singing styles in other countries, for example in the use of harmony?
- Are steps taken to overcome the feelings of children if they think that singing is not 'cool' or they are too shy to sing in front of anyone?
- Do lessons exploit the contribution that singing and knowledge of lyrics can make to literacy?
- Do children learn to write lyrics?
- Do children learn how to write and perform their own and each other's songs, for example about personal, national, local or school events?

Dance

- Do children learn a variety of dance styles?
- Are children encouraged to find their own preferred dancing style?
- Are dancers and dancing schools encouraged to share their skills in the school?

Story-telling

- Are children encouraged to develop powers of story-telling?
- Do children use their knowledge of story-telling in their homes and communities?
- Do children's developing powers of story-telling contribute to their story-writing?

Literature

- Do adults at the school share their varied appreciation for poetry, fiction and plays?
- Do children learn to appreciate a range of writing styles and develop their own style?

Poetry

- Are children encouraged to express themselves in poetry in a style with which they feel comfortable?
- Are children introduced to a range of styles of poetry writing?
- Are children encouraged to write, share and perform their poetry as a way of responding to feelings and events?

Drama

- Is a range of drama skills integrated into the curriculum, for example in puppetry and role play?
- Do children learn to invent, write and perform their own plays?
- Is drama used to encourage children to develop confident, strong voices?
- Does everyone learn that the magic of the theatre – the suspension of disbelief – can be produced in the simplest of surroundings?
- Do children learn the dramatic potential of adding lighting, music and other media to drama productions?

Film and television

- Are children exposed to a range of films made in English and other languages?
- Do children compare books and films of books?
- Do children use films and TV programmes as a springboard for their own stories?
- Do children learn to make their own films, producing a script, filming, editing and adding music?

Photography

- Do children learn to compose photographs?
- Do children discuss what they like and dislike about photographs?
- Do children use photographs to illustrate stories, for example about their locality, and to produce fictional photostories?

Art business

- Do children investigate who makes a living from making and performing art?
- Do children learn who makes money from staging and buying and selling art?

Arts and ethics

- Do children consider how some art forms are inaccessible to many people because of their cost?
- Do children consider the limits to the portrayal of scenes of violence and denigrating relationships?
- Do children consider the possibility that the portrayal of exploitative relationships involves exploitative relationships?
- Do children consider the value of distinction between arts and crafts?
- Do children consider the extent to which the character and actions of an author and artist affects the value of their art?
- Do children consider the relationship between the value of art and its cost?

Linking past, present and future

- Do children consider how the use of books and literacy have developed?
- Do children consider the way printing has developed?
- Do children consider the changing nature of popular music?
- Do children consider how classical music has changed?
- Do children consider the effect of the internet and electronic equipment on the way people engage with literature and music and how this will change in the future?
- Do children investigate the development of a variety of art forms?
- Do children consider how art forms have developed differently in different places?

C1.12 Children learn about work and link it to the development of their interests

B1.9 Children are well prepared for moving on to other settings.

Linking locally and globally

- Do children learn about the work that people do in their locality, in their country and around the world, related to food, clothing, building, transport, energy, finance, legal and illegal drugs, health, education and child-care, the physical and natural environment, travel, leisure, the arts, government?
- Do children explore how the jobs in one part of the world are dependent on those in another?
- Do children explore how jobs can be moved from one country to another?
- Do local people, of a mix of genders, with a variety of occupations contribute to learning activities in school?
- Do children keep a record of the different activities in which they engage in a week or month?

The nature of work and activity

- Do children learn about the skills required in different occupations and how they are acquired?
- Do children learn that many people do a number of different jobs over the course of their lives?
- Do children learn how they might move on from a job or occupation that they dislike?
- Do children learn about the differences between public and private sector work?
- Do children learn that important work, in homes and in caring for others, is often unwaged?
- Do children learn about the variety of voluntary work in which people engage?
- Do children learn how work becomes a source of identity for many people?
- Do children explore the meaning of retirement for people who work hard caring for others but are not paid for it?
- Do children engage with the meaning of retirement for those who have a range of activities to take up time freed by ending full-time paid work?

The meaning of unemployment

- Do children learn to distinguish between unemployment, inactivity and not being in paid employment?
- Do children understand why some people are unemployed and how this changes with changes in the strength of the national economy?

Developing interests and activities

- Do people learn how some people's work is based on their particular interests while others follow their interests outside of their paid work?
- Are children helped to develop a set of activities related to their interests that they do outside school and might continue when they are no longer in formal education?

Work, wages and finance

- Do children learn about budgeting income and expenditure?
- Do children learn how and why money is deducted from wages for tax and pensions?

- Do children consider the advantages and disadvantages of having a debit card or credit card?
- Do children learn how profits and losses are made through buying and selling commodities and goods?
- Do children explore the relationship between the amount of work that goes into a product and its price?
- Do children explore ideas of productivity?
- Do children learn about the work of banks and how they make money from more or less risky investments?
- Do children learn about public companies, bonds, stocks, shares, shareholders and dividends?
- Do children explore gambling industries including the national lottery and who gains and loses money from them?

Work, ethics and politics

- Do children explore a variety of perspectives on work, wages and profit?
- Do children learn how exchanges of work or services, as well as paid work, take place outside of an official economy?
- Do children learn about the wages that are attached to various jobs?
- Do children consider how the value of work relates to the wages that are received for it?
- Do children explore the meaning of a living wage, what it means to live in poverty, wealth or to have a 'good' standard of living?
- Do children consider the purpose and desirable level of a minimum wage?
- Do children consider the possibility that there is a level after which a salary ceases to be legitimate income and becomes theft?
- Do children learn about equality, inequality, bullying and discrimination at work?
- Do children consider differences in pay between men and women and between ethnic groups and whether and how this should be reduced?
- Do children learn about rights in the work-place?
- Do children learn about exploitation and how it is prevented?
- Do children learn how inequalities in the workplace can be challenged?
- Do children examine why some people think of the money for the work they do as a wage and others a salary?

Linking past, present and future

- Do children consider how occupations have changed over the last fifty years and over longer timescales, in their country and other countries?
- Do children learn about the way inequalities of income have changed?
- Do children learn about past campaigns to improve work conditions including pay for holidays, sick pay, maternity and paternity allowances and equal pay for women and what these campaigns achieved?
- Do children explore occupations within their own families and interview older members of their families about their past work?
- Do children consider how working lives have changed in relation to life-expectancy and starting and retirement ages?
- Do children consider how work patterns might change in the future?

C1.13 Children learn about ethics, power and government.

A1.7 The school is a model of democratic citizenship; A2.1 The school develops shared inclusive values; A2.2 The school encourages respect for all human rights; C1.12 Children learn about work and link it to the development of their interests.

Linking locally and globally

- Do local philosophers, politicians, bankers, union officials, humanists, religious leaders contribute to the curriculum?
- Do children explore the way forms of government in other parts of the world are similar and different from the form of government in their own country?
- Do children explore the similarities and differences between the way legal systems operate in their own country and in other countries?
- Do children explore the meaning of corruption and the extent to which it affects the government and other institutions in their own and other countries?
- Do children consider the form of government that best describes their school, families and other institutions that they know?

Who has power?

- Do children consider who has power to make things happen that affect their lives in families, schools and neighbourhoods, locally, nationally and globally?
- Do children explore the ways in which power and influence may be distributed between national and local governments, legal systems, the military, corporations, shareholders, businesses, financial institutions, the media, unions, classes, communities, families and citizens?
- Do children learn the extent to which corporations may have greater influence over the lives of citizens than some governments?
- Do children consider the relative power of different countries?

Nations and borders

- Do children consider how nations come into being and how borders are decided?
- Do children consider how borders are disputed?
- Do children learn how countries have been and are colonised and occupied?
- Do children learn how people have been (and continue to be) treated as commodities and bought and sold as slaves?
- Do children consider movements for secession and independence?
- Do children investigate the nature of alliances between governments and how and why other countries are seen as allies or enemies?
- Do children explore the meaning of sovereignty or state independence, and how it is affected by international and European law, the European parliament, the movement of money, debt, newspaper ownership, food, fuel and energy security and the ownership of land and utilities?

Democracy and other forms of government

- Do children consider how people are governed in monarchies, theocracies, dictatorships and democracies?
- Do children explore what local and national governments do?
- Do children explore the meanings of democracy?
- Is democracy understood as always in development?
- Do children learn about the variety of voting systems?

- Do children learn what local councillors, Members of Parliament and Members of the European Parliament do?
- Do children learn why people vote and do not vote in local, national elections and European elections?
- Do children learn how democratic rights can be exercised and thwarted?
- Do children learn about the relationship between the Church of England, other religions and the state?
- Do children consider how prioritising one religion may imply that other religions and non-religious beliefs are of lesser value?
- Do children learn about political parties and who joins them?
- Do children learn about the ownership of the media and the interests of owners in directing politics in particular ways?
- Do children investigate the merits of the private and public ownership of a variety of services, such as clothing manufacture, transport, haulage, banking, education, water supply, telephones, gas and electricity?
- Do children learn about the importance to national cohesiveness and collective action of the development and loss of public space?
- Do children explore the relationship between wealth, poverty and participation in society?

Legal systems

- Do children learn how their lives are affected by national laws?
- Do children learn about the workings of the courts?
- Do children learn about the extent to which breaking of the law is punished?
- Do children learn about the different forms of punishment handed out by courts, their purposes and effects?
- Do children learn how fairly the law is applied?
- Do children learn how they are affected by international laws?
- Do children learn about the power of international courts and who they bring and don't bring to justice?

Public and private finance

- Do children find out how governments get income?
- Do children consider how governments decide how much money to print?
- Do children learn about income and wealth distribution nationally and globally?
- Do children learn what governments spend money on and how this is decided?
- Do children investigate who governments borrow money from when they are in debt?
- Do children learn about the International Monetary Fund and how it is financed?
- Do children consider how government finances are affected by the international financial situation?
- Do children consider transactions with other countries (Balance of Payments) and the implications of importing more than is exported or earned in other countries?
- Do children find out how bank interest rates are decided?
- Do children investigate how people and countries acquire a credit rating?
- Do children learn about the causes and consequences of inflation, its desirable level and how it is measured and controlled?
- Do children explore the different ways of measuring inflation and deflation and how do decide on an ideal level of inflation?
- Do children learn how currencies are valued against other currencies?
- Do children examine loans and grants their government gives in aid to other countries?

Personal and political ethics

- Do children consider whether the same or different values should govern action in personal and work life, including politics?
- Do children consider what countries do and what they do not do if they have an ethical foreign policy?
- Do children explore the values they wish to underlie their own actions and those of others?
- Do children develop their capacity to relate values to actions?
- Do children develop a capacity to make judgements when values provide conflicting impulses for action?
- Do children learn to engage in moral argument?
- Do children explore the different values that inform the actions of different people?
- Do children consider the nature of punishment and what punishments they think are appropriate within schools, families and prisons?
- Do children investigate how their desires, choices and ethics are influenced by government, religion, family, friends, media, and advertising?

Linking past, present and future

- Do children learn about the histories of democracy in the UK and internationally?
- Do children learn about the struggles of people to achieve their democratic rights?
- Do children learn about what has been achieved through collective action?
- Do children learn about the roles of political parties, unions and collective action in developing democracy?
- Do children explore the nature of the monarchy in the UK, how this came about and whether it represents a stage on the route to a more mature democracy?
- Do children explore what would make their country, communities, schools and families more democratic?
- Do children consider how power might be distributed in their country in the future?

C2.1 Learning activities are planned with all children in mind.

C2.2 Learning activities encourage the participation of all children.

a) Are activities planned to support learning rather than to deliver a curriculum?
b) Do curriculum materials reflect the backgrounds, experiences and interests of all learners?
c) Do learning activities reflect the variety of interests of children?
d) Is there a range of activities involving oral presentation and discussion, listening, reading, writing, drawing, problem solving, drama, use of library, audio/visual materials, practical tasks, ICT?
e) Do learning activities provide opportunities for paired and group activities as well as individual and whole-class work?
f) Do activities involve experiences outside the classroom, in the grounds and surroundings of the school and in visits further afield?
g) Do activities extend the learning of all children?
h) Do activities develop the capacity of children to think, talk, write and learn?
i) Do activities encourage a view of learning as continuous rather than completed with particular tasks?
j) Are learning arrangements flexible so that, for example, it is possible for children to have an intensive foreign language course or literacy course?
k) Are interpreters available for deaf children or others for whom English is an additional language?
l) Does planning identify and minimise barriers to learning and participation for particular children?
m) Do staff encourage activities which appeal to the variety of ways in which children view their gender?
n) Do staff draw on opportunities provided by topics given media attention which may motivate particular groups of children, such as men's or women's football and rugby, and provide equally considered alternatives for those uninterested in a particular topic?
o) Can children participate in lessons such as science and physical education in clothes appropriate to their religious beliefs?
p) Is the curriculum adapted for children who do not participate in, for example, art or music, because of their religious beliefs?
q) Are lessons adapted, if necessary, for children with physical or sensory impairments to develop their skills and knowledge in physical education, understanding of light and sound or practical work?
r) Do staff recognise the additional time required by some children with impairments to use equipment in practical work?
s) Is particular attention given to involving children in learning who are unsettled, disengaged or disaffected?

t) ______________________________

u) ______________________________

v) ______________________________

C2.2 Learning activities encourage the participation of all children.

C2.1 Learning activities are planned with all children in mind.

a) Do learning activities involve shared experiences that can be developed by children in a variety of ways?
b) Do teachers avoid specifying expectations for learning as lesson objectives?
c) Do lessons regularly take the form of enquiries guided by open-ended questions?
d) Do teachers limit asking questions to which they expect a single right answer?
e) Do lessons build on the experience, knowledge and skills children have acquired outside school?
f) Do lessons involve children emotionally?
g) Do lessons convey a sense of excitement and pleasure in learning?
h) Do teachers demonstrate their own love of learning?
i) Is the spoken and written language used in lessons made accessible to all children?
j) Is technical vocabulary only used where necessary and explained and practised during lessons?
k) Are children encouraged to say when they do not understand something?
l) Can children record their work in a variety of ways, using drawings, photographs, videorecording and sound recording as well as writing?
m) Do lessons encourage dialogue between staff and children and between children?
n) Do children learn how to question each other in order to support each other's learning?
o) Do lessons encourage children to talk about the processes of thinking and learning?
p) Do children initiate further independent work when they have finished a task suggested by a teacher?
q) Do adults and children improve their Internet skills to assist learning at school and home?
r) Are any worksheets clearly written so that they extend the learning of children?
s) Do children learning English as an additional language have opportunities in lessons to speak, write or sign in their first language and use their skills of translation?
t) Do staff make the adjustments necessary for the participation of children with impairments?
u) Do staff recognise the physical effort expended on tasks by some children with impairments or chronic illness, and the tiredness that can result?
v) Do staff recognise the mental effort involved in lip-reading and using aids to vision?
w) Are technological advances exploited, such as speech recognition programmes, to support children who experience severe difficulties in writing?

x) ______________________________

y) ______________________________

z) ______________________________

C2.3 Children are encouraged to be confident critical thinkers.

C2.4 Children are actively involved in their own learning.

a) Do staff support each other to be confident, critical thinkers?
b) Is it understood that dialogue works best when people set aside differences of power and perceived status?
c) Do staff demonstrate that they respect and value alternative views?
d) Are children and adults encouraged to express their point of view assertively without aggression?
e) Are debates encouraged so that people get to hear, and practise expressing, points of view other than their own?
f) Are children encouraged to develop and express views and feelings about important local, national and international events, such as when their country is at war or there has been a catastrophe in their own or another country?
g) Are children encouraged to ask challenging questions?
h) Do those on different sides of arguments recognise the importance of other views in clarifying opinions and reaching joint solutions to problems?
i) Do children learn to detect contradictions in their own and other people's arguments?
j) Do children and adults learn to weigh up the strength of arguments including their own?
k) Do children learn when the truth of an assertion or argument requires supporting evidence?
l) Do children learn how to use examples to support an argument?
m) Do children learn how carefully chosen examples can show the limits to generalisations?
n) Do children learn to ask 'to what extent..?' and 'under what circumstances...?' questions when people assert that something is true about the world (for example about differences between genders)?
o) Do children learn how to assess the audience to which a piece of writing is intended to appeal?
p) Do children learn how people take for granted that certain arguments are correct, even when they are not, because they seem to carry the voice of authority?
q) Do children and adults identify the beliefs and values that underlie differences of view?
r) Are children and adults helped to increase their fluency in argument?
s) Do children learn about the pressures on them to think and act in particular ways?
t) Do children explore the reasons for the opinions they express?
u) Are all those taking part in dialogue supported to retain their self-esteem?
v) Do people avoid triumphalism when they feel they have won an argument?
w) Do child and adult mentors help others to contribute their views?
x) Is particular attention paid to helping those who are shy about speaking up, to make a contribution?

y) ______________________________

z) ______________________________

aa ______________________________

C2.4 Children are actively involved in their own learning.

A1.11 Staff link what happens in school to children's lives at home;
C2.3 Children are encouraged to be confident, critical thinkers.

a) Is it evident that adults in the school are active learners with a range of interests?
b) Are children encouraged to believe that they can increase their capacity to learn independently?
c) Is it recognised that as some children increase their capacity to learn and collaborate independently this frees staff to help others to do the same?
d) Are children encouraged to identify what they want to learn and take responsibility for learning it?
e) Are children encouraged to develop interests in learning which they pursue outside school?
f) Do staff increase the occasions when children can make choices about what they learn?
g) Are children helped to write their own titles and headings to structure a piece of work?
h) Are children encouraged to ask challenging questions to which no-one has an immediate answer?
i) Are curriculum plans shared with children so that they can choose to study at a faster pace or in greater depth?
j) Does the support given to children help them to move on in their learning while drawing on the knowledge and skills they already possess?
k) Are children taught how to research and write up a topic?
l) Are children able to use the library and information technology resources independently?
m) Are children taught how to take notes from lectures, books and the Internet?
n) Are children helped to investigate a topic by having clear questions they are trying to answer?
o) Do children learn to help each other with investigations by listening to what one of them is trying to do and then asking questions to clarify that person's thinking?
p) Do children learn to write brief summaries of a piece of work in order to grasp the structure of it?
q) Are mechanical copying activities avoided?
r) Are children taught how to present their work in spoken, written and other forms, individually and in groups?
s) Are children helped to plan and manage revision for tests and examinations?
t) Are children consulted about the support for learning that they need?
u) Do children provide constructive comments on how to improve learning activities?
v) Does the feedback children give about learning activities make a difference?
w) Are children involved in finding ways to overcome their own and each other's barriers to learning?

x) ______________________________

y) ______________________________

z) ______________________________

C2.5 Children learn from each other.

A1.3 Children help each other

a) Do children see helping each other as routine?
b) Is everyone encouraged to listen carefully to others without interruption?
c) Do children learn how to seek clarification from each other to better understand what is being said and to help the speaker to develop their ideas?
d) Do children avoid laughing at the contribution of another unless they are making a joke?
e) Do children disagree with another's ideas without denigrating them?
f) Do children recognise when they are changing a topic of discussion rather than contributing to a previous one?
g) Do lessons regularly contain opportunities for group work?
h) Do children learn how to chair discussions so that everyone contributes?
i) Do children use the same signal to contribute in group work as in class discussion?
j) Do group learning activities draw on the differences in children's knowledge and experience, such as of countries, local geography and family histories?
k) Do group activities allow children to divide up tasks and pool what they have learnt?
l) Do students compile joint reports from the different contributions of a group?
m) Are activities planned so children of different ages and attainments can support each other's learning?
n) Do children learn how to tell and teach others about something they know or have done?
o) Is teaching understood to involve high level skills which benefit a child or adult teacher's own learning?
p) Is it understood that everyone can make a contribution to teaching and learning irrespective of their attainment or impairment?
q) Do children brainstorm ideas and solutions to problems without judging each other's contributions?
r) Do children enjoy learning through group activities?
s) Do children share responsibility with teachers for helping to overcome the barriers to learning experienced by some children?
t) Do children mention the contributions of others in reports of their work?
u) Do children comment critically and constructively on each other's learning?
v) Do children share their skills, for example, in speaking a language, juggling, chess, origami, cricket, at break and lunchtimes and in after school clubs?
w) Is the variety of languages spoken by children used to develop the languages of everyone?
x) Do children share their experience of overcoming problems in learning and relationships?
y) Do children's design and problem solving projects involve imaginative solutions to barriers they and others experience, such as in access to buildings or curricula?

z) ______________________________

aa) ______________________________

ab) ______________________________

C2.6 Lessons develop an understanding of the similarities and differences between people.

A1.8 The school encourages an understanding of the interconnections between people around the world.

a) Do learning activities develop an understanding of differences of background, culture, ethnicity, gender, impairment, sexual orientation, belief, religion and politics?
b) Are there opportunities for children to work with others who differ from themselves in background, ethnicity, impairment and gender?
c) Do materials used in lessons represent human diversity?
d) Do children question stereotyping in curriculum materials and in discussion?
e) Do children recognise the similarities to themselves of those they see as very different?
f) Do children recognise the differences from themselves of those they see as very similar?
g) Do children recognise the differences between people they see as similar to each other?
h) Are children encouraged to see present and past parallels in their own country with actions elsewhere seen to be extremely uncaring, discriminatory or anti-democratic?
i) Do activities regularly make links to events and lives of people in other countries?
j) Do children learn about the origins of differences in geographical spread of religions and political systems?
k) Does the school convey an understanding of differences in poverty, health, life expectancy, welfare and safety for people in different parts of the country and the world?
l) Do children explore the legacy of the negative treatment of, and persistent discrimination towards, people historically, for example through slavery, or the colonisation of indigenous peoples?
m) Do children learn how easily people deny and reject aspects of themselves, such as older people forgetting what it was like to be young?
n) Do children identify with elderly people by understanding that they, too, will grow old?
o) Do children who do not have an impairment identify with those that do, by recognising their own possibilities for acquiring an impairment?
p) Do children investigate how past injustices can contribute to present inequalities?
q) Is the deep identification with place recognised for those whose families have lived in one area for generations?
r) Do adults and children understand the way a belief in a single national culture discriminates against people and limits understanding between people?
s) Do lessons challenge gender generalisations such as that boys are stronger or run faster than girls?
t) Do children have opportunities to communicate with children in both economically richer and poorer parts of the world?

u) ______________________________

v) ______________________________

w) ______________________________

C2.7 Assessments encourage the achievements of all children

C1.4 Children are actively involved in their own learning;
C2.12 Homework is set so that it contributes to every child's learning.

a) Is assessment of children's learning always seen to involve reflection on teaching?
b) Do adults draw on their own experiences of being assessed to improve the way they assess children?
c) Are children helped to reflect on their own written, oral, and other contributions to lessons, so that they know how to make their own improvements?
d) Are children involved in supporting and commenting on the learning of others?
e) Does assessment of children involve identifying barriers that impede learning?
f) Do assessments identify how relationships with adults and children can impede and support learning?
g) Do staff assess how a child's relationships with adults and other children can support or impede their learning?
h) Are comments on children's work encouraging and respectful?
i) Does the assessment of children involve an attempt to understand learning from their viewpoint?
j) Do teachers and teaching assistants attempt to understand the learning of children by careful observation and description?
k) Do adults help each other to understand the implications of their observations for the learning of children?
l) Do assessments of children lead to modifications in learning activities?
m) Is assessment directed at helping children to reflect on their learning?
n) Is assessment used to increase the capacity of children to assess themselves?
o) Do staff avoid allowing assessments to include judgements of ability or potential that lower expectations, or limit the opportunities, of children?
p) Are adjustments made in public examinations, in terms of time, assistive communication devices or interpreters, to make them fairer for children with impairments?
q) Are parents/carers involved in commenting on the learning of children?
r) Are there a variety of ways of assessing learning that engage with differences in children's characters, interests and range of skills?
s) Do staff and children regularly assess work produced in collaboration with others?
t) Do children understand the reasons for teacher initiated and national assessments?
u) Are children informed honestly about the purpose of national assessments to measure school performance?
v) Are children informed about the consequences of being entered for an examination at a particular level and how this is perceived by people, including employers?
w) Are the achievements of different groups of children (boys/girls/ethnic minority children/children with impairments) monitored so that barriers to learning can be uncovered, investigated and addressed?
x) Are records of achievements produced in collaboration with children so that they reflect all their skills, knowledge and experience?
t) ______________________________

C2.8 Discipline is based on mutual respect.

A1.4 Staff and children respect one another;
B2.7 Pressures for disciplinary exclusion are decreased.

a) Is the way children and adults behave towards each other in lessons a reflection of a positive culture of respect in the school?
b) Does the approach to discipline encourage self-discipline?
c) Do children help teachers to create an atmosphere that supports learning?
d) Do staff support each other to be assertive without being angry?
e) Do staff share responsibility for overcoming difficulties with discipline experienced by an individual colleague?
f) Do staff pool their knowledge and skills in overcoming disaffection and disruption?
g) Is discipline seen to depend on good relationships with children?
h) Is a good atmosphere for learning seen to depend on avoiding a sense that children and adults are on opposite sides of a conflict?
i) Do staff avoid conveying a view that children should blindly follow authority?
j) Is the way children are expected to behave in lessons consistent with a values framework developed with the support of staff, parents/carers and children and young people?
k) Do children view learning outside and inside classrooms as involving similar ways of behaving?
l) Do staff and children feel comfortable in admitting a lack of knowledge or that they have made a mistake?
m) Do children contribute their ideas for improvement when children are inattentive in lessons?
n) Do adults and children distinguish between quiet busy chatter and disrupting talk?
o) Do children modify the loudness of their voices when asked, so as to allow everyone to learn?
p) Do children recognise that every child should have their share of the limelight?
q) Do children help to calm others down rather than wind them up when they are troubled or disturbing lessons?
r) If there is more than one adult working with children do they share responsibility for the smooth running of lessons?
s) Are there clear procedures, understood by children and teachers, for responding to extremes of challenging behaviour?
t) Do children feel that they are treated fairly irrespective of gender, class or ethnicity?
u) Is it recognised by staff and children that it is unfair for one gender to take up more of a teacher's attention or more time in class or group discussion than another?

v) ____________________

w) ____________________

x) ____________________

C2.9 Staff plan, teach and review together.

A1.2 Staff co-operate; C2.10 Staff develop shared resources to support learning.

a) Do groups of teachers and teaching assistants plan lessons and homework together?
b) Are teaching activities planned to make full use of all adults present in the classroom?
c) Is planning informed by the knowledge teaching assistants may have of the way a child responds in lessons with different teachers?
d) Do teachers plan activities so that they make use of each other's knowledge and skills?
e) Do teachers use collaborative teaching as an opportunity for learning from each other?
f) Do staff help to improve each other's use of technology such as computers and interactive white boards?
g) Do staff reflect on instructive practice in other schools to review and adjust their own practice?
h) Do staff draw on ideas from colleagues in teacher education and elsewhere in higher education?
i) Do teachers and teaching assistants review their practice in relation to a shared framework of values?
j) Is mutual observation followed by shared reflection used to improve teaching and learning?
k) Do teachers video parts of each other's lessons and review lessons together?
l) Do teachers welcome comments from colleagues on, for example, the accessibility of the language they use and the quality of the participation of children in activities?
m) Do teachers modify their teaching in response to the feedback from their colleagues?
n) Do staff help each other to view learning and support from the perspective of children?
o) Are staff able to join a child or groups of children taught by several teachers in a day to better understand their experience of education?
p) Do staff working in the same class share responsibility for ensuring that all children participate?
q) Do staff engage in joint problem solving with colleagues, within and outside the school, when the progress of a child or group is a cause for concern?
r) Do staff feel confident to challenge each other's thinking about how problems arise?
s) Do staff encourage each other to try out new approaches and activities?
t) Do staff consider their feelings about a child's learning and how these can hinder or help to remove barriers for that child?

u) ______________________________

v) ______________________________

w) ______________________________

C2.10 Staff develop shared resources to support learning.

C2.14 Resources in the locality of the school are known and used.

a) Is there an area in the staffroom where staff place information about favourite resource books and websites?
b) Does the school community develop a website which links the interests of staff, children and parents?
c) Does the school website link the school with other schools locally/nationally and in other countries?
d) Do staff and students share in the creation of a newspaper about events and issues important to them, which is integrated into learning activities?
e) Are classrooms developed as stimulating learning environments that reflect the knowledge and interests of adults and children, which can be used by other classes to stimulate their learning?
f) Do staff share classroom plants, hatching insects, wormeries etc?
g) Is play equipment or material to stimulate imagination for younger children made available to older children and young people?
h) Do staff collaborate over the creation of a school garden, orchard, and allotment?
i) Do adults and children share a dedicated story area, room or shed?
j) Do adults and children collaborate over the collection of the school's museum of artefacts and the stories that go with them?
k) Do staff organise a library so that it supports the learning of all?
l) Is the library organised to support the independent learning of children?
m) Is there an easily accessible collection of DVD/CDs?
n) Are library staff involved in the planning of learning and teaching?
o) Is there a system for recording, organising and sharing TV programmes?
p) Do children have access to digital books and electronic book readers?
q) Are there fiction and non-fiction books which appeal to the diversity of learners?
r) Are books available in the variety of languages spoken and learnt by children?
s) Are appropriately adapted curriculum materials available for children with impairments, for example in large print, audio or Braille?
t) Do primary classrooms have access to a puppet theatre and a range of large and small puppets?

u) ______________________________

v) ______________________________

w) ______________________________

C2.11 Teaching assistants support the learning and participation of all children.

A1.2 Staff co-operate; B1.4 Staff expertise is known and used.

a) Are teaching assistants attached to a classroom or curriculum area rather than particular children?
b) Are teaching assistants concerned to increase the participation of all children?
c) Do teaching assistants demonstrate that they too are learners with a range of interests?
d) Do teaching assistants aim to make children independent from their direct support?
e) Do teaching assistants encourage peer support of children who experience difficulties in learning?
f) Do teaching assistants contribute their particular understanding of the barriers to learning and participation experienced by children and young people in the school?
g) Do teaching assistants contribute any particular knowledge of the locality and communities of the school?
h) Are teaching assistants involved in planning and reviewing learning activities?
i) Do teaching assistants avoid getting in the way of children's relationships with their peers and other staff?
j) Is the space in classrooms organised so that teachers and teaching assistants can work with groups as well as a range of individuals?
k) Are attempts made to recruit male as well as female teaching assistants?
l) Are the views of teaching assistants sought about the nature of the tasks they are expected to carry out?
m) Do teaching assistants negotiate a job description which reflects the range of duties they undertake?
n) Are all teachers familiar with the range of activities which teaching assistants expect to undertake?
o) Are teaching assistants paid for all the time they give to working for the school, including attendance at meetings, preparation of teaching materials and for staff development?
p) Is it recognised that some children with impairments may need a personal assistant, rather than a teaching assistant?
q) Are teaching assistants with impairments welcomed into employment by the school?
r) Do personal assistants have the same concerns as teachers and teaching assistants in supporting a child to participate with other children inside and outside classrooms?
s) Are children with impairments consulted about the support they might need and the characteristics of the person who might provide it?
t) Is it recognised that personal assistants and teaching assistants may need to take on an advocacy role for some children and young people?

u) ______________________________

v) ______________________________

w) ______________________________

C2.12 Homework is set so that it contributes to every child's learning.

C2.7 Assessments encourage the achievements of all children;
C2.1 Learning activities are planned with all children in mind.

a) Do staff consider under what circumstances homework makes a contribution to, or detracts from, learning?
b) Do staff consider whether there is an age below which homework is commonly inappropriate?
c) Do staff have an understanding of the kinds of things children learn at home when they are not doing homework?
d) Is homework only suggested in order to contribute to learning rather than for other reasons such as learning conformity to routines?
e) Do staff work with parents and children to review the school's approach to homework?
f) Do teachers have an accurate idea of the time it takes to complete homework?
g) When homework is set does it help to develop the skills and knowledge of all children?
h) Do staff consider how to encourage children to engage in their own interests rather than set homework?
i) Do teachers support each other on how to set useful homework?
j) Is homework integrated into curriculum planning for the term/year?
k) Do teachers check that all children understand what they need to do for homework?
l) Do children have choices over homework so that they can relate it to the development of their knowledge and interests?
m) Are homework tasks modified if discussion reveals that they are not meaningful or appropriate for some children?
n) Can children extend their learning by setting their own homework questions?
o) Does homework encourage children to take responsibility for their own learning?
p) Do staff know who completes homework with and without assistance from siblings, parents or carers?
q) Do staff know who has books and access to computers at home to assist with homework?
r) Do staff provide alternative help for children who do not have assistance at home?
s) Are there opportunities to do homework and get help with it on the school premises out of school hours?
t) Can children use homework to sustain an area of interest over a period of time?
u) Does homework encourage children to collaborate?
v) Are there opportunities for recording homework in a variety of ways?

w) ______________________________

x) ______________________________

y) ______________________________

C2.13 Activities outside school lessons involve all children.

C2.14 Resources in the locality of the school are known and used.

a) Is there a wide range of activities available before school, at lunchtime and after school?
b) Do games in break times and playtimes reflect the interests of all children?
c) Do children learn a repertoire of playground games so that no-one feels excluded?
d) Are children consulted about the activities that are available at break times and before and after school?
e) Are there opportunities for adults and children to learn together, for example, additional languages, computing, literacy?
f) Is transport available so that children who live far from the school can take part in events before and after school?
g) Are all children encouraged to take part in extra-curricular music, drama and physical exercise?
h) Is an effort made to make activities in which a particular gender predominates attractive to all children?
i) Can boys and girls take part in single-sex groups if there are activities in which one gender predominates, such as computer club, chess club or choir?
j) Are there opportunities for single-sex groups where mixed activities are prohibited on cultural or religious grounds?
k) Are particular groups of children and young people discouraged from monopolising the space in the playground, for example for football?
l) Do sports days include activities in which everyone can take part, irrespective of skill level or impairment?
m) Do children who are chosen to represent their classes or school in sports, drama or other activities reflect the diversity of children in the school?
n) Do overseas visits appeal to the diversity of children within the school?
o) Are school trips, including overseas visits, made accessible to all children in the school irrespective of attainment, impairment or parental income?
p) Are all children given opportunities to take part in activities outside the school?
q) Are all children given opportunities to take part in activities which benefit local communities?

r) ______________________________

s) ______________________________

t) ______________________________

C2.14 Resources in the locality of the school are known and used.

C1.1 – C1.13 and C2.1 – C2.13

a) Do members of local communities contribute to teaching in school?
b) Do parents/carers and other community members support learning in school?
c) Do community organisations help in the support of learning outside of classrooms and the school?
d) Do people working in the neighbourhood mentor children experiencing difficulties?
e) Is it recognised that some adults such as those with impairments, Traveller families, or those speaking a minority language, might play a special role in supporting children who may feel vulnerable?
f) Are resources in some homes, such as special knowledge and skills, computers and reference materials, allotments, made available, at times, to a wider group of children?
g) Is there a regularly updated record, readily accessible to staff, of resources in the locality to support teaching and learning?

Resources might include:

allotments
ambulance service
art galleries
charities and campaigning organisations
childbirth organisations
cinemas
citizens advice bureaux
city and rural farms and farmers
community groups
countryside authorities
dance centres/dance groups
environmental groups
ethnic minority leaders and organisations
national events such as: black history month, LGBT history month, disability history month
garden centres
health visitors
social workers
heritage and ancient building authorities
hobby clubs
homes for the elderly/day centres
lesbian gay bisexual and transgender organisations
libraries
local authorities/children's departments
local events and exhibitions
National Trust
organisations of disabled people
other schools, further and higher education
parents/carers and community members
parish, town, city and county councils
parks and gardens
police service, fire service, hospitals
politicians and political parties
recycling services and centres
religious centres
Royal Mail centres
shops and other businesses
singing groups
sports clubs and sports centres
street entertainers
study centres
swimming pools
telephone/mobile companies
theatre/theatre groups
train stations, bus stations, airports, ports
unions
water, river and canal authorities
yoga and meditation centres
youth groups
etc, etc, etc.

5 Planning Framework and Questionnaires

Planning Framework and Questionnaires

Part 5 of the *Index* contains a planning framework and four questionnaires. The Planning Framework has been included here so that it can be easily photocopied and used to reflect on a development plan in which changes made in each dimension and section of the *Index* become mutually reinforcing (see activity 13 on page 61).The questionnaires can be used to prompt adults and children to work out what needs to be developed next within their school. They can help to involve a wide group of people in reviewing what is going on and how to improve it. But they are best used as part of continuing dialogues which deepen the participation of teaching and non-teaching staff, governors, parents/carers, children and young people and others involved in the school.

Questionnaire 1 might be most commonly used with teaching and non-teaching staff and governors. Parents and children who have an interest in the way the *Index* is structured and how indicators connect with questions might also use it as part of a process of engaging with the *Index* materials. Questionnaire 2 is for parents/carers. Questionnaires 3 and 4 are for children and young people. The language in questionnaire 3 may feel young to older children. It can be explained that it was written to appeal across the age range – or the wording can be changed so that it feels as if it speaks more directly to them. Questionnaire 4 has been adapted for use with the youngest children.

PLANNING FRAMEWORK

Please enter your priorities for development into the sheet, expressed in any way that seems sensible to you. You will need to consider how change within one section might need to be supported by changes elsewhere if it is to be sustained. You might base your suggestions on an indicator, a question or group of questions or other ideas about barriers to learning and participation and what resources need to be mobilised to overcome them. If this sheet is used as part of a workshop you might indicate your relationship to the school by ticking the box for any of the following that apply to you:

☐ teacher ☐ teaching assistant ☐ other member of staff (please specify) ________

☐ governor ☐ parent/carer ☐ child or young person ☐ other (please specify) ________

PLANNING FRAMEWORK	
Creating inclusive cultures	
Building community	**Establishing inclusive values**
Producing inclusive policies	
Developing the school for all	**Co-ordinating support**
Evolving inclusive practices	
Constructing curricula for all	**Orchestrating learning**

QUESTIONNAIRE 1: INDICATORS

Please tick the boxes for the groups below which describe your involvement with the school:

☐ teacher ☐ teaching assistant ☐ other member of staff ☐ parent/carer

☐ child or young person ☐ governor ☐ other (please specify) ____________________

Please tick the box that best reflects your opinion

			Agree	Agree and disagree	Disagree	Need more information
Dimension A – Creating inclusive cultures						
A1: Building community	1	Everyone is welcomed.				
	2	Staff co-operate.				
	3	Children help each other.				
	4	Staff and children respect one another.				
	5	Staff and parents/carers collaborate.				
	6	Staff and governors work well together.				
	7	The school is a model of democratic citizenship.				
	8	The school encourages an understanding of the interconnections between people around the world.				
	9	Adults and children are responsive to a variety of ways of being a gender.				
	10	The school and local communities develop each other.				
	11	Staff link what happens in school to children's lives at home.				
A2: Establishing inclusive values	1	The school develops share inclusive values.				
	2	The school encourages respect for all human beings.				
	3	The school encourages respect for the integrity of planet earth.				
	4	Inclusion is viewed as increasing participation for all.				
	5	Expectations are high for all children.				
	6	Children are valued equally.				
	7	The school counters all forms of discrimination.				
	8	The school promotes non-violent interactions and resolutions to disputes.				
	9	The school encourages children and adults to feel good about themselves.				
	10	The school contributes to the health of children and adults.				
Dimension B – Producing inclusive policies						
B1: Developing the school for all	1	The school has a participatory development process.				
	2	The school has an inclusive approach to leadership.				
	3	Appointments and promotions are fair.				
	4	Staff expertise is known and used.				
	5	All new staff are helped to settle into the school.				
	6	The school seeks to admit all children from its locality.				
	7	All new children are helped to settle into the school.				
	8	Teaching and learning groups are arranged fairly to support all children's learning				
	9	Children are well prepared for moving on to other settings.				
	10	The school makes its buildings physically accessible to all people.				
	11	The buildings and grounds are developed to support participation of all.				
	12	The school reduces its carbon footprint and use of water.				
	13	The school contributes to the reduction of waste.				

Please tick the box that best reflects your opinion

Section	No.	Statement	Agree	Agree and disagree	Disagree	Need more information
B2: Organising support for diversity	1	All forms of support are co-ordinated.				
	2	Professional development activities help staff to respond to diversity.				
	3	English as an additional language support is a resource for the whole school.				
	4	The school supports continuity in the education of children in public care.				
	5	The school ensures that policies about 'special educational needs' support inclusion.				
	6	The behaviour policy is linked to learning and curriculum development.				
	7	Pressures for disciplinary exclusion are decreased.				
	8	Barriers to attendance are reduced.				
	9	Bullying is minimised.				
Dimension C – Evolving inclusive practices						
C1: Constructing curricula for all	1	Children explore cycles of food production and consumption.				
	2	Children investigate the importance of water.				
	3	Children study clothing and decoration of the body.				
	4	Children find out about housing and the built environment.				
	5	Children consider how and why people move around their locality and the world.				
	6	Children learn about health and relationships.				
	7	Children investigate the earth, the solar system and the universe.				
	8	Children study life on earth.				
	9	Children investigate sources of energy.				
	10	Children learn about communication and communication technology.				
	11	Children engage with, and create, literature, arts and music.				
	12	Children learn about work and link it to the development of their interests.				
	13	Children learn about ethics, power and government.				
C2: Orchestrating learning	1	Learning activities are planned with all children in mind.				
	2	Learning activities encourage the participation of all children.				
	3	Children are encouraged to be confident critical thinkers.				
	4	Children are actively involved in their own learning.				
	5	Children learn from each other.				
	6	Lessons develop an understanding of the similarities and differences between people.				
	7	Assessments encourage the achievements of all children.				
	8	Discipline is based on mutual respect.				
	9	Staff plan, teach and review together.				
	10	Staff develop shared resources to support learning.				
	11	Teaching assistants support the learning and participation of all children.				
	12	Homework is set so that it contributes to every child's learning.				
	13	Activities outside formal lessons are made available for all children.				
	14	Resources in the locality of the school are known and used.				

Three things I like best about this school:

1 ______________________

2 ______________________

3 ______________________

Three things I would most like to change:

1 ______________________

2 ______________________

3 ______________________

QUESTIONNAIRE 2: MY CHILD'S SCHOOL

	Please tick the box that best reflects your opinion	*Agree*	*Agree and disagree*	*Disagree*
1	My child usually looks forward to coming to school.			
2	My child has good friends at the school.			
3	I feel part of the school community.			
4	The school keeps me well informed about what is going on.			
5	I have been asked to make a contribution to lessons.			
6	I think this is the best school in the area.			
7	The school and the playground are attractive.			
8	The toilets are clean and safe.			
9	The children get on well together.			
10	The teachers get on well together.			
11	Adults and children get on well together.			
12	The teachers and parents get on well together.			
13	All families are equally important to the teachers at the school.			
14	I have friends among the other parents.			
15	I like the teachers.			
16	The teachers take an interest in what I tell them about my child.			
17	It's good to have children from different backgrounds at the school.			
18	Just by being at the school my child learns how to get on with people.			
19	My child learns what democracy means just by being at this school.			
20	My child learns the importance of caring for the environment.			
21	My child eats healthily after school.			
22	I have been involved in making the school a better place.			
23	Any child who lives near to this school is welcome to come here.			
24	When my child started at this school there was an effort to make me feel involved.			
25	Every child is treated with respect.			
26	Disabled children are accepted and respected at the school.			
27	Boys and girls get on well together.			
28	Being gay or lesbian or transgender is seen as an ordinary part of life.			
29	You are respected irrespective of the colour of your skin.			
30	You are an equal part of the school whatever your religion or if you have no religion.			
31	People do not look down on children because of what they wear.			
32	You are respected for your effort not for the scores you get on tests.			

	Please tick the box that best reflects your opinion	Agree	Agree and disagree	Disagree
33	Children should avoid calling each other hurtful names.			
34	Bullying is not a problem.			
35	If anyone bullied my child I know that I would get help from the school.			
36	If children have been away for a day a teacher wants to know where they have been.			
37	Teachers do not have favourites among the children.			
38	I think the teachers are fair when the praise a student.			
39	I think the teachers are fair when the punish a student.			
40	When children are interrupting lessons other children help to calm them down.			
41	My child learns how to settle disagreements by listening, talking and compromise.			
42	The school sends children home if they have behaved badly.			
43	Lessons make good use of what my child has learnt outside school.			
44	The school has a good system for supporting children when they have a problem.			
45	My child learns a lot at this school.			
46	Children are often trusted to learn on their own.			
47	The school is good about saving energy.			
48	My child learns to care for the environment in the school and the area around it.			
49	The children help each other when they are stuck with their work.			
50	My child knows how to get help with his or her work when it is needed.			
51	The school is a place where people really listen to each other's ideas.			
52	My child always understands what to do next in lesson.			
53	My child usually understands what to do when he or she is given homework.			
54	Homework helps my child to learn.			
55	At lunchtimes my child sometimes joins in clubs or practices a sport.			
56	After school, my child sometimes joins in clubs or practises a sport.			

These are the three things I like best about this school:

1 ______________________________

2 ______________________________

3 ______________________________

These are the three things I would most like to change about this school:

1 ______________________________

2 ______________________________

3 ______________________________

QUESTIONNAIRE 3: MY SCHOOL

Please note that in this questionnaire when we use the word child or children we mean to older children and young people too.

	Please tick the box that best reflects your opinion	*Agree*	*Agree and disagree*	*Disagree*
1	I look forward to coming to school.			
2	I feel part of a big community.			
3	The school and the playground look attractive.			
4	The toilets are clean and safe.			
5	The children get on well together.			
6	The adults get on well together.			
7	Adults and children get on well together.			
8	I have some good friends.			
9	I like my teachers.			
10	The school helps me to feel good about myself.			
11	The school helps me to feel good about the future.			
12	We are encouraged to stand up for what we believe is right.			
13	It's good to have children from different backgrounds.			
14	Just by being at the school you learn how to get on with people.			
15	I have learnt what democracy means by being at the school.			
16	I have learnt how my actions affect others in the school.			
17	I have learnt how my actions affect others around the world.			
18	I have learnt how my values affect the way I act.			
19	I eat healthily at school.			
20	My family feel involved in what goes on at the school.			
21	When teachers say they are going to do something they do it.			
22	People admit when they have made a mistake.			
23	There is a comfortable place inside the school I can go to at lunchtimes.			
24	I have been involved in making the school a better place.			
25	Any child who lives near to this school is welcome to come here.			
26	When I first came to the school I was helped to settle in.			
27	You are respected regardless of the colour of your skin.			
28	You feel an equal part of the school whatever your religion or if you have no religion.			
29	Children do not look down on others because of what they wear.			
30	Boys and girls get on well together.			
31	Being gay or lesbian is seen as an ordinary part of life.			
32	Disabled children are respected and accepted.			

	Please tick the box that best reflects your opinion	*Agree*	*Agree and disagree*	*Disagree*
33	Children avoid calling each other hurtful names.			
34	If anyone bullied me or anyone else, I would tell a teacher.			
35	Teachers do not have favourites among the children.			
36	If I have been away for a day a teacher wants to know where I have been.			
37	I think the teachers are fair when they praise a child.			
38	I think the teachers are fair when they punish a child.			
39	Teachers know how to stop children interrupting lessons.			
40	When children are interrupting lessons other children calm them down.			
41	We learn how to settle disagreements by listening, talking and compromise.			
42	In lessons children often help each other in pairs and small groups.			
43	In lessons children share what they know with other children.			
44	If I have a problem in a lesson, a teacher or teaching assistant will help me.			
45	I enjoy most of my lessons.			
46	I learn about what is going on in the world.			
47	I have learnt about the importance of human rights.			
48	I learn how suffering in the world can be reduced.			
49	I learn a lot at this school.			
50	At times children are trusted to learn on their own.			
51	We learn how to save energy at the school.			
52	We learn to care for the environment in the school and the area around it.			
53	We learn to respect planet earth.			
54	When teaching assistants are in the classroom they help anyone who needs it.			
55	Teachers are interested in listening to my ideas.			
56	Children are interested in listening to each other's ideas.			
57	In lessons I always know what to get on with next.			
58	I know myself when I have done good work.			
59	Teachers don't mind if I make mistakes in my work as long as I try my best.			
60	My work is displayed on the walls in the school.			
61	When I am given homework I usually understand what I have to do.			
62	I find that homework helps me to learn.			
63	At lunchtimes or after school I sometimes join in clubs or do sports practice.			

QUESTIONNAIRE 3: MY SCHOOL

Do you agree or disagree? Please put a line on the face that shows what you think.

1	I am happy at school	☺	😐	☹
2	I like the way the school looks.	☺	😐	☹
3	I have good friends at the school.	☺	😐	☹
4	Children are kind to each other at the school.	☺	😐	☹
5	Adults are kind to children at the school.	☺	😐	☹
6	I like my teachers.	☺	😐	☹
7	I eat food that is good for me at school.	☺	😐	☹
8	I like to tell my family what I have done at school.	☺	😐	☹
9	When I first joined the school I was helped to feel happy.	☺	😐	☹
10	Boys and girls get on well together.	☺	😐	☹
11	Children do not get hit or called hurtful names at school.	☺	😐	☹
12	I feel safe in the playground and in the toilets.	☺	😐	☹
13	Teachers stop children making a fuss in lessons.	☺	😐	☹
14	Children often help each other in lessons.	☺	😐	☹
15	If I have a problem I can ask an adult for help.	☺	😐	☹
16	I learn all sorts of interesting things at school.	☺	😐	☹
17	I learn about people in other parts of the world.	☺	😐	☹
18	We learn how to save energy at school.	☺	😐	☹
19	We learn to care for the environment.	☺	😐	☹
20	Teachers are interested in listening to my ideas.	☺	😐	☹
21	I always know what to do in lessons.	☺	😐	☹
22	Teachers don't mind if I make mistakes as long as I try my best.	☺	😐	☹
23	My work is sometimes put up on the wall in my school.	☺	😐	☹
24	I sometimes join in clubs before or after school.	☺	😐	☹

What are the three things you like best about your school?

1 ______

2 ______

3 ______

What are the three things you would most like to change at your school?

1 ______

2 ______

3 ______

6 Resources

Resources

Abdi, A. and Shultz, L. (2008) *Educating for human rights and global citizenship*, Albany: State University of New York Press.

Actionaid (2008) *Power down: save energy, be the solution*, Chard: Action Aid.

Alexander, R. (2010) (ed.) *Children, their world, their education: final report and recommendations of the Cambridge Primary Review*, London: Routledge.

Andreotti, V. and de Souza, L. M. (2008) *Learning to read the world through other eyes*, Derby: Global Education.

Au, W. and Tempel, M. (2012) *Rethinking high-stakes testing and accountability in public schools*, Milwaukee, Rethinking Schools.

Baginsky, W. (2004) *Peer mediation in the UK, a guide for schools*, London: NSPCC.

Balshaw, M. (1999) *Help in the classroom* (2nd edition), London: Fulton.

Barnes, J. (2011) *Cross-curricular learning 3-14* (2nd edition), London: Sage.

Bigelow, B. and Swinehart, T. eds. (2014) A people's curriculum for the earth, Milwaukee, Rethinking Schools.

Bigelow, B. and Swinehart, T. eds. (2014) A people's curriculum for the earth, Milwaukee, Rethinking Schools.

Black, M. and King, J. (2009) *The atlas of water: mapping the world's most critical resource*, Brighton: Earthscan.

Blair, M. and Bourne, J. with Coffin, C., Creese, A. and Kenner, C. (1999) *Making the difference: teaching and learning strategies in successful multi-ethnic schools*, London: HMSO.

Boaler, J. (2010) *The Elephant in the Classroom: helping children learn and love maths*, London: Souvenir Press.

Bohm, D. (1996) *On Dialogue*, London: Routledge.

Brighton and Hove City Council (2005) *Biodiversity Action Plan*, Brighton: BHCC.

Buckingham, S. and Turner, M. (eds.) (2008) *Understanding environmental issues*, London: Sage.

Centre for Equity in Education (2007) *Equity in Education: new directions, second annual report on the state of equity in the English education system*, Manchester: The University of Manchester.

Centre for Studies on Inclusive Education (2010) *Developing a single equality policy for your school: a CSIE guide*, Bristol: CSIE.

Clark, A. and Moss, P. (2001) *Listening to young children*, London: National Children's Bureau.

Clutterbuck, P. (2008) *Values: a programme of study for primary schools*, Carmarthen: Crown House Publishing Ltd.

Collaborative Learning Project: www.collaborativelearning.org

Craig, D. (2009) *The weather book: why it happens and where it comes from*, London: Michael O'Mara Books.

Dahlberg, G., Moss, P. and Pence, A. (2007) *Beyond quality in early childhood education and care*, London: Routledge.

Denman-Sparks, L. and the A.B.C. Task Force (1989) *Anti- Bias Curriculum, tools for empowering young children*, Washington: National Association for the Education of Young Children.

Department for Children, Families, Lifelong Learning and Skills, (2008) *Careers and the world of work: a framework for 11-19 year olds in Wales*, Cardiff: Welsh Assembly.

Department for Children, Schools and Families (2008) *Top tips for developing the global dimension in schools*, London: DCSF.

Department for Children, Schools and Families (2008) *Top tips for sustainable purchasing in schools*, London: DCSF.

Department for Children, Schools and Families (2008) *Planning a sustainable school: driving school improvement through sustainable development*, London: DCSF.

Department for Children, Schools and Families (2009) *S3: Sustainable school self-evaluation*, London: DCSF.

Department for Education and Employment (1999) 'Inclusion: providing effective learning opportunities for all pupils', in *The national curriculum handbook for primary teachers in England*, London: DfEE.

Department for Education and Employment (2000) *Working with teaching assistants: a good practice guide*, London: DfEE.

Department for Education and Employment (2000) *Guidance on the education of children and young people in care*, London: DfEE.

Department for Education and Skills (2002) *Accessible schools: planning to increase access to schools for disabled pupils* [Guidance] London: DfES.

Department for Education and Skills (2006) *Implementing the Disability Discrimination Act in schools and early years settings*, London: DfES.

Department for Education and Skills (2006) *Learning outside the classroom manifesto*, London: DfES.

Department for Education and Skills (2007) *Top tips to reduce energy and water use in school*, London: DfES.

Dow, K. and Downing, T. (2006) *The atlas of climate change, mapping the world's greatest challenge*, Brighton: Earthscan.

Dressner, S. (2008) *The principles of sustainability*, London: Earthscan.

Drummond, M. J. (2003) *Assessing children's learning*, London: David Fulton.

Durbin, G., Morris, S. and Wilkinson, S. (1990) *A teacher's guide to learning from objects*, London: English Heritage.

Egan, K. (1988) *Teaching as Storytelling, an alternative approach to teaching and the curriculum*, London: Routledge.

Farrer, F. (2000) *A quiet revolution, encouraging positive values in our children*, London: Ebury Press.

Fielding, M. and Moss, P. (2011) *Radical education for the common school*, London: Routledge.

Fisher, R. (2003) *Teaching thinking*, London: Continuum.

Flowers, N. (2000) *Human rights education handbook: effective practices for learning, action and change*, Minneapolis: Human Rights Resource Centre, University of Minnesota.

Forest Schools: www.forestschools.com

George, S. (2010) *Whose crisis, whose future? Towards a greener, fairer, richer world*, Cambridge: Polity.

Hart, S. (1996) *Beyond special needs: enhancing children's learning through innovative thinking*, London: Paul Chapman Publishing.

Hart, S. (2000) *Thinking through teaching: a framework for enhancing participation and learning*, London: David Fulton.

Hart, S., Dixon, A., Drummond, M.J. and McIntyre, D. (2006) *Learning without limits*, Buckingham: Open University Press. http://learningwithoutlimits.educ.cam.ac.uk

Hatcher, R. (2006) 'Social class and schooling: differentiation or democracy?' in Cole, M. (ed.) *Education, equality and human rights: issues of gender, race, sexual orientation, disability and social class* (2nd edition), London: Routledge.

Hawkes, N. (2003) *How to inspire and develop positive values in your classroom*, Cambridge: LDA.

Higgins, P. (2010) *Eradicating ecocide*, London: Shepheard-Walwyn.

Holmes, T., Blackmore E., Hawkins, R. and Wakeford, T. (2011) *The common cause handbook: values and frames*, Machynlleth, Public Interest Research Centre.

Klein, N. (2014) This changes everything, capitalism versus the climate, New York, Simon Schuster.

Knight, S. (2011) *Forest School for All*, London, Sage.

Kohn, A. (2006) *The homework myth: why our kids get too much of a bad thing*, Cambridge, MA: Da Capo Press.

Language and Curriculum Access Service (LCAS) (1999) *Enabling progress in multilingual classrooms*, London: London Borough of Enfield.

Leggett, J. (2005) *Half gone: oil, gas, hot air and the global energy crisis*, London: Portobello Books.

Lesbian, Gay, Bisexual and Transgender History Month (2009) Toolkit for schools, London: LGBT.

www.lgbthistorymonth.org.uk

Mackay, M. (2008) Sustainable energy without the hot air: www.withouthotair.com

McNamara, S. and Moreton, G. (1997) *Understanding Differentiation: A Teacher's Guide*, London: David Fulton.

Marlowe, B. A. and Page, M. L. (1998) *Creating and sustaining the constructivist classroom*, London: Corwin Press/Sage.

Martin, F. and Owens, P. (2008) *Caring for our world: a practical guide to education for sustainable development*, Sheffield: Geographical association.

Millstone, E. and Lang, T. (2008) *The atlas of food: who eats what, where and why?* Brighton: Earthscan.

Noddings, N. (2005) *The challenge to care in schools, an alternative approach to education*, New York: Teachers College Press.

Noddings, N. (2005) *Critical lessons: what our schools should teach*, New York: Cambridge University Press.

Norfolk County Council (2009) February is Lesbian, Gay, Bisexual and Transgender History Month, Ideas for primary schools, Norwich: NCC.

Norfolk County Council (2009) February is Lesbian, Gay, Bisexual and Transgender History Month, Ideas for secondary schools, Norwich: NCC.

Northern Ireland Curriculum (2009) *Clothes conscious, learning for life and work*, Belfast: CCEA.

Noyes, A. (2007) *Rethinking school mathematics*, London: Paul Chapman Publishing.

Office for Standards in Education (2008) Learning outside the classroom, London: Ofsted.

Office for Standards in Education (2009) Education for sustainable development, London: Ofsted.

Ollerton, M. and Watson, A. (2004) *Inclusive mathematics 11-18*, London: Continuum.

O'Neill, O. (2002) A question of trust, BBC Reith Lectures, Cambridge, Cambridge University Press.

Open spaces for dialogue and enquiry, critical literacy in global citizenship education, Nottingham: Centre for the study of social and global justice.

Orr, D. (2004) *Earth in mind: on education, environment and the human prospect*, Washington: Island Press.

Owen, J. (1991) *The ecology of a garden, the first fifteen years*, Cambridge: Cambridge University Press.

Pearl, A. (1997) 'Democratic education as an alternative to deficit thinking', in Valencia, R. (ed.) *The evolution of deficit thinking: educational thought and practice*, London: Falmer Press.

Potts, P. (ed.) (2002) *Inclusion in the city*, London: Routledge.

Qualifications and Curriculum Authority (2007) *The global dimension in action: a curriculum planning guide for schools*, London: QCA.

Rich, D., Casanova, D., Dixon, A., Drummond, M.J., Durrant, A. and Myer, C. (2004) *First hand experience, what matters to children*, Clopton: Rich Learning Opportunities.

Rich, D., Drummond, M.J. and Myer, C. (2008) *Learning: what matters to children*, Clopton: Rich Learning Opportunities.

Rustemier, S. and Booth, T. (2005) *Learning about the Index in use, a study of the use of the Index in schools and LEAs in England*, Bristol: CSIE.

Save the Children (2000) *The school council: a children's guide*, London: Save the Children.

School councils UK: www.schoolcouncils.org

Schools out classroom: www.schools-out.org.uk/classroom

Scoffham, S. (2010) (ed.) *Primary Geography Handbook*, Sheffield: Geographical Association.

Scoffham, S., Bridge, C. and Jewson, T. (2006) *Keystart World Atlas*, London: Harper Collins.

Scottish Health Promoting Schools Unit (2004) *Being well, doing well*, Dundee: Learning and Teaching Scotland.

Steel, C. (2008) *Hungry city: how food shapes our lives*, London: Vintage Books.

Stibbe, A. (2009) *The handbook of sustainability literacy: skills for a changing world*, Dartington: Green Books.

Stone, M. (2009) *Smart by Nature: schooling for sustainability*, Healdsburg: Watershed Media.

Stone, M. and Barlow, Z. (2005) *Ecological Literacy: educating our children for a sustainable world*, San Francisco: Sierra Club Books.

Sustain: the alliance for better food and farming (2010) *Every school a food growing school*, London: Sustain.

Sustainability and environmental education: www.se-ed.co.uk

Sustainable Development Commission (2009) *Prosperity without Growth? The transition to a sustainable economy*, London: Sustainable Development Commission.

Swann, M. and Peacock, A. (2012) *Creating learning without limits*, Buckingham: Open University Press.

Swann, M., Peacock, A., Hart, H. and Drummond, M. (2012) *Creating learning without limits*, Maidenhead, Open University Press.

UNICEF UK (2008) *Rights respecting schools in England*, London: Unicef.

UNICEF/UNESCO (2007) *A human rights based approach to education for all*, New York, Paris: UNICEF/UNESCO.

Wallace, B. (2001) *Teaching thinking skills in the early years/across primary years*, London: David Fulton.

Warwick, I. and Douglas, N. (2001) *Safe for all: a best practice guide to prevent homophobic bullying in secondary schools*, London: Citizenship 21.

Watson, A. (2006) *Raising achievement in secondary mathematics*, Maidenhead: Open University Press.

Winter, R. (1989) *Learning from experience: principles and practice in action research*, London: Falmer.

World of Inclusion: www.worldofinclusion.com

Wrigley, T. (2006) *Another school is possible*, London: Bookmarks Publications.

Young, M. (2002) *Global Citizenship, the handbook for primary teaching*, Cambridge: Oxfam.

Internationally Ratified Human Rights Documents

Because of a degree of separation of the legal systems of England, Scotland, Northern Ireland and Wales, the adoption in law of these instruments varies in each country of the UK.

Documents include:

- Universal Declaration of Human Rights 1948 (voted for at UN General Assembly by UK in 1948)
- International Convention on the Elimination of All Forms of Racial Discrimination 1965 (UK ratified 1969)
- International Covenant on Civil and Political Rights 1966 (UK ratified 1976)
- International Covenant on Economic, Social and Cultural Rights 1966 (UK ratified 1976)
- UN Convention on the Elimination of All Forms of Discrimination against Women 1979 (UK ratified 1986)
- Convention on the Rights of the Child 1989 (UK Ratified with reservations 1991, fully 2006)
- Convention on the Rights of Persons with Disabilities 2006 (UK Ratified 2009 with reservation about inclusion in mainstream education)
- European Convention on Human Rights 1950 (Included in English Law 1998)

Universal Declaration Of Human Rights 1948

This is the founding declaration for all other human rights documents. It grew out of the aftermath of the World War 1939-1945 and led to the founding of the International Criminal Court. It was produced by a committee chaired by Eleanor Roosevelt wife of the US president. It was adopted by the United Nations General Assembly in 1948. To assert something as a right is to say that it is universal but not everyone is in agreement that all articles of the Declaration represent rights. Although the right to life might be seen to include the need for environmental protection, there is little reference to the environment in the declaration.

Extracts:

Article 1:

All human beings are born free and equal in dignity and rights. They are endowed with reason and conscience and should act towards one another in a spirit of brotherhood.

Article 2:

Everyone is entitled to all the rights and freedoms set forth in this Declaration, without distinction of any kind, such as race, colour, sex, language, religion, political or other opinion, national or social origin, property, birth or other status. Furthermore, no distinction shall be made on the basis of the political, jurisdictional or international status of the country or territory to which a person belongs, whether it be independent, trust, non-self-governing or under any other limitation of sovereignty.

Article 3:

Everyone has the right to life, liberty and security of person.

Article 17:

1. Everyone has the right to own property alone as well as in association with others.
2. No one shall be arbitrarily deprived of his property.

Article 26:

Everyone has the right to education. Education shall be free, at least in the elementary and fundamental stages. Elementary education shall be compulsory. Technical and professional education shall be made generally available and higher education shall be equally accessible to all on the basis of merit.

Education shall be directed to the full development of the human personality and to the strengthening of respect for human rights and fundamental freedoms. It shall promote understanding, tolerance and friendship among all nations, racial or religious groups, and shall further the activities of the United Nations for the maintenance of peace.

Parents have a prior right to choose the kind of education that shall be given to their children.

Convention on the Rights of the Child

The United Kingdom ratified the Convention in December 1991, but said that it would not comply with requirements concerned with the treatment of children of asylum seekers and the age of criminal responsibility. In addition, the UK was criticised by the UN Committee on the Rights of the Child in 1995 for the growth in child poverty and inequality and the lack of opportunities for children and young people to express their views. The 2002 report of the Committee stressed concerns about the welfare of children in custody, and the negative impact of poverty on children's rights. There was mention of the continuation of corporal punishment in private schools in Northern Ireland, where it was finally abolished it in 2003. The 2002 report had described the UK's view that parents should be able to engage in 'reasonable chastisement' of children as 'a serious violation of the dignity of the child'. This was not accepted by the UK Government. Although the government removed its 'reservations' in 2008, in 2011 it remained legally permissible for parents to discipline children by hitting and the age of criminal responsibility was lower than elsewhere in Europe (10 in England, Wales and Northern Ireland, 12 in Scotland up from 8 in 2011).

Extract:

Article 29: States Parties agree that the education of the child shall be directed to:

a) the development of the child's personality, talents and mental and physical abilities to their fullest potential;

b) the development of respect for human rights and fundamental freedoms, and for the principles enshrined in the Charter of the United Nations;

c) the development of respect for the child's parents, his or her own cultural identity, language and values, for the national values of the country in which the child is living, the country from which he or she may originate, and for civilizations different from his or her own;

d) the preparation of the child for responsible life in a free society, in the spirit of understanding, peace, tolerance, equality of sexes, and friendship among all peoples, ethnic, national and religious groups and persons of indigenous origin;

e) the development of respect for the natural environment.

Extracts from the Universal Declaration of the Rights of Mother Earth[53]

This declaration was adopted by the World People's Conference on Climate Change and the Rights of Mother Earth on April 22nd 2010, in Bolivia and submitted to the United Nations for Consideration.

Article 2: Inherent Rights of Mother Earth

(1) Mother Earth and all beings of which she is composed have the following inherent rights:
- (a) the right to life and to exist;
- (b) the right to be respected;
- (c) the right to regenerate its bio-capacity and to continue its vital cycles and processes free from human disruptions;
- (d) the right to maintain its identity and integrity as a distinct, self-regulating and interrelated being;
- (e) the right to water as a source of life;
- (f) the right to clean air;
- (g) the right to integral health;
- (h) the right to be free from contamination, pollution and toxic or radioactive waste;
- (i) the right to not have its genetic structure modified or disrupted in a manner that threatens its integrity or vital and healthy functioning;
- (j) the right to full and prompt restoration the violation of the rights recognized in this declaration caused by human activities;

(2) Each being has the right to a place and to play its role in Mother Earth for her harmonious functioning.

(3) Every being has the right to wellbeing and to live free from torture or cruel treatment by human beings.

Article 3: Obligations of human beings to Mother Earth

(1) Every human being is responsible for respecting and living in harmony with Mother Earth.

(2) Human beings, all States, and all public and private institutions must:
- (a) act in accordance with the rights and obligations recognized in this Declaration;
- (b) recognize and promote the full implementation and enforcement of the rights and obligations recognized in this Declaration;
- (c) promote and participate in learning, analysis, interpretation and communication about how to live in harmony with Mother Earth in accordance with this Declaration;
- (d) ensure that the pursuit of human wellbeing contributes to the wellbeing of Mother Earth, now and in the future;
- (e) establish and apply effective norms and laws for the defence, protection and conservation of the rights of Mother Earth;
- (f) respect, protect, conserve and where necessary, restore the integrity, of the vital ecological cycles, processes and balances of Mother Earth;
- (g) guarantee that the damages caused by human violations of the inherent rights recognized in this Declaration are rectified and that those responsible are held accountable for restoring the integrity and health of Mother Earth;
- (h) empower human beings and institutions to defend the rights of Mother Earth and of all beings;
- (i) establish precautionary and restrictive measures to prevent human activities from causing species extinction, the destruction of ecosystems or the disruption of ecological cycles;
- (j) guarantee peace and eliminate nuclear, chemical and biological weapons;
- (k) promote and support practices of respect for Mother Earth and all beings, in accordance with their own cultures, traditions and customs;
- (l) promote economic systems that are in harmony with Mother Earth and in accordance with the rights recognized in this Declaration.

53 http://therightsofnature.org/universal-declaration/